What People Are Saying About
Chicken Soup for the Caregiver's Soul . . .

"*Chicken Soup for the Caregiver's Soul* is a heartwarming book that captures the essence of what it means to care and what it means to give. I definitely recommend it."

Suzanne Mintz
president/co-founder,
National Family Caregivers Association

"*Chicken Soup for the Caregiver's Soul* shares the stories of caregivers who represent us all. From the up-front, right-next-to-you caregiver to the long-distance caregiver, the messages are ones that will resonate with caregivers everywhere. If you have ever been a caregiver or will be a caregiver, you will find yourself in this book, which portrays the challenges and rewards faced by us all in one of life's most important roles."

Ronda C. Talley, Ph.D., MPH
executive director & professor, Rosalynn Carter Institute
for Caregiving

"This great book truly captures the heart and soul of the family caregiver within these pages. It's sure to be a classic and help a lot of caregivers along the way."

Gary Barg
editor-in-chief, *Today's Caregiver* magazine
author, *The Fearless Caregiver*

"The miracle of humanity at its best is portrayed here in these stories. *Chicken Soup for the Caregiver's Soul* draws you into a world of gentle, intimate compassion filled with hope to face the brutal realities of life events. I recommend this inspirational book—not only to caregivers—but to anyone who wants to know life's meaning in a deeper way."

Paul Falkowski
Desert Ministries Radio Hour

"The word 'caregiver' encompasses a great deal: choices, responsibilities, emotions and even hidden joys. *Chicken Soup for the Caregiver's Soul* embraces all of these, leaving you with the greatest emotion of all—laughter through tears. You'll find yourself giggling while choking back a sob, realizing that through any circumstance you can still find hope. A perfect gift for a friend or yourself."

Lisa Copen
Rest Ministries

"Caregiving is primarily an act of love and one of life's worthiest endeavors, and these wonderful words and stories will help dedicated caregivers with their task. They offer the special blessing of tenderness for those who tend and nourishment for those who nourish. What a gift!"

Gretchen Thompson
author, *God Knows Caregiving Can Pull You Apart:*
12 Ways to Keep It All Together

"Beautifully written, like a book of great fiction filled with laughter and tears, but with real voices of courageous caregivers who share their triumphs and sorrows, helping make your caregiving journey an easier one. These amazing stories, written with passion and delightful humor, will warm your heart and have you nodding in recognition, as you gain valuable insight, solutions and hope. Captivating and edu-taining—you won't be able to put it down!"

Jacqueline Marcell
author, *Elder Rage -or- Take My Father . . . Please!*
How To Survive Caring For Aging Parents
host, "Coping with Caregiving" radio program

"Inspiration, tears, even laughter—I experienced them all in *Chicken Soup for the Caregiver's Soul.* A beautiful salute to caregivers —ordinary people performing extraordinary service."

Gloria Cassity Stargel
author, *The Healing: One Family's*
Victorious Struggle with Cancer

"The stories are fabulous! This is exactly what caregivers need! When they do have a moment to themselves, to be able to pick up a book that contains stories just like their own is priceless. They are reminded that they are not alone. It provides them with the means for laughter and tears; both so essential in the caregiver journey."

Jo Huey
author, *Alzheimer's Disease: Help and Hope*

"For twelve years I had the privilege to care for my wife, who died from the debilitating impact of multiple sclerosis. During those twelve years, I searched for all the inspirational material that I could put my hands on that would emotionally help me through those trying times of being a caregiver. I found many books that talked about the subject of the disease that she and I were battling, but very little that directly was written to help and inspire me. Finally, the book has been written. You have it in your hands. You will be helped, informed, encouraged and inspired in your life by *Chicken Soup for the Caregiver's Soul.*"

Glenn Mollette
author, *Silent Struggler: A Caregiver's Personal Story*

"The support of caregiving families centers on relationships and community. We learn more about the challenges and joys of caregiving relationships in the stories and reflections shared in *Chicken Soup for the Caregiver's Soul.*"

Brian M. Duke MHA, MBE
WHYY Wider Horizons
Caring Community

CHICKEN SOUP
FOR THE
CAREGIVER'S SOUL

Chicken Soup for the Caregiver's Soul
Stories to Inspire Caregivers in the Home, Community and the World
Jack Canfield, Mark Victor Hansen, LeAnn Thieman

Published by Backlist, LLC,
a unit of Chicken Soup for the Soul Publishing, LLC. www.chickensoup.com

Front cover design by Andrea Perrine Brower
Originally published in 2004 by Health Communications, Inc.

Back cover and spine redesign by Pneuma Books, LLC

Distributed to the booktrade by Simon & Schuster. SAN: 200-2442

Publisher's Cataloging-in-Publication Data
(Prepared by The Donohue Group)

Chicken soup for the caregiver's soul : stories to inspire caregivers in the
  home, community and the world / [compiled by] Jack Canfield, Mark
Victor Hansen, [and] LeAnn Thieman.

  p. ; ill. ; cm.

  Originally published: Deerfield Beach, FL : Health Communications, c2004.
  ISBN: 978-1-62361-020-3

  1. Caregivers--Religious life--Anecdotes. 2. Anecdotes. I. Canfield, Jack,
1944- II. Hansen, Mark Victor. III. Thieman, LeAnn.

BL625.9.C35 C48 2012
158.1/28   2012944184

PRINTED IN THE UNITED STATES OF AMERICA
on acid free paper
24 23 22   09 10

CHICKEN SOUP
FOR THE
CAREGIVER'S SOUL

Stories to Inspire Caregivers in the Home, Community and the World

Jack Canfield
Mark Victor Hansen
LeAnn Thieman

Backlist, LLC, a unit of
Chicken Soup for the Soul Publishing, LLC
Cos Cob, CT
www.chickensoup.com

Contents

3. ANGELS AMONG US

4. THE TRUE MEANING OF HEALTH CARE

5. ACTS OF KINDNESS

6. OVERCOMING OBSTACLES

7. INSIGHTS AND LESSONS

8. A MATTER OF PERSPECTIVE

9. UNEXPECTED BLESSINGS

CONTENTS xiii

Foreword

Chicken soup is everyone's recipe for anything that ails you. From mothers to scientists, from folklore to data, this familiar food has been prescribed for hundreds of years to relieve the symptoms of the common cold. Recipes handed down from one generation to the next contain the ingredients that University of Nebraska Medical Center scientists have documented as "good medicine" for our bodies. Now the authors of *Chicken Soup for the Caregiver's Soul* have brought that "good medicine " to support caregivers and help them as they carry out their vital roles.

Today, there is a serious and rapidly growing crisis in caregiving over the lifespan in America. Nationwide, an estimated 52 million caregivers currently provide continuous care each year to their loved ones. This figure includes ill or disabled family members or friends. Caring for others, despite its challenges, is often rewarding for both those who give care and those who receive it.

For more than 30 years, I have been involved in efforts to improve the quality of life for people with mental illnesses and those who care for them. In the course of my work, I have heard from so many people who were caring for a loved one, neighbor or member of their congregation, and not only for mental disorders but for all sorts of illnesses or disabilities. Because of these messages, in 1987, we established the Rosalynn Carter Institute for Caregiving to study the issues and take action to ease the burdens and recognize the rewards of caregiving.

The Rosalynn Carter Institute stands as the only university-based center in the United States dedicated to helping both family and professional caregivers. We research critical caregiving needs, provide education, raise public awareness of the issues and advocate for policies and legislation that support caregivers to help them as they fulfill one of the most important challenges they will ever face.

At the Institute, we have found that sharing the poignant experiences of caregivers is powerful therapy. Like chicken soup, these stories soothe and nourish family members and professionals devoting themselves to the care of those who are ill or disabled. *Chicken Soup for the Caregiver's Soul* is a potent resource for encouragement, advice and empathy, and I am confident readers will find comfort and strength in the following pages.

Rosalynn Carter

Introduction

Over fifty-two million people in the United States and more than a quarter of the adult population worldwide help care for ailing family members and friends. Millions more selflessly give of themselves in day-care, elder-care, community and international settings. While rewarding, caregiving requires tremendous emotional, physical and spiritual stamina. That's why we created *Chicken Soup for the Caregiver's Soul*—to offer care for the caregiver, a respite where you can read real-life stories of encouragement and inspiration.

Mother Teresa, one of the greatest caregivers of our century, said she never looked at the masses as her responsibility but only at the individual. She could, she claimed, love only one person at a time. And that, dear caregiver, is what you do. We included her stories and those of caregivers from all over the world to show you that you are among an international league of caregivers, and your efforts are no less important.

This collection of inspirational stories will lift your spirits, nourish your soul and remind you that others understand. Like caregiving, these stories celebrate life and death. Read them one at a time, savoring the hope, the healing and the happiness they offer.

It is our sincere wish that *Chicken Soup for the Caregiver's Soul* gives back to you a portion of the love and caring you give to others. We honor you for your daily contributions and thank you for making a difference in another's life— and in the world.

1

SPECIAL MOMENTS IN CAREGIVING

I am one, but still I am one. I cannot do everything, but still I can do something.
I cannot refuse to do the something I can do.

Helen Keller

That's Why I Am Here

What gift has providence so bestowed on man that is so dear to him as his children.

Cicero

My children have always been involved in 4-H. Heavily into the animal divisions with a few other projects, they took their county fair presentations very seriously. I was a professional dog trainer and handler, and one year my two youngest children entered our registered dogs in the Beginner Obedience class. My fourteen-year-old son, Jeremy, wanted to do something with the dogs too, but he was very independent and didn't want to do something that everyone else was doing. He came to me in the spring, several months before the fair, and said, "I've decided to make my dog project count." He proceeded to show me his detailed plan for his Citizenship project, which was to provide therapy-dog visits to local nursing homes.

In the north-central portion of Minnesota, where we lived, this was an unheard-of concept. Jeremy told me he had already done some of the legwork by asking his brother, sister and two members of the 4-H club to come along and assist. What he most needed from me was to choose the appropriate dogs and teach the handlers how to present a dog to an elderly, and perhaps bedridden, person. We contacted several nursing homes and finally found one that agreed to allow our therapy dogs to visit. Jeremy called his 4-H buddies and set up a training schedule. When all five kids were comfortable presenting the dogs, we made an appointment with the nursing home.

The first day we visited, I went along as driver, photographer and supervisor. We went from room to room, sharing our smaller trained therapy dogs and puppies with as many people as possible. Each child carried a dog and a towel to place on the bed in case someone wanted the dog there. We were a hit! The joy these folks exhibited was genuine and wonderful. They all asked us to visit again.

On our next outings, we left earlier so we could visit more residents. Jeremy enjoyed watching people's faces light up as we entered a room, but there seemed to be something disturbing him. I asked if he was having a problem with the project. He became solemn. "I love coming here, but I want to make an even bigger difference. I'm not sure how, but I know there is something more I can do."

Each time we visited, the residents anticipated it with greater enthusiasm. Some even had family members bring in photos of their own dogs to share with us. We listened to stories about their pets, their families and their lives when they were young. Each sat constantly petting one of the dogs, gaining the comfort and unconditional love only an animal can give so freely.

One day, we ventured into an area we hadn't been to before. As a nurse's aide led the way, we came upon several rooms that were quieter than most and not decorated. The aide motioned for us to continue following her to the residents down the hall who had requested visits. Jeremy stopped and peered into one of the rooms. The aide reprimanded, "There is no use going into that room; that lady hasn't moved or spoken in months. She is unresponsive and pretty much alone." Jeremy looked at her and then at the French bulldog he held in his arms. Calmly, he replied, "That's why I am here." He proceeded into the room and stood hesitantly. The woman was ghost-white and showed no signs of life. She lay prone and didn't move so much as her eyes when we entered. Jeremy took a deep breath and moved to the side of the bed. "My name is Jeremy, and I am here with my therapy dogs. I brought a dog to see you. Since you can't come to see the dog, I'd like to place it on your bed. I have a towel so no hair will get on your blankets."

The woman did not move. Jeremy looked to me for approval. I nodded. He moved to the side of the bed where her arm was exposed and placed the towel on the bedspread. While all this was happening, the aide left to get a nurse. By the time Jeremy was ready to put the dog beside the woman, two nurses and the aide were in the doorway. As one began to tell me we were wasting our time, I raised my hand to silence her. She huffed but was otherwise quiet.

Jeremy placed the dog against the woman's arm. He spoke softly. "She won't hurt you. She came here just to see you." As he spoke, the woman's head shifted slightly. The glaze in her eyes seemed to disappear. Jeremy allowed the dog to nestle close. The woman raised a weak arm and placed it on the dog's back. Although she had no words, she began to make sounds. Tears brimmed her eyes as she moved her hand along the hair. The nurses rushed to the bedside and began pressing the nurse-call button. More people rushed into the room. There was not a dry eye in the group. Jeremy looked at the aide and reiterated, "This is why I am here." Then he looked at me, tears flowing unashamedly down his face, and he said, "I made a difference." I hugged him and acknowledged that he certainly had. When it was time to leave, Jeremy gathered up the dog and the towel and said to the woman, "Thanks for letting us come into your room—and into your life." She smiled at him and touched his arm.

Jeremy received the highest award for his Citizenship project and went on to the state level, where he earned Grand Champion. But for Jeremy, the ribbons were nothing compared to his biggest award—the touch of a hand and the smile from a woman who was said to be a waste of time.

Loretta Emmons

The Day Wishes Came True

There is nothing more properly the language of the heart than a wish.

Robert South

My mother was very hard-of-hearing for almost all of her life. As a child, I became her hearing aid before the precious invention was made available to her. Even after she began wearing one, I spent a lot of time repeating myself or the words of others so she knew what was happening. In those days, the contraption buzzed and squealed so loudly it hurt *our* ears. No matter, the device was there to stay. She thought hearing aids were the greatest. Many times I wished for her to be able to hear me without speaking loudly, or having to stand where she could read my lips. I used to see other mothers and their little girls whispering secrets, and I would think, *When Mother and I get to heaven, she will be able to hear me whisper secrets.*

Daddy died when Mom was only forty-five, so I served as her caregiver her last years. Despite her near deafness, she kept up on current events from the newspaper, local news and the blaring television. But her favorite pastime was recalling the past.

One day, she recounted to my daughter, Debbie, "I married your grandpa two days before my seventeenth birthday. On July 19, 1928, we went into Lake City, Arkansas, to buy me a new dress for our wedding. He wanted me to have a pretty white dress, but we couldn't find one. So, he bought me a blue dress with white lace, new white shoes and a hat." She chuckled as she told how they were wed that day and then hurried back to their respective homes in time to milk the cows!

Mother always told her wedding day story with humor—especially that they had to split up and go back to their parents' homes to do their chores. However, she always admitted her regret that she didn't have a white dress for her special day. This time, she concluded, "I married in blue, but when Albert sees me, I want to be in white."

Mother and Debbie shared a love for catalogs. In between Debbie's visits, Mother created a stack and had them waiting for her. One day when Debbie came over to help me, as she often did, she said, "By the way, Mom, Grandma and I ordered her a long white dress." She went on to explain that she had ordered and paid for the gown of Mother's choice for her burial.

When the dress arrived, Mother loved it. She even asked for a new slip to go with it. She had wished for that dress for so many years; like a youthful bride, she looked forward to wearing what Albert had wanted for her long ago.

Mother suffered from congestive heart failure, and in her last days, her kidneys failed so her body was retaining water; she was a little woman and had put on close to twenty pounds within a few days. One day, she was in pain and couldn't eat, and we didn't place her hearing aid in her ear that morning. Losing her mobility made her angry, so she stood up from her chair without help and began trying to walk. Of course, she did not move far in her attempt to defy death. Later in the day, she absolutely could not pull herself to her feet, so she asked me to please help her stand. Just Mother and I were in the house. By then, she was quite heavy and I was sixty-four years old. I picked her up as if she were a child and had her stand on top of my feet. I laid her head on my shoulder while I walked her around.

Absentmindedly, I began to sing softly as we walked. When I was young and lived on a farm, I sang at the top of my voice as I pumped water by hand for our thirsty, hardworking farm animals. Some of our neighbors would say to me, "You have a beautiful, clear voice. You should be a singer." I had not sung in years except in the congregation of our church. I didn't even know a complete song. But while walking Mother, I began to sing some of those long-ago songs.

"Lula, where is that beautiful singing coming from?" she asked.

"Me," I said, almost surprising myself. Then, in a hushed tone, I started quoting scripture. I said, "You know, Mother, you will not always be trapped in this old, sick body, but you will walk on streets of gold, pure gold."

She said back to me, "Pure gold, Lula."

Then it dawned on me: She was hearing *every* word I said to her, without her hearing aid! God was giving Mother and me that precious day I had longed for since I was a kid. In spite of that miracle, it didn't dawn on me that my precious mother was only minutes from being on those streets of gold.

That evening, in her beautiful white dress, she walked down the eternal aisle to Albert.

Lula Smith as told to Kim Peterson

A Musical Eye-Opener

Music is the medicine of the breaking heart.
Alfred William Hunt

My father had been diagnosed with dementia and lived in a nursing home. He became ill enough to be admitted to the hospital, so I stayed with him. He was confused and rarely spoke, but that didn't keep me from chatting away, trying to communicate with him.

One day, I ran out of things to say, so I decided to sing. Unfortunately, I inherited my daddy's musical ability. Neither of us could carry a tune in a bucket. I crooned, "I love you. You love me. We're a great big family."

Daddy opened his eyes, turned and looked at me. For the first time in days, he spoke. "I love you too, honey," he said. "But you don't have to sing about it."

Nancy B. Gibbs

Christmas Eve Devotions

A song will outlive all sermons in the memory.

Henry Giles

It was Christmas Eve 1997, my first working at the Good Samaritan Home. It was the custom there for the supervisory and administrative staff to conduct Christmas Eve devotions for the residents. I was looking forward to participating, but I didn't know quite what to expect.

There was no set program, but all the supervisors came prepared to share something. Some read scripture; others shared special Christmas memories. I love to sing, so, naturally, that's what I decided to contribute.

Before we started the services on each unit, we greeted the residents, wishing them all a Merry Christmas. They welcomed us with smiles and even some tears as a feeling of warmth and love filled the air.

We arrived at the Special Care Center for those suffering from Alzheimer's disease. As we had done on all of the other floors, we spent time visiting with the residents prior to the devotions. Most of them, however, were very disoriented and confused.

I noticed one particular woman, Mary, sitting alone, and I went over to speak to her. She had a distant look in her eyes, a look you might find on the face of a small child lost from her parents—scared and utterly helpless.

When I reached for her hand, she said in a raspy voice, "Is Tom here yet? He should be here any minute."

I could tell that Tom was someone very special to her. I wondered, *Who is he? Is he a relative coming to spend the holiday with her?* I hoped so.

As I moved on to greet another resident, a nurse who had seen me talking with Mary walked past. "Who is Tom?" I asked.

The nurse pulled me aside and with sadness in her voice said, "Tom was her husband. He's been dead for at least five years now."

My heart just broke. It was all too sad. So many of the people here didn't even know it was Christmas Eve. Could they truly appreciate this service?

We began the devotions, reading scriptures and reciting poetry. Then it was my turn to sing. I began, "O Holy Night, the stars are brightly shining . . ." And then suddenly, I heard it—another voice singing with me. I turned my head and saw it belonged to Mary! With a radiant smile on her face, she sang strong and clear, as if she were performing as a soloist. The words just flowed from her lips, "It is the night of our dear Savior's birth . . ."

I sang past the emotion welling up in my throat, and our voices blended together. This woman who had lost so much showed us that somewhere deep inside her, the flame of life still burned brightly. Although ravaged by Alzheimer's disease, her spirit had not been vanquished. She was alive with song.

Mary kept singing, and gradually, everyone in the room joined in. "Long lay the world, in sin and error pining . . ."

As I wiped the tears from my eyes, I noticed that a nurse—our activity director—and a visiting family member did the same.

I'm sure the Lord was looking down and smiling on us all as we sang, "Fall on your knees, and hear the angel's voices . . ." Because that's exactly what we were hearing.

Amy Ross Vaughn

Daddy's Dance

Dancing . . . the body and the mind feel its gladdening influence.

William Ellery Channing

I loaded the last of my retreat supplies in the back of my minivan then kissed my husband and son good-bye. Not only was I excited about the overnight ladies' retreat where I would be speaking, but I had mapped out a driving route that took me right through the town in which my parents lived. I planned to stop and spend a few hours with them, welcoming any opportunity to visit my mother and father, now eighty-three and eighty-six years old. Often, though, these visits were difficult.

Daddy was in the throes of Alzheimer's disease, and his comprehension and communication were severely impaired. The progression of the illness was devastating, especially to my mother, his mate of sixty-six years. She was now more a caregiver than a wife, and Daddy was often unable to even recognize her face. I grieved for both of them as well as for myself. I wasn't ready to let go of the father I had known forever, the one who was so full of life—smiling, singing, joking, laughing. Where had he gone? How did those "tangles" in the brain rob him of words, faces and places?

Many times, Mama wanted to tell me of personal incidents, thinking I would understand, me being the mother and caregiver of an adult son with special needs. But I didn't want to hear humiliating details of Daddy's debilitating disease. This was still my father, the man who held me on his lap and rocked me as a child, who put me on my first horse to ride, and taught me to drive in an old 1948 Ford pickup truck. This was the daddy who used to show up unexpectedly at my college dormitory to bring me home on weekends when he thought I had stayed away too long. There was no way to divorce myself from those memories, nor did I want to. I held them close to my heart.

Once when I presented him with a framed picture of me, Mama asked, "Do you know who's in that picture?" He smiled and pointed directly at my face, and said, "That's my baby." Indeed, I would always be his baby girl.

But today, after arriving at my parents' home, Daddy gave me a quick hug then went to the bedroom to take a nap while I sat at the kitchen table with Mama. She spilled out her fears, resentment and pain. She had no idea how to cope with Daddy's anger when she didn't fulfill his requests. How could she possibly know what he wanted when she couldn't understand his words or gestures?

Because of my own son's lack of communication, I could identify with her frustration, but it seemed harder for my mother. This was her husband, and it wasn't supposed to be this way. This was the time she had dreamed of traveling and relaxing after many years of hard work.

Daddy got up several times from his nap to make trips to the bathroom, always requiring Mama's help with snaps and zippers on his clothing. Neither of them liked this situation, and both were argumentative and irritated with each other.

Finally, I left for the retreat, but my heart was heavy.

As I drove, I thought of the anger, fatigue and emotional pain that my parents were experiencing, and I wondered if they ever had a happy moment. I loved them and wanted to help, but had no idea what to do. As I guided the car along the highway, I prayed for peace, harmony, love, health and even joy in their lives.

The retreat provided a refreshing respite for my body and soul, and I was in great spirits as I headed back home. Again, I stopped for a visit with my parents, hoping things had improved.

I pulled into the driveway just ahead of my brother, and we congregated in the living room with his guitar. Monte played and sang several songs, then Mama and Daddy joined in. By the time they hit the old hymn, "I Saw the Light," Daddy was singing every word from memory and smiling from ear to ear. I sat in awe as I watched his whole countenance change.

Suddenly, Daddy, who normally shuffled and slumped when he walked, jumped up from the couch and began to dance a jig to the music, his face alive with pure joy and fun. Then, he put his hands out toward my mother. She stood up, and together they two-stepped across the living room floor, both of them laughing and gliding like I remember them doing when I was a child.

I sat clapping my hands in time to the music and wiping away tears. I had forgotten how much music had been a part of our family while growing up. I couldn't count how many times Mama and Daddy had stood beside our old upright piano and sang while I barely plunked out a melody. Daddy also led the singing at our little country church and even sang while he worked in the fields, often letting me ride on the horse's broad back while he guided the plow behind. My mind was flooded with wonderful memories. Good times and hard times, but happy times.

Soon, Daddy plopped down on the couch, a smile still lighting up his face.

I left for home with a new peace and joy in my heart, and while I drove, I again prayed for my parents, thanking God for allowing me to witness the love and happy times they still enjoy.

I know there will still be hard times in the future. But I'm thankful for this beautiful memory and reminder to celebrate every moment in life—perhaps even dance in it.

Louise Tucker Jones

My Sunshine

The world goes up and the world goes down, and the sunshine follows the rain; and yesterday's sneer and yesterday's frown can never come over again.

Charles Kingsley

I looked out the window of the plane thinking, *Is this it? Will Dad be okay again, or will this heart attack make me face the inevitable?* When I arrived, I went straight to the intensive care unit. Dad was hooked up to numerous tubes and machines. He smiled when he saw me, and I took his hand. The look on his face said more than his words. This was going to be a tough one.

The next day, the doctor met with Mom, my sister and me outside Dad's room. "I have good news and bad news. The good news is we got his heart started again. The bad news . . . his kidneys are failing." He paused a moment as we tried to figure out what it all meant. "We could put him on dialysis, however, he'd need surgery to implant a shunt in his arm for the treatments. I'm not sure his heart would make it through that surgery. He's eighty-one and has lived a good life. I suggest you unhook the machines and let him go."

The doctor's words floated off into space like clouds passing over. All I could hear was, "Let him go." I thought, *I'm not making that decision. My sister can. My mother can.*

But Mom didn't want to. Neither did my sister. They turned to me. I said, "I'm not going to make the decision. Dad should. He's coherent, and after all, it is *his* life."

I went to Dad.

There was a mutual admiration between Dad and me that formed in my infancy and strengthened in me in adulthood. He was my adviser, my counselor, my father, but more important, my friend. I knew the love we had for each other would get us through the experiences ahead.

I walked into his ICU room. "Dad, the doctor says they got your heart started again, but there is scar tissue, and it's pretty damaged. And your kidneys are failing. You could go through dialysis to try to keep them going, but the doctor doesn't feel your heart is in any shape to handle even the initial procedure."

I stopped talking and waited. I saw him grow still and speculative. He looked up at me and said, "If I do this dialysis thing, will I ever get out of the hospital?"

"I don't know, Dad."

"Will I be dependent on a machine for the rest of my life?"

"Yes."

My throat ached during the long pause that followed, and I swallowed back tears. His eyes met mine and there was a slight smile on his face. He said pointing to the machines. "Then, unhook 'em."

We informed the doctor of his decision. Dad was disconnected from all the lifesaving devices and moved to a private room. The doctor told us Dad would last twenty-four to forty-eight hours. Bracing ourselves for the inevitable as best we could, we spent the next two days by his side, falling into bed at night in total emotional exhaustion. The third day, Dad was still hanging on.

Day after day, I drove Mom to the hospital. Fifteen days passed. I was really stressed. I'd been away from home three weeks now. I was worried about my family, my business, my life. Dad had been in and out of a coma for days, and he seemed oblivious to my presence. As I drove into the parking lot, I talked to the higher power above, trying to negotiate a deal. Tears streamed down my face as I pulled into the parking space. I had to tell Dad I needed to go home to my family and work.

I walked into his room to find him sleeping with his arms folded across his chest. I looked down at his loving face and hands. This was the man who had supported me in everything I endeavored. This was the man who never missed a concert, athletic event, graduation or the birth of a baby. This was the man who had been there for me every day of my life. How could I even think about going home? He had walked through forty-four years with me. The least I could do was walk the last mile with him.

I held his hand and started humming. My dad loved music and had a beautiful tenor voice. He always sang to me as a child. He'd bounce into my room every morning to wake me. Enthusiastic and happy, he sang, in his most operatic tenor voice and to the tune of "Oh My Papa," these lyrics: "Oh my Suzanne, to me you are so wonderful!" He made sure it reached a decibel that not only woke me but half the neighborhood. I would usually put my pillow over my head and beg for mercy. What an awesome message he gave every morning before I went off to school and work. What a positive reinforcement his songs were.

Now it was my turn. I began humming "You Are My Sunshine," as it was a favorite of ours often sung around the family piano. When I finished, Dad didn't budge. His eyes remained shut. He didn't hear a thing. I started to cry.

Dad opened his eyes, "Oh Suzi, I'll never take your sunshine away." He closed his eyes and went back into that familiar deep sleep.

Five hours later, he died.

My dad was the sunshine in my life and continues to be so in spirit. There have been dark moments and days since he died, but I always look up and say, "Okay, Dad, send me some sunshine."

Without fail, the sun always comes out.

Suzanne Vaughan

Caregiver's Handbook

Pretty much all the honest truth-telling there is in the world today is done by children.

Oliver Wendell Holmes

I heard the sounds of car doors opening and shutting, and nine-year-old Ellen's eager hop-skippity. In the flick of an eyelash, she stood at the door, arms stretched wide. "Grandma, I've been missing you!" The radiance of that smile made me forget the punishing weight of relentless July heat.

Her arms locked around my waist, her head pressed against my chest.

I looked down. "New shoes?"

She nodded. "Fast ones," she said, then announced, "I came to give Grandpa a big hug."

Red flags whipped from my caregiver's antennae. For the be-zillionth time in the past three years, my frustration level shot off the chart. I needed a caregiving how-to book, where I could run my finger down the table of contents, point to a key word, flip to that page and read the answer. Should I let her see him?

I drew Ellen closer and gazed over her to meet my son's eyes. She'd seen her grandpa two days ago, but . . .

"He's much worse," I mouthed. "Seeing him might frighten her."

My son's gaze held steady. "She'll be all right, Mom. She needs to hug him."

I felt compelled to protect her. Would she store up nightmare images that frightened away memories of his healthy years?

And I felt just as compelled to protect my husband. Yesterday's words from our hospice nurse still echoed sharply inside me. "He needs to relax and let go," she'd advised. "Distractions now will disrupt the dying process."

How could I take responsibility for even a single-minute's extra suffering? Yet, how could I deny either of them a last hug? I teetered on the edge of denial and consent.

Where *was* that caregiver's handbook?

My son's arm circled my shoulders. "She'll be okay, Mom, I know."

My emotional teetering steadied. I nodded at Ellen, whose face glowed with expectation. "He's sleeping," I said, "but he'll wake when he knows you're there."

Tiptoeing into the bedroom, she gazed at the still, slight form beneath the covers. In seconds, she was on the bed beside him, arms gentle around his neck. He turned to her with a sun-and-stars smile that matched hers. "Hello, Ellen. How's my buddy?"

"I love you, Papa," she said.

"I love you, too."

She snuggled beside him, stroking his face. "I have new sneakers."

"They'll help you run faster," he said. His eyelids grew heavy.

My son signaled Ellen, and with a farewell pat on Grandpa's shoulder, she climbed down.

"Did I help him feel better, Grandma?"

"Yes, you did. Much better." I watched as he rolled again to the place where his body rested more at ease.

Leaving him, the three of us moved to the cool shade of the deck for ice cream bars.

"I *wish* he could get well," Ellen said. "But I'm glad I made him smile."

"Yes, and he gave you the best smile ever."

The previous week, she'd asked when he would get better. I'd tried to explain that he couldn't get well, that his body had used up all its strength. The cancer, I told her, was taking his body, but it could never take away who he really is—his sparkling smile, the light in his eyes, his love for her.

Looking back on the countless teams of caregivers— the teams shifting and changing with each new twist and turn, every team giving its all to his care—I saw that Ellen herself had been a constant. For the entire three years of his illness, her steel thread of caregiving never wavered. She brought a kind of caregiving no one else could offer, partly out of the innocence of childhood. There was more, though. She and her grandfather had always shared a special bond, but his illness had deepened their connection.

Since infancy, Ellen herself had been in and out of clinics, emergency rooms and hospitals, but the summer her grandpa underwent major surgery, she seemed to set aside her own fear of hospitals. During the month of his stay, she often rode the elevator to his fourth-floor room and blended into the sterile atmosphere with the nurses and doctors bustling in and out, the beeping monitors, the medicinal smells, the tubes and needles attached to his body. With a clinical interest, she inspected each object, asking how it would help Grandpa get better, the way she'd gotten better.

He explained, "I'm trying to be brave, just like you, Ellen."

How do you tell a child about dying? How do you tell her that soon Grandpa won't be with us?

How I yearned for that caregiver's book.

As she ate her ice cream bar, she said, "I'll miss him, Grandma. It makes me sad." After a moment, her brown eyes grew round. "Will he be an angel soon?"

"Yes, he'll be an angel watching over us even when we can't see him. And, he'll stay in our hearts always."

My son knew his little girl. She had needed to see her Grandpa one more time.

I thought about how as a teenager I'd felt hurt and left out when my parents kept me from seeing my dying grandmother. Now I'd nearly repeated history, trying to protect my own granddaughter.

Did her visit disrupt his dying process? Maybe. But her farewell touch gave a loving grandfather a last moment's earthly treasure. He, in turn, gave the gift of that moment back to her, to our son and to me.

Ellen didn't need a caregiver's handbook. She opened her heart and followed it.

Beverly Haley

When All Hope Is Lost

"Don't you know? There will never be a cure!" my teenage daughter screamed from the backseat of the car.

I steadied my hands on the steering wheel while Jenna continued to rant and rave. I tried to swallow the lump in my throat. Not finding a single word that could or would change the situation, I remained quiet and tears stung my eyes. *God, you have to help the scientists find a cure soon. My daughter is losing all hope.*

"It's just too hard! I'm tired of feeling sick! I'm tired of being tired! I'm sick and tired of being sick and tired!" Jenna sobbed from behind. "Mom, I just don't think I can do it anymore . . ." she said as her voiced faded off into silence.

Jenna's words cut deep, for I knew that without hope, her heart would break. Wishing that this conversation wasn't occurring on a freeway, I fought traffic and slowly made my way to the off-ramp, checking my rearview mirror only to see the penetrating look in Jenna's eyes as she stared back at me. The unnerving silence was only interrupted by the sound of my turn signal.

It had been twelve years since Jenna truly "felt good." For twelve years, she had lived courageously, fighting her chronic disease. I understood her feelings of defeat. I, too, was tired of daily watching my daughter tend to her catheter site, injecting herself with the proper medications and experiencing the unpredictable side effects. I, too, wanted to join her in screaming, "I'm sick and tired of you being sick and tired!"

Watching her in such emotional and physical pain made me ache all over. If only I could take her illness upon me, I'd give her my health and bear her infirmity. But I felt helpless not knowing how to console her.

I pulled into the first parking lot I could find. I parked the car, stepped out and crawled into the backseat, where Jenna lay motionless. I brushed her hair from her eyes, hoping she'd open them and look into mine. She didn't move. For five minutes, I just sat and held her, praying that God would renew her strength and will to live.

What does a mother say to her child who is living a nightmare, praying that she'd someday soon wake up and it would be over? What words could bring comfort when all hope is lost?

Not knowing the answers, I spoke from my heart, hoping to reach Jenna's. "Jenna, look at me. I need to know that you really understand what I am about to say."

She turned her head towards me and opened her eyes. Immediately, she began to repeat her words of hopelessness. Gently, I placed my finger against her lips.

"Honey, today you're tired and you've lost all hope. Today, you can rest in my arms and let me hope for you. You can be assured that my hope is endless and so is my love."

"Mom," Jenna interrupted me, smiling slightly. "If you can hope for me, I guess I can too." She draped her arms around me. "Tell me again, Mom, that your hope is forever."

"It's forever, baby. My hope is forever."

Janet Lynn Mitchell

Daddy's Little Girl

*You are the bows from which your children are
as living arrows sent forth.*

Kahlil Gibran

When I accepted a new nursing home patient, my hospice volunteer coordinator said, "This patient really needs a caregiver who will help him cope with his depression. I hope you can reach Allen."

I was surprised at his name. Allen. My father's name.

I glanced over at him. Even from across the room, his body looked tense. Walking to his bedside, I looked down on his sleeping face, and froze. I was looking at my father. I couldn't look away. His face had the same distinctive features, with weathered skin stretched over strong jaws and cheekbones. His hair was gray and white, long enough to wave. The resemblance was uncanny.

Common sense took hold, making me admit this was a different Allen. Dad had died years ago, but I had stubbornly held on to the guilt in me.

Looking down at Allen's hands, emotions assaulted me yet again. Unbelievable! The same golfer's hands as Dad's;

muscular with sun-worn, stubby fingers. I reached out to touch him but stopped short. I could have sworn I saw the Masonic ring Dad always wore.

Brushing away tears, I choked on the word, "Allen." I almost said Daddy. Clearing my throat, and getting back in control, I repeated clearly, "Allen." His eyes opened immediately, as though he'd been expecting me. Taking his hand in mine, I smiled into his beautiful eyes. "Well," I said, "I already know what I'll call you—Old Blue Eyes." He grinned, and his wide eyes welled to the brim. As I'd hoped, the phrase "Old Blue Eyes" was meaningful to him, he being one who'd lived through the 'sentimental journey' years of Frank Sinatra and his music.

I introduced myself, explaining that I'd visit him often if he'd like. Keeping a strong grip on my hand, his eyes searched mine and he nodded.

During the first visits, I needed to do most of the talking. Allen was in the advanced stages of Parkinson's disease, which made his voice soft and low, and difficult to understand. But we came to sense what each other meant by using our own shorthand of words. I knew he needed to recall the good times of his life. Music became our bond. I took my tape recorder with a selection of cassettes—including the Sinatra favorites and other oldies—guaranteed to evoke emotions. "Fly Me to the Moon" and "One for My Baby" performed their magic. As we reminisced, memories decorated the room. It became a dance floor, a candlelight dinner or a bus station to see a loved one off to war. When I played "Near You," Allen's eyes overflowed. Choking and trying hard to swallow, he said, "My girl and I . . . we danced . . . hotel ballroom . . . proposed." His voice drifted off.

Although the music brought tears, it also brought emotions out in the open, where they could be felt and shared, not buried or denied. His depression eased.

Because of his strong resemblance to my father, spending time with Allen satisfied my intense yearning to be with my dad again. Over the weeks, we became good friends, yet I sensed there was some deep, unlabeled ache within him. "Are you afraid to remember too much?" I asked.

He shook his head and muttered, "No, no one lets me . . . here. I'll tell . . . about my daughter . . . but not today."

Some days were pure joy, as the music brought fun flashbacks. We laughed and joked as we tried to remember the words of songs that triggered our memories.

One day, I played a mixed cassette of titles. When one song began, I quickly glanced at Allen to see if we were sharing the same impact. We were. "Daddy's Little Girl." The endearing words proclaimed the loving connection between father and daughter.

"I've loved this song my whole life," I said.

"Me too," he whispered.

I pulled my chair closer, took Allen's hand, and his tormenting story poured out. His daughter, a young woman who while in her teens, had been the victim of a long, painful illness. Months of heartbreak and dedicated caring vanished when she abruptly died while he was away on a business trip. As he confessed unnecessary guilt, it echoed mine. Late in my father's terminal illness, after years of separation, we'd come together and had shared several memorable evenings forgiving each other and renewing our love. But then I felt guilty when I hadn't been there for his last moments.

Allen and I talked through the grief we had both shelved for so long. As we shared, what he heard were a daughter's words. What I heard was a father's love.

Ruth Hancock

Saving Him

It is one of the most beautiful compensations of this life that no man can sincerely try to help another without helping himself.

William Shakespeare

BOYS HOME, read the sign over the entrance. Twenty years ago, I entered this one-hundred-year-old orphanage to install wood-burning stoves in the dormitories so the children could have heat for the winter. Now, on this hot summer day, my wife, Judy, and I were coming to meet her friend Chelsey, who hoped I'd be a surrogate parent to one of the boys there.

As we walked around the grounds, I noticed the old orphanage had really lost its luster. In the old gymnasium building, I could hardly believe it when the temperature was over one-hundred degrees! The air conditioner had given out many years ago, and there simply were not enough funds to have it replaced or repaired. Yet, the boys were playing basketball as if they hadn't a care in the world. As we stepped back out into the ninety-eight-degree weather, it felt almost cool.

"Roger, this is the young man I told you about," said Chelsey.

"Hi, my name is Bill." The fourteen-year-old extended his hand. His limp handshake felt like a rubber glove full of pudding. "Thank you for coming to visit my home."

"Well, I am very glad to be here."

"Miss Chelsey, can we show them our kitchen and where we eat our food?" asked Bill.

"Maybe some other time," she told him. He smiled, then turned and walked away. I watched him as he slowly disappeared around the corner of the building, his shoulders and head down. I knew very well what the young man wanted to show me—the only thing he truly owned, the chair where he ate his meals. I knew because that was the only thing I could ever call my own when I lived in an orphanage.

Chelsey said, "That is one of the nicest kids I have ever known. He has absolutely no one on the face of the Earth except himself."

I excused myself and walked into the bathroom. I locked the door behind me and bent forward on the sink. For about a minute, I slowly looked at every wrinkle and sag on my face, yet, it was still the face of that same little boy I was when I lived in my orphanage, almost forty-five years ago.

I groaned, "Roger, I don't know if you can do this again."

Then, I placed my right hand into my left hand and shook it. It was a bit firmer than that of young Bill's, but it still lacked the feeling of someone who felt they were worth loving.

Biting my lip, I stared deep into my own eyes and said to myself, "Let's go save that boy."

From out of nowhere came a great big, wonderful smile.

Let there be no doubt that when we save a child, in the process we may also save ourselves.

Roger Dean Kiser, Sr.

In the Sack

"You want to go *where*, Grandma?"

"You heard me. Here. Right here." She pointed.

"*Here?* Are you *sure?*"

"Here." Grandma Vic was adamant.

With a sigh, Jenna shrugged the strap of her purse higher on her shoulder as she steered the wheelchair up the mall ramp. She turned toward the store Grandma indicated, but she paused at the entrance.

"Grandma, you *do* understand what they sell here, don't you?"

"I'm neither blind nor stupid, dear. And, contrary to what you might be thinking, I still have all my marbles. I know exactly what I'm doing." Victoria—Grandma Vic— took a deep, audible breath, cocked her silvered head even higher and ordered, "Now, push me in."

Jenna shook her head in dismay. In all the years she'd cared for her grandparents, run their errands and taken them on excursions, nothing had prepared her for this demand. Nothing. It was downright embarrassing. Grandma was asking too much of her this time. What would people think? What if they saw someone they knew? This was . . . awkward.

She sighed again then wheeled her stubborn grandma right into . . . Frederick's of Hollywood, but Jenna stalled just inside the door, her own jaw dragging the floor.

While her arms hung limp at her sides, Jenna absorbed the displays of intimate apparel. She hadn't been in Frederick's in a few years herself. A lot had changed. *A lot.* Everything was skimpier. More transparent. More daring. Why, some might even call it obscene! She should never have agreed to escort an elderly . . .

It was several moments before she realized that Grandma Vic had impatiently self-propelled the wheelchair to a mannequin. She studied the risqué lingerie.

"Hmm. That's the new-fangled underwear? Why, I've got Band-Aids that cover more," Grandma Vic "tsked" with an ornery grin into Jenna's stunned face. "I want to see it all—everything in the store."

"Grandma Vic . . . " Jenna was amazed to find a blush staining her own thirty-three-year-old cheeks.

"All of it, dear."

Row after sexy row, rack after sensuous rack, the two toured the store, Grandma delivering more spicy one-liners than a standup comic.

"A 'thong?' How odd. We used to wear those on our feet!

"Bustiers? They look as painful as my mother's corset. Of course, hers didn't come in leather . . . or leopard skin.

"Why would they call it a teddy? The trim doesn't look like bear fur to me.

"Flavored lotions and edible undies? Why don't they just print up a menu?"

Jenna flinched. Customers grinned. Sales clerks eyed them doubtfully. At last, Jenna leaned into Grandma's face and looked her squarely in the eyes. "Now, are you ready to tell me what this is all about?"

"Jenna, you've always been so good to tend to our

needs. Shopping, chauffeuring, even putting up the Christmas tree so we can celebrate the holidays. You're the only one in the family I could trust with this errand."

Grandma's chin sank a little further onto her ample bosom and she sighed. After a thoughtful silence, she spoke low and falteringly into her lap.

"Our sixty-fifth wedding anniversary is just around the corner. I want to surprise Grampa. For just a few hours, I want to be young and whole again. Or, at least, *look* that way. For Grampa. For . . . me."

Grandma glanced up with new determination. "I might be old and . . . broken . . . but I'm not dead. I need a new nightie, something . . . suggestive . . . and I want to buy it here. At Frederick's."

Jenna bit her lip—not in vexation, not in embarrassment, certainly not to stifle a giggle—to prevent it from trembling and hinting at the tears that threatened.

"Why, you old romantic!" She hugged Grandma. "I guess it's never too late to re-invent love."

Without hesitation, Jenna pushed the chrome wheelchair to a display of naughty nightwear and watched a pair of aged, corded hands lovingly caress diaphanous baby dolls, sheer chemises, and velvet camisoles.

"This one." Grandma's dove-gray eyes sparkled.

With a conspiratorial smile, the middle-aged salesclerk folded the full-length, spaghetti-strapped nightgown, rang up the sale and complimented them on their choice. As Jenna steered her out the door and through the mall, Grandma Vic wore a smug look. And she made certain the sack from Frederick's of Hollywood perched prominently on her lap. When shoppers turned to stare, she winked devilishly. "Let them guess—this Victoria's not keeping anything secret!"

Carol McAdoo Rehme

Lunch with Grandma

Laughter is the sun that drives winter from the human face.

Victor Hugo

Although uncertain, unprepared and unaware of the challenges of Alzheimer's disease, I headed to Charlotte, North Carolina, to help Mom care for Grandma.

With my usual upbeat, positive attitude, I arose the first morning full of enthusiasm and knowing exactly what to do, or so I thought. Before my first cup of coffee, I entered the bathroom to find Grandmother attempting to brush her teeth with a razor! Shocked and near hysterics, I yelled for Mother while trying to retrieve the razor without hurting Grandmother or myself. Mom quietly walked into the room, took the razor with a smile, and what looked like an invisible tear. Tears were many as the day went on. The "tough one," as I had been called, had met her match.

As the days passed, Mom and I realized that Grandmother did things born of habit. So we began playing on her habits—messing up the living room so she could straighten it up again and again, assigning her the chore of sweeping the porch, having her wash unbreakable plates and cups as I dried them and put them away.

Convinced I could handle any situation with ease, not to mention that Mother was impressed with my ability to keep Grandma busy, my confidence grew. So I decided to take Grandma to lunch, just the two of us. Against Mother's better judgment, I planned to take Grandma to a steakhouse with a salad bar, so she could pick out what *she* wanted to eat.

Riding to the restaurant was no problem; she just loved these new-fangled vehicles. Happily, we entered the steakhouse, got our plates and ventured to the salad bar. But Grandmother didn't know what anything was, not even a roll. She refused to eat anything except the pretty "red stuff" that wiggled. Finally, with only gelatin on her plate, we sat down and had a wonderful lunch. She swirled the good red stuff around in her mouth, thoroughly enjoying herself.

All of a sudden, without warning, she grabbed my arm and yanked me to the floor, pulling me under the table. I was too shocked to scream or I would have. I took her arm and gently coaxed her to stand, but she clutched my arms with a strength I couldn't imagine and jerked me back to the floor. "Indians!" she cried out in a hushed tone. "We must escape!"

Trying desperately to understand, I said, "Where are the Indians?"

Frightened, she pointed to a group of people that had just entered the restaurant. Then, she started crawling on the floor, dragging her purse behind and motioning me to follow her. I knelt still.

"Come on!" she commanded, her irritation and my embarrassment mounting.

What the heck, I thought, swallowing any pride I had left.

I crept behind her between and under empty tables, making our way through the great Wild West toward the salad bar. Once we arrived safely to our "cover," she pulled me toward her and said, "That way, to the door! We can make it," she said. "Be brave!"

Off we went at a fast crawl, she in her dress, me in cut-off blue jeans, both of us dragging a purse and turning our heads from side to side. She was looking for danger, and I was looking to see who was staring. Just as we neared the door, the manager came from behind the counter. Terrified, Grandma flung herself over my body to protect me.

The manager gazed down at the two of us piled in a heap on the floor and asked, "Can I help you ladies?"

I burst out laughing. Grandma pulled herself up and bent over to help me, since I was laughing so hard I couldn't stand. She brushed me off and asked me, "Are you okay, honey?"

The confused manager asked the obvious question. "Is anything wrong?"

"Of course, everything is quite all right," Grandmother said, "now that you're here, Marshall Dillon."

With tears of hysterical laughter streaming down my face, Grandmother pulled me along to the door. Once she got there, she turned back to the manager and said, "I'm sorry sir, we forgot to pay." She took a dime out of her purse and placed it on the counter.

"Thank you, ma'am," he said and gave her a big smile.

By now, I was laughing so hard I could hardly breathe. My Grandmother gripped my arm and jerked me toward the door. "We have to get out of here, Teri," she said. "You're embarrassing me."

Teri Batts

Too Late

I like the laughter that opens the lips and the heart, that shows at the same time, pearls of the soul.

Victor Hugo

My ninety-year-old mom, Bert, is in the late stages of Alzheimer's disease and has been in a nursing home for twelve years.

I am her only family, and I love being with her as much as I can. We find meaningful, loving times together. I sing to her. We hug. We speak primarily through touch. Once a fun, witty woman, now she rarely has lucid moments when we can communicate. I am simply that "nice lady." She cannot move herself at all. Her hands are atrophied, and the only movement of her body is when the nurses turn her in bed every two hours.

One day, an aide went to check on my mother, who had been sleeping. She was shocked to find Mom on the floor, with no apparent injury, still asleep and snoring. The aide called to the nurse, "Bert has fallen out of bed!" The nurse immediately headed to her room saying, "Bert doesn't move. She doesn't roll. This can't be."

Even when in the room, looking at my mother on the floor, she was amazed and repeated, "This can't be! Bert doesn't move or roll."

The aide wondered out loud, "Maybe we should pull up the bed rails."

From my mother came, "Don't you think it's a little late for that now?"

Mom grinned. The staff burst into laughter.

Esther Copeland

2

ON LOVE

And now abide in faith, hope, love, these three; but the greatest of these is love.

1 Corinthians 13:13

Love in the Land of Dementia

So ought men to love their wives as their own bodies. He that loveth his wife loveth himself.

Ephesians 5:28

"There's my man," my mother says to the nurse, beaming at my father. He has been out of the room for five minutes, but Mom greets him like it has been days.

Shyly, my father comes up to her and takes her hand. They look at each other.

"Fifty-two years married," my father tells the nurse as she checks the IV.

She shakes her head. "And still in love," she marvels. She adjusts her blond ponytail, pulls the stethoscope out of the pocket of her smock and leans over to listen to Mom's heart. "Your main man, huh?" she says to Mom.

"Yes." Mom smiles, then makes a noise right out of a Donald Duck cartoon. Then, Mom picks up a corner of her hospital gown and tugs at it. She pleats it into little sections and tugs again. "Well you so and so," she says to the gown. "If you aren't going to cooperate, you can't come with me."

I hand a blanket to mom. "Here," I say. She stares into the blanket like there's a child cradled inside. "What a sweet baby," she says. "I love you, baby."

I look at Dad, and he shrugs and smiles.

With Mom's advancing Alzheimer's, much has been lost. Rising up and sitting down are complicated events of gymnastic proportion. All foodstuffs, except for chocolate, which has always been Mom's favorite, are foreign substances. Dressing, conversing, bathing, teeth brushing—all the events of everyday life are neatly erased from Mom's scope.

But when my dad walks in, for a moment she remembers this is her husband. For those few seconds, happiness floods her.

"I wish I had a relationship like you two have," the evening nurse says wistfully. She's a thin, vigorous brunette who's already been through two husbands, she tells us as she gently wraps the blood pressure cuff around Mom's arm. "Neither one of them was worth the polish on my toenails," she says.

My parents don't have the perfect romance. Most of the time, Mom doesn't know Dad's there. Most of the time, he has to stand right in front of her to talk. Most of the time, Mom's her own entertainment center, bouncing off his words but not truly interacting with him.

But when he first enters the room, light fills her face. Her eyes are luminous, and her silvery hair seems to glow. The distracted, anxious look leaves her, and there's an angelic purity to her expression. For that moment, she is present and filled only with love.

All who see this—the med tech, the certified nurse's aide, the registered nurse, the lab tech, the transportation aide, the social worker—look with awe and envy. They coo and sigh. "Ahhh," they murmur. "That's the way it's supposed to be."

Even the doctor looks up from his clipboard, seemingly perplexed. When he continues his charting, I wonder if he will write, "Patient exhibits symptoms of deep dementia and signs of true love." I wonder how far apart these two conditions are.

When she was my age, my mother used to say, "I want to die if I lose my mind." According to her diagnosis, my mother has officially "lost her mind." She came to the hospital from a nursing home. The "worst," as she then envisioned it, has happened.

This disease is devastating for all of us, and our hearts are torn apart by the living loss of this great woman. But her greatness remains in this simple gift she shows us: When all the ordinary things are gone, true spirit can still remain. Love doesn't necessarily conquer anything or all, but it can outlast the rational parts of life.

Tomorrow, everything could change. Dad could walk in and Mom might not ever look up from her pleating, plucking and picking. She might stare at him like she sometimes stares at me, knowing he's a nice person, but not knowing just who he is.

But we no longer think of tomorrow. We are happy with the fact that Mom laughs, even if it's at a bowl of vanilla pudding. We are thrilled with the fact that she talks, even if she's addressing invisible children in a language that makes pig Latin seem scholarly. And we are awed by the fact that she loves.

"So where's your husband?" the nurse's aide says as she organizes Mom's dinner tray.

Mom doesn't answer. She examines the pink-plastic arm bracelet on her left wrist.

"Let's scoot up in the bed," the aide says. Mom doesn't move. She fiddles with the plastic.

Dad walks into the room and stops in front of the bed. Mom ceases her fiddling. She looks at him and smiles.

"My husband," she says in an awestruck voice. "My husband's here," she says to the nurse and to me.

"That's right," Dad says. I hear the joy and anguish in his voice. I hear the depth of his grief and the strength of his love.

Deborah Shouse

Love's Own Language

Love is never lost. If not reciprocated it will flow back and soften and purify the heart.

Washington Irving

It had been a long, tiring day caring for my husband, who suffered from Alzheimer's disease, and when he spit the pill out, I was upset and said in an unkind voice, "Why did you do that?"

I got down on the floor to look for the pill and heard him softly say, "But that's what you told me to do, isn't it?"

I began to cry. How could I have been so cross with him, when he had done exactly what he understood me to say? The doctor had told me that he might begin processing language in reverse; that his "yes" could be "no," and a "no" could be "yes." Obviously, when I asked him to swallow the pill, he had understood me to say just the opposite.

When he saw me crying, he reached out to me. "Don't cry. Come here," which caused me to cry even harder. Moving over by his wheelchair, I put my head on his knee, and he patted my shoulder.

Although he didn't understand my asking him to swallow the pill, he did understand my distress and pain, and in spite of all the confusion and damage the disease had done to his mind, his love caused him to reach out to comfort me.

Eventually, the disease left him unable to speak, except for an occasional word here and there. And even when he could not express in words what he was thinking, in his own way he still communicated. When I did something to make him more comfortable, he would look at me with a soft expression in his eyes, acknowledging what I had done. When I straightened the bedclothes or changed his gown, he would take hold of my hand and caress it.

These gestures spoke to me as eloquently as if he had spoken out loud, proving where there is love, there will never be an insurmountable language barrier.

Dorothy Snyder

Dear Precious Husband

If ever two were one, then surely we. If ever man were loved by wife, then thee.

Anne Bradstreet

God gave me the greatest and most unique treasure when I married you. Little did we know what lay ahead those twenty-one years ago when we said, ". . . for better, or worse, in sickness and in health." Multiple sclerosis has become an all-too familiar term in our lives. What began as simple fatigue and a slight limp became over the years a wheelchair, long visits to the doctor, and surgeries to help spasticity and bladder problems. Thank you for traveling this unpredictable road with me and loving me despite the tremendous costs. Our children and our friends look at you and see an unselfish and giving child of God. Many times, I have cried when I hear the song "You Are the Wind Beneath My Wings," because it describes what you are to me. I have been blessed in so many ways, and the greatest blessing is you.

"Caregiver" is a word that was foreign to me when I was young. Growing up and being independent was my goal. I flourished in school and in athletics. I was captain of my high school tennis team, third in my class and had hopes of a career in physical therapy. Then, in college, I met you in Greek class, of all places. We began dating and learning about each other, and before long we made our vows in a lovely garden wedding, with birds singing as the sun set by the lake. We shared days of playing golf together, tennis, even basketball at night, with car lights illuminating the court. When our first child was born, we loved being parents.

When I awoke with double vision just months after our wedding, I called my brother-in-law, who is an internist. He suggested a neurologist, and I awkwardly began dialing. We were young, naive newlyweds hearing the words "demyelinating disease" for the first time. It wasn't until my brother-in-law, who had talked to the doctor, told us that it was probably multiple sclerosis, did I really understand. I was stunned, not believing what I heard. I had only known one guy with multiple sclerosis. He lived in a nursing home, hardly able to speak, unable to walk and with little hope to go on. So my first reaction was to move back home with my mom, send you back home to yours and forget we were ever married. Solidly grounded in God's word and in your commitment to our marriage, you said we would pray, forge ahead and make it.

Now that I've had multiple sclerosis for twenty-one years, my admiration for you has grown more than words can express. My daily needs are now your daily activities: stretching my legs, putting on my socks and clothes, lifting me into my electric wheelchair, getting my meds, serving my breakfast and taking the kids to school. You do these things without complaint, without hesitation and with consistent dedication. At night, the routine begins again, only backward. Then, after putting on my nighttime ankle brace, you get me into bed. During the night, you awaken to my whisper and tend to my needs.

Holly Baker

Banishing Cancer from the Bedroom

Life is a flower for which love is the honey.

Victor Hugo

"It's like an elephant in the bedroom," my husband, Rudy, said of his advanced prostate cancer. "We can't get rid of it."

"Yes we can," I said, with a bravado I didn't feel. "Let's make a pact. We won't let this cancer consume us. You're still Rudy, my loving husband," *not Rudy the cancer patient,* I thought. *But how do we kick the intrusive cancer elephant out of the bedroom?* Months of fatigue weighed heavily on my shoulders, dragging me down. Sometimes I felt so exhausted I could hardly move my feet.

Rudy's cancer had spread to his bones, causing excruciating pain that lessened when he lay on our queen-size bed, propped against pillows piled at his back. He raised his left hand, his wedding ring dangling loosely. I clasped his pale hand in both of mine. Rudy had played the violin with that hand as a child; he was sensitive and artistic. But now, his poetic sense of joy was being beaten down. I knew it was up to me to keep this cancer elephant from dominating our lives and destroying our marriage.

One day before lunch, I went out to our yard. I looked up at the bright late-summer sky with its wisps of clouds. Silently, I prayed for the strength to help us both preserve the love we felt for each other. *God, I prayed, please don't let this illness destroy our marriage.* I lowered my eyes. There was a delicate dark-red rosebud just beginning to open by our front walkway. It looked so fragile, just like our love. I picked it and put it in a small glass vase on Rudy's lunch tray. He rarely ate, and coaxing him had been so hard.

"Oh, what a lovely rosebud," he said. "Look how it's just starting to open. It looks like a baby's mouth." Rudy smiled for the first time in days. He lifted the small vase to his nose. Since chemotherapy had dulled Rudy's sense of smell, I didn't know whether he could catch the scent of the fragile flower. But he seemed to absorb its presence in some way of his own.

Taking small, precise bites, he ate more lunch than usual. When he finished, I set the little rosebud on his tray table and put the food tray on the dresser instead of taking it to the kitchen. Dirty dishes could always wait.

I stretched out beside Rudy on the bed, and we held hands as I stroked his head.

The pain that often dominated his arms and legs seemed to have receded as he rested. I lay there feeling the warmth of his body next to mine, listening to him breathing quietly. I felt the tension leaving my shoulders; I let myself go limp. I closed my eyes, and we both slept, holding hands.

That night, before I brought Rudy his dinner, I went back out to the yard, walking with more energy, looking for flowers. I thought as I looked around the yard, *What will I find to make him smile?* The bright-yellow heads of marigolds shone in the slanting afternoon light. I selected one. I perceived it to be the color of hope, because it had the brilliance of the sun.

When I took Rudy his dinner tray, it had a small glass with the yellow marigold on it.

"Oh," he said, "look how cheerful it is. Just like a little sunbeam." He chuckled. I hadn't heard Rudy chuckle in weeks, although before, he had loved to laugh. Now I laughed with him. "Yes," I said, "it's greeting you." He raised the little glass to his nose; I wondered if he caught the pungent scent of the marigold, so much stronger than the rose.

"This is good applesauce," he said, consuming the last bite. I set the marigold on his tray table next to the rosebud and put his dinner tray aside on the dresser. Again, I lay down next to him on the bed, stroked his forehead and held his hand. The bedroom was very quiet. Nothing intruded on our togetherness. I could hear nothing but Rudy's even breathing. I felt his warmth and nearness. Again, we both fell into a peaceful sleep.

From then on, Rudy's breakfast, lunch and dinner trays always held a flower or a small sprig of fresh holly or greenery. His anticipation turned his mealtimes into a happy ritual. It became our intimate game. I loved to go hunting for just the right bloom from our yard. I loved to see the light in his eyes as he saw the blossoms of hope I brought him with his food. I loved hearing his comments. "Oh," he might say, "just look at the shade of orange of that leaf. It flames like a sunset."

Yes, we did banish the elephant from the bedroom . . . with flowers. And I learned that even the elephant of terminal cancer can't stomp out love.

Peggy Eastman

Level the Playing Field

Next to a good soul-stirring prayer, is a good laugh.

Samuel Mutchmore

My husband, Terry, had performed the 6:00 A.M. and midnight wet-to-dry dressings on my abdomen and chest for several months. I battled post-operative gangrene following mastectomies and reconstruction surgery six months earlier. What was supposed to be an eight-day hospital stay and single surgery had turned into four surgeries, three months in the hospital, and then a nursing home because of aggressive infections and related complications. Now, visiting nurses came to our home twice each day while Terry was at work.

I knew living with me had not been a picnic. My pain and immobility kept me housebound and frustrated. I'm sure Terry wondered why he pulled so many strings to get me out of the nursing home early.

One night, we had an argument. It wasn't over anything significant, but it was the first since the surgeries. By bedtime, we had yet to make up. Terry still had the complicated dressing changes to complete. He had no medical training, but the nurses had taught him how to clean and dress the wounds that covered my front from hip to armpit.

Terry helped me roll onto my side. I sensed the tension in the air and still felt hurt from our disagreement. I didn't know how he felt, because he is quiet when upset. That night was no different.

I looked up at him and said, "This isn't fair. I feel too vulnerable here with nothing on while you take care of my wounds when you're still mad at me."

He walked away. A few minutes later he returned and stood in front of me, still silent with a half-smile on his face. He was stark naked.

"Terry, what are you doing?" I shrieked with laughter.

"Just leveling the playing field," he smirked—then tenderly changed my dressing.

Linda S. Lee

Kite Season

*Love is all we have, the only way we can help
the other.*

Euripides

"Why don't you just grab hold of my arms and stand
up?"

My wife looked up from where she lay on the floor, her
eyes filling with tears of anger and frustration. "Don't you
think if I could do that I would've done it half an hour
ago?"

She crumbled.

Before my eyes I saw her will leave her, like a kite string
falling to the earth after being snapped by an angry gust
of wind.

My own feelings of impotence broke the calm. I grew
furious.

"Don't you give up on me, Laura! Don't you dare give
up on me!" The house echoed with my anger. I flushed,
embarrassed at my own outburst. I felt the ache begin in
my chest, that tightness that precedes tears. No, I would
not fall apart. She needed strength, not a wet Kleenex. I

drew in a deep breath and turned away, wiping my eyes with the knuckles of my clenched fist.

"Why are you mad at me? What did I do? You don't know what this is like, Bret. To know I've ruined your life, ruined the kids' lives, I've . . ."

"Let's not get into the self-pity thing, honey. I hate it when you do that."

"It's not self-pity," she sobbed. "It's reality. Look at this," she waved a limp hand around from side to side. "I'm on the bathroom floor half-naked, and I have to call you home from work to help me up. Your job is on the line, and I can't even go to the bathroom by myself. Now, tell me I'm not ruining your life!"

I swallowed hard. There was no easy answer to this. The reality was here, all around me: the crumpled and balled-up floor rugs, which she had used in vain attempts to regain her footing; the shampoos and conditioners scattered on the bottom of the tub; the broken towel bar that had betrayed her and caused this fall. Seeing the towel bar stung me. I stared at it with guilt. I had meant to replace it with a sturdier grab bar designed for just such circumstances, but I hadn't. I had just been too tired. Now . . . here we were. Stupid, stupid, stupid. There's just no time to be tired in this household. Now, it was my turn to throw the pity party.

It was true, in a sense. Not that she was ruining my life, certainly not that. The multiple sclerosis was ruining our life together. I hated it, this disease that turned our lives into a daily hell. What had we done to deserve this? What unfeeling god had pointed its finger in our direction? Why us? Why me? Sure, I could choose to walk away from it all. The thought had even crossed my mind occasionally. Statistically, I'm in the minority among men. It seems my gender is easily discouraged when faced with an unwelcome guest such as this. Who would want a guaranteed life of turmoil? Something in me won't let me walk away, though. We've come too far, loved too much and too well. No, this woman on the floor before me deserved better. True, she wasn't the woman I had run with through Golden Gate Park. Not the woman serving cocktails at the Comedy Club in Long Beach, where this lonely sailor had caught her eye. Yet, she was. It's hard to explain. This woman still had the same wry sense of humor, the same love of old movies, the same gleam in her eyes. She had changed, yes. But, so much of her was still there, and she shared it with me every day.

"Honey, we're where we are. That's all," I answered. "You're not the reason life sucks. You're one of the bright spots. You're the reason I go on. You haven't ruined my life. M.S. has caused us some problems but nothing that warrants . . .," I spread my hands out helplessly, "this."

She looked at me for a long while, not saying a word. It seemed like forever in that small, unventilated bathroom. I had an aching back, quivering arms, mushy legs, sweat-soaked clothes, and still, she looked at me. My wife. The woman I had sworn to love, honor and cherish in sickness and in health. There had been a lot more of the former than the latter. I tried to read her thoughts from the expressions on her face. I saw hurt. I saw anger and a sense of futility. But then, I saw her soften. She seemed to be thinking much the same thoughts as I was. Maybe not the specifics. Maybe she was thinking of our walks along North Beach or Chinatown, or about all those wonderful times before multiple sclerosis.

Maybe she was thinking of times more recent. That was entirely possible—there were many. Sure, spur-of-the-moment outings were a thing of the past. But the spark was still there. The fun was still there. We still laugh at the same jokes, and I still screw up the same meals, try as I may to get them right. Our lives have changed irrevocably, but the warmth remains. These things, no doubt, were what she was thinking.

"Honey, tell me you still love me," she pleaded.

My heart skipped. Yes! "Yes, I do. I love you more than ever. You know that, don't you?"

"Yes, I guess I do. I don't know why, but you do." She looked up at me, still hurt, still weak, but with a new determination. "Well, let's do this. Where do you want me?"

I grinned and motioned to the bedroom. "Well . . ."

She smiled back and slapped my leg. "You've got a one-track mind, mister!" She laughed. It sounded like a song to me. "How 'bout a rain check on that one?"

"Deal!"

The kite was again dancing in the breeze.

B.R. Wright

A Hero for the Books

The heart of him who truly loves is a paradise on earth: he has God in himself, for God is love.
Abbe Hugo Felicite de Lamennais

His grin and twinkling eyes were the first thing I noticed. I was a regular at the public library and had seen librarians come and go like Heinz goes through tomatoes, but this guy was different. He talked to patrons like they were special and the most important people ever to grace the earth. It didn't take many visits to feel like we were old friends, and trips to the library became social events.

Sharing New York humor made for some belly-grabbing laughs; Mark's deadpan quips made tears roll down my face. I never tired of leaning against the front desk to hear his latest spin on some inane happening, which only he could make into a comedy routine. My book returns were notoriously overdue, but it was so much fun to visit with Mark that promptness became my habit.

Over time, though, Mark seemed tired. He would rub his eyes while in the middle of a story, and his quips weren't as frequent. Yet, he never lost his smile and always made a point of asking about my family. We still discussed books and motorcycles and religion, but I could tell something was wrong in his life. I couldn't just blurt out, "What's wrong?" based solely on a gut feeling. Or, could I?

It was during one of our chitchats that Mark let slip that he had taken his wife to the doctor. Not wanting to lose the opportunity, I pursued the subject. What did he mean by sick?

"ALS, Lou Gehrig's disease," he replied. His answer shoved me into the proverbial brick wall. As a nurse, I had seen the destruction wrought by the disease and knew there was no cure. For once in my life, I was speechless.

Heartbroken for his situation, I gently pressed him for more details. He was willing to talk, and talk he did. His words gushed like water from a crack in a dam, flowing until there was nothing left. He had kept his secret well hidden behind the jokes, the stories, the exchange of wit, but he couldn't mask the pain any longer. The lump in my throat prevented any reply. The tears in my eyes reflected his.

The debilitating disease was diagnosed shortly after their second child was born. Mark and his wife were sucked into the quicksand of illness in the prime of their lives.

They were fast-forwarded through the marriage experiences, living out their vows "in sickness and in health." While other young mothers taught their babies to speak, their little boy translated his mother's increasingly slurred speech. She was now at the point where one blink of the eye meant "yes," two blinks, "no."

After working all day, Mark rushed home to oversee homework, prepare dinner and drive the children to their activities. He survived his first shopping trip with his pre-teen daughter, and, when their son was old enough to play ball, he purchased a van so his wife's wheelchair could be rolled into it. As long as she had breath in her body, she was determined to see every game. She loved being a mother.

When Mark exhausted his monologue, he poignantly added, "Did you know we both love the beach? One of our favorite things to do together was to sit on the sand at sunset. We'll never be able to do that again." Now, their dates were trips to the hospital during bouts of pneumonia or wild-goose chases to doctors, hoping for a new solution.

On subsequent visits, I learned how draining the responsibilities of caring for a spouse with ALS are. After carrying her into the bathroom and preparing her for bed, Mark then wakes up at least once every hour to turn his wife so she doesn't choke. The muscle activity in her body has diminished, and she has to be physically lifted, rolled over, suctioned and repositioned. He gently rubs her legs to ease the pain, and he whispers in her ear as he wedges pillows around her. A little smile peeks up at him in gratitude, and they drift off for a few minutes sleep, until the routine is repeated. He is up at dawn to send the children off to school, greet the aide and leave for work at the library.

It's been a gift to become a part of his life, to witness the incredible bond of a man's love for a woman. His commitment to her shines like a beacon in a dark world where marriage is devalued. He is a testimony to what men and women are called to do in their lives—to love unconditionally, selflessly and without end.

A lesson that's long overdue.

Irene Budzynski

Traveling with Visitors

He shall give his angels charge concerning thee: and in their hands they shall bear thee up, lest at any time thou dash thy foot against a stone.

Matthew 4:6

My mother's face was illuminated, free of signs of anxiety or pain. Her eyes were wide open and brilliantly clear, their lids no longer shuttering from acute spasms of pain. A wonderful, bubbling laughter spilled forth from her lips while she conversed with her visitor.

Standing unseen in the doorway of her bedroom, I peered silently at the miraculous transformation in my terminally ill mother, watching her wait patiently for a reply from her visitor then continue with her animated words and laughter. My mother was quite lucid, and her aphasia (difficult speech) improved when she spoke with her visitor.

This wasn't the first time I'd noticed this strange, baffling phenomenon. Physically, her body lay in a hospital bed in my home, ravaged by breast cancer, which spread to her bones, brain and other organs. She required complete care for every daily need, which I provided with the help of hospice. But I knew she was slowly traveling away from this physical earth, preparing to take her final journey. It had started the day she called me into her room with a voice that was coherent and clear as a bell. "Claire, tell that man to move away from the television. I can't see my soaps."

I, of course, saw no one, but my mother's head was tilted, trying to watch her shows. I yelled out anyway, "Hey, move it! My mom can't see around you!"

"He's not moving," Mother chuckled. She waved her hand at me and just continued to watch her show, peering around her visitor. I asked her who he was, and she gave me a look that intimated I was the one who was utterly confused. "You know who. Now be quiet, I'm watching my show." She wrinkled her face at me then ignored me, keeping her head tilted at that strange angle.

During the past weeks, a man came to play cards in a chair in her room. Her deceased mother stood there shaking her finger at her. Her deceased aunt sat on her bed, talking about past days when they were young. And there were others who she wouldn't introduce me to. Sometimes I interrupted their talks, questioning Mother about her visitors. She tried to include me in their conversations, but soon I got an exasperated look thrown my way before she turned and explained to her visitor that I was her strange daughter.

But I knew my mother was leaving me and starting to travel closer to her new home. Were her visitors guides, helping her begin her journey to her new home as she leaves her tired worn-out body behind? Some days I asked her if she wanted to go with them. Her reply was, "They're visiting me, Claire. I'll go visit them soon. Now I'd like something to drink."

The past days, her visitors have been coming more frequently, spending more time in her room. Between visits she sleeps, restless, moving her hands and legs. I even whisper in her ear, "Go to the light, Mother." How can I be selfish and try to keep her here when there is a better place for her where she won't suffer any longer?

Today, my mother was staring up at one corner of the ceiling as I encouraged her to eat at least three spoonfuls of food. I inquired what she was staring at. Very calmly, she answered, "I'm just watching those three angels fly around. Each time they come, I know I'm going to have another visitor."

My mouth dropped open in shock. Angels. I watched her glazed eyes clear up once again, her facial features smooth out and a warm smile appear on her lips.

Her death quickly approaches, but my mother, her angels and her visitors have shown me not to be fearful or upset about her next step of leaving this earth. I know now she won't be alone.

Claire Luna-Pinsker

Lisa

*Be ever gentle with the children God has given
you. Watch over them constantly; reprove them
earnestly, but not in anger.*

Elihu Burritt

The steam rising from the sudsy dishwater clouds the
window, blurring my view of the backyard. But I know
she is out there. I can tell by the rhythmic squeak of the
swing set. I can tell by the abandon in her high-pitched,
singsong voice. I know she is there, all right.

I take a deep breath and turn my attention back to the
dirty dishes. There will not be time enough to finish before
she comes running through the yard, dogs in tow, consumed with high drama and frantic energy, needing and
demanding all the energy I have left.

Nothing productive happens when Lisa is around; she
fills a room to bursting with her presence. Every breath,
every word, every shrugged shoulder captures her attention. "Why?" "How come?" "What does that mean?" "What
did I do?" she demands constantly.

Lisa talks loudly and incessantly. She is constantly in

motion. She walks into walls. She trips over her own feet. Once, midstream in endless dinnertime chatter, her entire chair tipped over. My husband and I exchanged glances. Lisa kept right on talking.

When Lisa first came to live with us, I thought I was a terrible grandmother. She was always getting hurt. She fell from gymnasium bleachers and broke her new front tooth. She backed into the iguana's heating lamp and scorched her backside. She peeked through the crack of an open door just as I shut it and got her lip and nose pinched. She got her finger stuck in a pop bottle. She reached for a ball in the swimming pool and nearly drowned herself. A somersault from her bed required four stitches to her scalp. Pretty soon, I figured out that I was not doing anything wrong with Lisa; Lisa is simply out of synch with her own body.

I'm nearly finished with the dishes when I hear Lisa let out an ear-splitting whoop. She comes running for the back door with the dogs, her beautiful long, woolly braids a tangled mess. "I'm bored," she exclaims loudly, her soft, full lips forming a perfect little pout. I take a long, calming breath that I wish I could somehow transfer to her. I pat her sweaty head and gently disentangle myself from her clutches. "How about watching a movie until dinner's ready?" I try hopefully.

Somehow, videos calm Lisa. Therefore, she owns dozens. She can recite them all, word for word, and act them all out perfectly—but not today. "Oh, pu-leeze!" She flaunts dramatically and rolls her eyes, behavior better suited to a sixteen-year-old rather than a six-year-old. She has practiced the look from her latest video. And then she is off again, already forgetting how "bored" she is.

I am the only one who loves Lisa; everyone else just yells at her. Even though she exhausts me, even though she can reduce me to a screaming, out-of-control maniac, even though my favorite pastime is fantasizing about a life without her, still, I am the only one who loves her. I am the only one who knows how unhappy she really is.

Lisa was expelled from two nursery schools, flunked preschool and could not pass the entrance exam at three different kindergartens. I enrolled her directly into first grade at a public school that could not turn her away. That year was a disaster. I fought her teacher daily. Susie wrote things like "violent and irrational behavior" instead of "high-strung" or "underdeveloped impulse control," which was, at least, equally true. Susie felt that Lisa should repeat first grade. I refused. I knew that Lisa would be the same difficult, hard-to-love, hard-to-teach child a year later. Besides, I will be sixty-five when Lisa graduates high school. I cannot hang on for "extra" years.

Lisa wishes she had a mommy like all the other kids, a mommy young enough to still be afraid of teachers instead of a granny, who sees her teacher as a girl young enough to be her own daughter. Lisa wishes for a mommy who will call her teacher "Miss King" instead of Susie. Lisa wishes for a lot of things, but mostly, she wishes for her mommy.

Pots are boiling all over the stove, dogs are chasing Lisa around the kitchen table, and my husband is trying to engage me in conversation when the telephone rings. Her cousins are coming over to play. I see a flicker of panic in Lisa's eyes.

Lisa is extremely social; she needs to be around people, and she usually seeks them out the way a diabetic seeks out sugar. But she knows her medication has worn off. She knows she is out of control. I try to calm her, reassure her. "You'll have fun playing with them," I tell her. She knows different. I know she is right.

The medicine was a concession to Teacher; in return she agreed not to recommend Lisa's dismissal from the school. Lisa knows the medication changes how she feels;

it's scary that she has made the connection between drugs and behavior. I am not so sure that is a good thing for the child of a drug addict to know.

Lisa's mommy is my daughter. She is a street person, a drug addict and a crack-head; a casualty of the failed war on drugs. Lisa idolizes her "Santa Claus, Tooth-Fairy Mommy." Lisa has created an imaginary Bestest Mommy Ever, and she loves her fiercely. It is heartbreaking to see, totally impossible to stop. I don't even know if I should try.

The cousins are here, the dogs are out of control and so is Lisa. She cannot cope with the excitement. One tattle of "Lisa hit me!" is followed by "Lisa pushed me!" followed by a crash that no one can identify but everyone is sure is Lisa's fault. Lisa is wound tight, ready to explode. I brace for it, too exhausted to plan an intervention. Then the lamp falls, crashes into a potted plant, which falls to the floor and breaks into a million pieces. The shards of glass pierce Lisa's fingers. Not badly enough to require stitches this time, I decide, but there is enough blood to make her hysterical. My husband handles first aid this time; I concentrate on cleaning up the mess and keeping calm. I will not lose control this time. I will not start yelling this time.

People accuse me of spoiling Lisa. They say I let her get away with too much. But I know when she is speaking disrespectfully, she is really reciting dialogue from a movie, because she doesn't know how to express herself. I know her frequent accidents are her way of getting loving attention, so different from the attention she usually gets. I know that the children at school are cruel to her and will not play with her. They tease her because she cannot read and has to sit at the blue table all by herself. They tease her because she does not have a mommy. I can't counter-balance all the hurt she has to endure, but I try. I really am the only one who loves her.

The cousins have gone home, the dogs have been fed, and Lisa has had a good cry and a warm bath. The tension is released from her little body, and she is exhausted. So am I. We cuddle on the couch, too tired to walk into her bedroom. "I'm sorry, Granny," she whispers in a tiny voice. She begins to cry all over again, her skinny shoulders shaking. I hug her tightly and let my tears mix with hers.

Tomorrow, I will call her teacher "Miss King."

Christina Miranda-Walker

"My toddler's going through this phase
where he's constantly testing me."

The Travelers

Patience is the art of hoping.

Vauvenargues

I watched as she led him by the hand to the bathroom at the airport terminal. Travelers surrounded them, rushing past, and although he seemed a little bewildered, he seemed secure as long as his hand was in hers.

Returning to their seats at the gate, she combed his hair and zipped his jacket. He fidgeted and asked, "Where are we going, Mommy? What time is it? When will we get to ride our plane?"

I marveled at the woman's patience and love. I watched her take him by the hand when they were finally allowed to pre-board.

Upon finding my seat, I discovered that the three of us would be together. I squeezed past the two of them to my window seat then told him how handsome he looked in his new coat. He smiled. She helped take off his jacket and buckle his seat belt. He said that he had to go to the bathroom again, and she assured him that he could last until the end of the flight. I hoped she was right.

As the jet engines started, he became frightened and reached for her hand. She explained what was going on and began talking to him about their trip. He was confused about the different relatives they would be seeing, but she patiently repeated who was who until he seemed to understand.

He asked many more questions about the time, what day it was, how much longer until they got there . . . and she lovingly held his hand and gave him her full attention.

We introduced ourselves and shared the usual things all mothers like to share with one another. I learned she had four children and was on her way to visit one of them.

The hour passed quickly, and soon we were preparing to land. He became frightened again, and she stroked his arm, reassuringly. He said, "I love you, Mom," and she smiled and hugged him. "I love you, too, Honey."

They got off the plane before I did, the mother never realizing how deeply she had touched me. I said a quiet little prayer for this remarkable woman and for myself . . . that I would have enough love and strength to meet whatever challenges came my way, as this extraordinary mother clearly had.

When I last saw them, she was still holding his hand and leading her husband of forty-four years to the baggage claim area.

"Where we going, Mommy?"

Bobbie Wilkinson

3

ANGELS AMONG US

Be not forgetful to entertain strangers, for thereby some have entertained angels unaware.

Hebrews 13:2

A Relay of Control

Death is the golden key that opens the palace of eternity.

John Milton

It was with sadness and dread that I received a phone call from one of our hospital discharge planners telling me a patient, Joyce, had gone home and wanted me to call her. Joyce was a former coworker with me in another agency and was, ironically, its first hospice nurse.

I knew Joyce had been living with breast cancer for the past five years and had undergone a bone marrow transplant and multiple courses of chemotherapy. I had renewed my relationship with her a few years earlier when she was chairperson for the American Cancer Society's Relay for Life. Our hospice team participated in this twenty-four-hour fund-raiser. Joyce's energy and enthusiasm were contagious.

I called this wonderfully vivacious and funny lady, and agreed, with a heavy heart, to come to her home. She said she understood that I managed the hospice program and would be coming in that context.

The next day, I visited her and spent about three hours with her and her mother. Her husband, Steve, came home on his lunch break, and we talked at length about Joyce's disease and the services of hospice. Joyce was not ready to give up the fight. She was only forty-seven (my age), a wife and the mother of three young children. She was still convinced she would beat this disease. About a week later, after several more calls from family and friends, Joyce agreed to hospice care. She asked if I would be her nurse, and I reluctantly told her I could not, because as the manager, I wouldn't be able to give her my full attention. However, I would come and see her as her friend.

And so began my once or twice a week visits. Each was a spiritual experience. Both Joyce and I practiced the same religion and strong faith. We also loved angels and believed in their presence and guidance. Despite her faith, Joyce struggled with accepting her impending death, determined she would live to see her three children grown.

During one of my visits, I told her that the hospice team would march in the St. Patrick's Day Parade to advertise the Relay for Life. I told her the Hospice Clowns (of which I am one) would also be there. "I hope you and your family can come and watch," I coaxed.

With that mischievous twinkle in her eye, she said, "I'll be marching with you. After all my years of working on that race, I'm not about to just watch it."

During the ensuing month, though, Joyce started to decline. She became weaker and weaker, and at times confused. She still insisted she was not going to die and was very frustrated when others tried to be more realistic. Finally, one day she cried out in anguish, "I can't die! I just can't!"

I held her bony hand in mine. "Joyce, please put yourself in God's hands and trust that He will lead you in whichever direction you should go. You can control what you can, and the rest you have to leave up to Him and His angels."

A remarkable sense of peace came over her, and from that day on, she seemed to accept her fate. She slept more and more each day until finally I received a call from her friend, Linda, asking me to come. Joyce was not responding and the family was unsure what to do.

"I'm in my car only about a mile from Joyce's house," I told Linda. "But I'm dressed as a clown because I was headed for the parade." I asked her to prepare the family for my appearance at this heart-wrenching time.

I arrived to find Joyce in a coma and knew by her symptoms that death was near. As the tears rolled down my face, I said, "Joyce, you're still in control; you couldn't get to the parade so you brought the parade to you." I made sure she was comfortable then told the family, "I need to walk the parade—for Joyce." Privately, I told Linda, "Page me if she dies before I get back."

Halfway through the parade, my pager rang. Ironically, I was again about one mile from her home. I removed my wig, wiped at my makeup and went back to Joyce's to perform the pronouncement and console her family.

As I drove home and the tears continued to flow, I had an overwhelming sense that Joyce had joined God and His angels in controlling the events of the day. They sent in a clown.

Flo LeClair

Lianna

A ministering angel shall my sister be.

Shakespeare

My son, Preston, was diagnosed with a benign brain tumor in his optic nerve at the age of nine. Three years of experimental chemotherapy left him permanently blind and faced with the struggle of relearning his world. Blessings noted, blindness was his only challenge—and it changed our family forever. His sister, Lianna, was only six when she became his "eyes," his helper, his teacher and his best friend.

Lianna Stacia was always a princess, not only in looks, as any mother would say, but in her sweet disposition, gentle voice, graceful moves and angelic charm. She was a quiet, unassuming child who willingly gave of herself in time and patience. Lianna loved her brother so much, I often worried she would sacrifice her own life, needs and desires to make sure his were fulfilled.

During Preston's lengthy absences, teachers at school often asked her how Preston was. One day, Lianna came home with a frown and stomped around the house. "Every day, my teacher asks me how Preston is. Just for once, wouldn't it be nice if she asked me how I was?" Yet, her devotion and attention to her brother never wavered.

The first sunny spring day after Preston's blindness, he went outside for the first time in months. Still weak from the pressures of chemotherapy, he bundled up, but no longer bolted out the door and charged full speed down our road. Instead, he opened the door and stepped out cautiously, sliding his feet and feeling ahead with his arms. He insisted on doing this alone, and I watched with motherly angst as he walked slowly down the road, stepping in the puddles and slipping on the ice. He stumbled and fell. I watched him mumble, stand up and continue.

Silently, I watched from the deck, tense with anticipation of what I would witness next. Then I heard laughter. Two happy voices giggling in the spring melt. The sound of two wanderers exploring their latest dig site in the pasture. Lianna was ahead, steering him around the old softened-up cow pies. I heard her crazy laughter as he stepped in one. I saw Lianna's arm go up. Carefully, he took her arm and allowed her to guide him through the pasture, stopping frequently to examine the relics found in the melting snow. Then she took his hand and ran with him in a spring frenzy. At the barbed-wire fence she placed her hand gently on his head and pushed down. I could hear her talking. From there, I watched them both come to the tree fort, where she guided him up the steps and in safely.

I cried and went inside the house. Lianna needed no asking. She knew, at six, that rewards come from within, with the simple pleasure of creating joy for others.

Preston and Lianna had their bedrooms in the basement. Many nights, he tiptoed in, patted the covers with his hand and said, "Lianna, I love you." What he really meant was, *Lianna, I can't sleep. I'm having nightmares about the tumor growing.* "Lianna? Are you awake? I forgot to tell you what else I did ..."

As his trusted confidante, she cuddled him beside her and listened. They laughed. She swore not to tell his secret fears. An innocent, empathetic soul rested within one whose life had also changed. The one who sat with, comforted, prayed for and read to her brother during the long three years of chemotherapy. The one who described every new sight in great detail so Preston could have the mental image. The one who was always there.

Trust is a huge word in our house. You need to trust in order to jump across large, round hay bales with your sister. "Okay, Preston. The next one is about two feet straight ahead," she'd say. And he'd follow.

Lianna challenged Preston, encouraging him to try new things and to never, ever let blindness be a disability. When Preston got ready for school or an outing, Lianna became his fashion designer, his hairdresser and critic. In six years, Lianna never walked ahead without turning around to check for her brother.

Today, Preston is considered an inspiration for other blind youth. People are amazed by his accomplishments, maturity and concern for others. Standing quietly, behind the pedestal, is the strongest one of all: his sister.

Lori Ulrich

God's Caregiver

*The smallest children are nearest to God, as the
smallest planets are nearest the sun.*

Jean Paul Richter

I rubbed my large belly as I entered the local Christian
bookstore in search of a wall hanging for the nursery. I
still couldn't believe Mike and I were going to be caring
for a newborn in less than a month.

A framed poem, with the colors of the baby's nursery,
caught my attention. I read it, and my heart ached for the
mother who wrote it. The poem, entitled "Baby Tears,"
was about a baby who died and was now with God. The
little one inside me shifted, and I thanked God for blessing me with a strong, healthy baby. I then continued on
my quest and found a different wall hanging, one for our
baby.

One week later, while at the movies, I went into labor.
When I arrived at the hospital, I was already dilated four
centimeters. They hooked me up to monitors to track my
contractions and the baby's heartbeat. As the pain inten-
sified, Mike held my hand, coaching me through each

surge. He soon noticed the baby's heartbeat went down during each contraction. Growing concerned, he summoned the nurse, who had me lay in different positions, hoping to regulate the baby's heartbeat. Nothing worked. The baby was in distress, but I trusted my doctor completely, so I wasn't worried. But he was. He recommended a C-section. The staff called the anesthesiologist and prepped me for surgery. It was then my water broke, and the look on the doctor's face told me instantly there was a problem. Still, my optimism and naiveté overshadowed my concern.

The baby's heartbeat plummeted, as my contractions and pain increased. They rushed me into the operating room only to find the anesthesiologist hadn't arrived yet.

"Lisa, we have to get this baby out," my doctor said in calm desperation. "We can't wait any longer! This is drastic measure, but it's our only hope. I can give you a local anesthetic, but an incision now will still hurt."

"Just get the baby out!" I panted. "Save my baby!"

They put a drape in front of me to block my view of the operation, but I could see it in the reflection of the silver light fixture. Eight painful shots of Novocaine were injected into my abdomen. I held Mike's hand and tried to take deep breaths. I felt God's presence, and I knew this would be over soon. We would soon see our baby. The incision seared pain through my body. The baby's heartbeat flatlined, and the doctor rushed to save the life inside me. I watched as he took out a limp baby and hurried it over to a table. Doctors and nurses swarmed around my little one. I heard no baby cry, just the frantic murmurs of the doctors and nurses. The anesthesiologist arrived. . . .

About an hour later, I opened my eyes.

A quiet stillness filled the white recovery room, and a supernatural peace came over me. Mike was right there. He looked worn out. "Lisa, are you okay? Wake up."

"Where's our baby?"

Mike caressed my face. Tears welled in his eyes, "Lisa, he didn't make it."

"It's okay," I said. "He's okay." The words flowed from my lips, mysteriously. I knew in my heart that he was with the Lord, and I felt at peace with that.

Then, as if reading my mind, Mike whispered, "Do you want to see him?"

"Can I?" I choked.

Mike left for a short time and then returned holding our son.

I gently took him. His face was beautiful and perfect. "He looks so peaceful," I told Mike, "like he's sleeping. He looks just like you."

I looked at my precious Tyler Michael and wished I had a camera. I wanted so much to remember him and how he looked. Gently, I put him on my lap and unwrapped the blanket. I soaked in all that I could about him. As the drowsiness again consumed me, I swaddled Tyler again and reluctantly handed him to Mike, who took him out of the room. I slumped back into the pillow, dazed and numb.

Soon after, my doctor came in. Tears streamed down his face as he took my hand and told me how sorry he was.

"It's okay," I told him. "It's okay." The words somehow kept coming out of my mouth. What I meant, though, was Tyler was okay because he was with God now. The doctor blamed himself, but I didn't blame him. He handed me a few Polaroid pictures he'd taken of Tyler. I consoled the doctor until sleep took over my body.

The reality of my loss, though, had not set in . . . until I awoke in the night. Emptiness consumed me. I relived the birth and death of our son as sobs wracked my body, and the immensity of my loss became clear. A wonderful nurse sat by my side the rest of the night, consoling me.

Sadness crept into the following days, trying to take

over. My arms felt empty. It seemed that for my entire life I had dreamed to hold and care for a baby. How could that dream be a nightmare? Even though I knew Tyler was in a better place, I missed him desperately. He had been a part of me for nine months, and now he was gone. I cried a lot at night as Mike held me, comforted me and cried with me.

Determined not to let this tragedy take over my life, I turned my grieving into healing. After doing some research, I found there were many moms facing the loss of a baby—through miscarriages, during delivery or soon after. Yet, there was nowhere for these women to get the support they needed to help them through the difficult times.

With the financial backing of local doctors, I started a group for mothers who had experienced the loss of an infant. I called this one-on-one support program HOP-ING—Helping Other Parents In Normal Grieving. I spent many hours in my basement organizing information, finding volunteers and holding mothers' hands while they grieved.

Today, fifteen years later, HOPING is still going strong. A social worker at my local hospital took it over and expanded it to include both parents. Hundreds have benefited from this caring program.

Losing Tyler brought Mike and me closer together. We are the proud parents of three more beautiful children, who were all delivered by the same doctor who delivered Tyler. We shared Tyler's special story with them, and they love his picture and other memories in his baby book.

The framed poem I'd seen in the store, "Baby Tears," now hangs in our home. God had an amazing plan for this one special child's life . . . and death.

Lisa Rossi as told to Kerrie Flanagan

Sisters

I was in the wrong place, and I knew it. When I walked into that coin laundry near Wallops Island, Virginia, I was the only white person. I couldn't leave, because my husband, Dave, had driven away.

I walked down the rows of machines in a vain effort to find an empty one. No one looked at me. No one spoke to me.

It had been years since I had been in Virginia or any part of the South, where I grew up. Since marriage, I had lived in Minnesota for thirty years. I remembered what the South had been like—places where blacks hung out and whites didn't go, places where whites hung out and blacks didn't go. That had all changed, hadn't it? Not here. I kept walking down the aisles looking for an empty washer.

When we had arrived in town earlier that week, we had been horrified to find my dad, age eighty-two, living in squalor. We scrubbed and repaired things in his tiny, rented house. Now, I planned to wash and mend his clothes, and go back to my teaching job. I had begged him to find someone to clean and help take care of him, but I knew he didn't want to spend his savings for that. I didn't know how to help him.

I found an available washer, lifted the lid and stuffed in Dad's clothes. They were stained from nosebleeds and riddled with pipe and cigar burns.

I slumped into one of the few worn chairs and thought about these past days—my dad. I had never felt so much like a stranger. Besides my husband, I had no one to talk to, no one to guide me. I wanted desperately to take care of Dad, but my family back home needed me. What could I do?

When the last cycle finished, I pulled out the yellowed sheets and clothes, and pushed them into a dryer. Involuntarily, I groaned as I dropped coins in the slot.

A pleasant-looking Afro-American woman about my age smiled at me. Encouraged, I explained, "My dad doesn't know how to take care of his laundry. And he burns holes in everything."

She smiled sympathetically. "My mom, too. I know what you're going through."

I was frantic to talk to someone. "I have to go home to Minnesota tomorrow," I said. "He promised to try to find someone to clean and help take care of him, but I know he won't—especially if it costs him any money."

"My mom, too. They're scared their money won't last," she said. "Someday, we'll be in their shoes."

"I know." I tried not to cry. "Our plane leaves tomorrow. I don't know what to do. If I only knew people in this community, I could find someone." I told her where his place was and that it was far from any town.

"I know where that's at. I go by his house every day," she said.

"He has the money; that isn't the problem. Do you know anyone around there who cleans? It would have to be someone special. He's half-blind and can hardly walk. It won't be long before he'll have to give up and come live with me. Right now, he refuses."

She smiled again. "I clean houses."

I gasped. It was too good to be true.

"I'm Florence," she said, taking my hand in hers. She agreed to come by Dad's place after church the next morning to meet him and decide if we could work out some arrangement for her to clean each week. I warned her that it could turn into caregiving because of his age and disabilities.

At exactly ten, she drove up with her elderly mother in the front seat and several young children in the back—her grandchildren, I assumed.

"God bless you. God bless you," the old woman waved her hand out the window. "God bless you."

Florence and I exchanged glances. We both knew exactly what the other was going through. The big difference was, she had her mom there and could take care of her, and I had to leave my dad. Florence talked to Dad, and he agreed with our plan and to pay Florence each week. We set it all up and exchanged phone numbers and addresses.

Florence and I looked into each other's eyes and knew, without a shadow of a doubt, that if our roles were reversed, I would take care of her parent and she would go back to her job.

Over the next three months, Florence not only cleaned Dad's house, but she also drove him to doctor appointments and shopping. When he finally agreed to come live with me, she packed up his useable clothing and keepsakes, and she escorted him to the plane.

See, Florence and I were sisters, and we knew that. God put her in that laundromat knowing I'd talk to her. And none of that black and white stuff had anything to do with it.

Isabel R. Marvin

An Act of Desperation

For love is as strong as death . . .

Song of Solomon 8:6

It was a day when defeat seemed complete, with one blow following another. I brought my daughter Rachel, who was severely disabled and battling yet another case of pneumonia, back from her pediatric appointment. The doctor had delivered the devastating news—Rachel most likely would die. She could no longer clear her lungs and would probably drown in her own fluids within a few days.

I felt numb, my mind still not comprehending what I had heard. I settled Rachel back in her bed and went to check my e-mail messages. I was reading distractedly, thinking about Rachel and what I was going to tell my family, when one message hit me with an unexpected impact: A friend I loved dearly had been killed early that morning in a car accident.

It was too much. I literally collapsed.

When Phyllis, my daughter's nurse, arrived a short time later, she found me sitting on the floor next to Rachel's bed, unable to move. After making sure Rachel was comfortable, she sat down on the floor with me and persuaded me to talk. She listened as my tears poured out.

Phyllis, who had been Rachel's caregiver for four years, had a special bond with my child. Even though Rachel could not speak, she and Phyllis developed their own way of communicating, even fighting. Her devotion to Rachel went above and beyond. Phyllis had become part of our family. As a single mother, I was very dependent on her help, and I knew losing Rachel was going to hit her hard, too.

As my tears dried, we talked about what to do next and decided that the most important thing was to make Rachel as comfortable as possible. We gave her something for her pain, hooked her up to the oxygen tank then turned her on her side. Rachel could no longer cough, so we wanted to make sure that any fluids from her nose and throat wouldn't choke her.

Phyllis stood over the bed for a few moments, stroking her, then started looking around the room.

"What do you need?" I asked.

She stood still for a moment then said, "Food."

Phyllis was a strong woman who worked part-time on a tobacco farm. She'd led a tough life, and it made her both loving and practical. I was surprised, but she pushed me toward the door. "I have an idea," she said, "and you need to get out of the house. Take a break; go get some food for us. The next few days aren't going to be easy. Go."

I was still not functioning on all burners, so I went, letting the sun wash over me as I drove the three blocks to a restaurant. I ordered the take-out and went home, my mind still very much on my friend, her family and what I was about to face with Rachel. Then, I walked in my front door and found that my living room had been transformed.

Phyllis had rolled up her sleeves, a sure sign that a lot of action was about to take place. She'd pushed the furniture out of the center of the room and turned a straight-backed chair upside down in the middle. Padding it with a comforter and cushions, she'd created a steep A-frame support, with the back legs of the chair forming the peak.

Rachel was lying face down across the frame, her hips braced between the legs of the chair and her head pointed toward the floor at a sharp angle. She looked up at me and grunted.

"What's going on?" I asked.

Phyllis was in the process of starting our cool-air mister. "She can't cough. So I thought that maybe gravity could give us a little help making her comfortable. It's probably not medically advisable, but what do we have to lose?"

I walked over and looked down at my daughter. Her face and chest were on a towel, already damp. "How long can she stay like this?"

Phyllis plugged in the mister, then dragged Rachel's aerosol machine over toward the chair. "We probably shouldn't leave her for more than thirty minutes at a time. I thought we'd do her Albuterol treatment here, then chest percussion. If we can suction some of that crap out of her, it might help her sleep."

I unwrapped the food as I watched Phyllis go to work on Rachel, not just with the professionalism of a nurse, but the love of a caregiver—and a friend.

The next three days were a blur. Phyllis didn't go home, and we slept in brief shifts, putting Rachel on her homemade A-frame every three to four hours. With every treatment, fluid from her lungs drained out of her mouth, soaking a thick bath towel. While one of us worked on Rachel, the other took care of the things that kept us going. It was so consuming that even my grief was set aside.

At about two in the morning, three days later, Rachel started to cough and fight on her own. We reduced the number of treatments, and finally, we all slept through the night. A week later, Rachel had cleared her lungs of the pneumonia, and in two weeks, she was off her oxygen. Four weeks after being told that my daughter was dying, I put her on her school van again, with a kiss and a breathless prayer.

I later asked Phyllis if she had really believed her treatment would save Rachel's life. She shook her head. "Nope. In fact, I thought it might make things worse. But I had to do something. I was ready to let Rachel go, but I didn't think you could have handled losing both of them at once. I don't think God did either. It was an act of desperation."

I call it an act of love.

Ramona Richards

Jesus Loves Me

Let the little children come to me, and do not forbid them; for of such is the kingdom of God.
Mark 10:14

One day, a beautiful but very troubled little girl came through the door of my day nursery. From the very beginning, I became captivated by this child who had so little but needed so much. I was heartbroken that a four-year-old could suffer such heartache and pain. She was born in prison after her mom had used marijuana, crack and cocaine her entire pregnancy. The little girl was non-verbal and had very little control. I knew her progress would be a mighty battle.

Whenever somebody approached her, she became violent for long periods and ended up in a fetal position on the floor crying out. I found myself praying for her day in and day out.

As months rolled on, I began to bond with this child that no one wanted. She and I worked very hard taking one step forward and four steps back. Daily, we sat in the big rocking chair in my office, swaying back and forth, back and forth. During our rocking time, I sang "Jesus Loves Me." She always settled down and became very still at the melody. Though she never spoke, peace seemed to fill her face as she listened to the song.

One day after a very long battle, I held my special girl to again calm her fears and pain. In silence we rocked back and forth and back and forth, back and forth. Then she looked at me with tear-filled eyes and spoke a complete sentence for the first time, "Sing to me about that Man who loves me."

Blinking back tears, I knew the battle had been won.

Alicia Hill

Songs of Love

Music, the greatest good that mortals know, and all of heaven we have here below.

Joseph Addison

Four-year-old Aspen greeted me at the door dressed in a pink ballerina outfit, complete with ballerina shoes, and waving a magic wand. All that was lacking was a tumble of blond curls falling into ringlets around her face. Her pretty mouth was grinning from ear to ear, and she giggled in delight when she saw me.

I had come to baby-sit for Aspen for a few hours. After she waved good-bye to her mother, she placed her tiny hand in mine then walked me into the kitchen, where we sat at the table.

"I want to draw you some pictures," she said. She grabbed a large crayon and began to draw a portrait of a little girl. "This is a picture of me when my hair grows back," she commented matter-of-factly. She then turned the picture over and scribbled my name on the back, "So you'll know it's for you!"

I leaned over and gave her a hug as tears welled up in

my eyes. I couldn't let her see me cry—this perceptive child would probably ask *me* what was wrong. I was really surprised by her energy. When Aspen and I first met, she was in preschool. Then she became ill. High fevers and unexplained bruises became cause for alarm. Her parents were shocked by the terrifying diagnosis: leukemia.

Overwhelming, intense emotions ravaged her family. Suddenly, they were thrust into a new world populated by an ever-changing cast of characters—interns, residents, oncologists, nurses and social workers.

Aspen's parents explained the situation to her, telling her that she was seriously ill, that she had leukemia—"bad guys" in her blood. The medicine would get rid of the bad guys and keep them from coming back. Spending time at Children's Hospital, going through lots of tests and having chemotherapy became a part of her routine.

When Aspen's hair fell out, her mom reminded her it would grow back again. Meanwhile, Aspen collected hats for indoors when she played dress-up and bonnets for when she went outside.

During this time, my husband came across on the Internet an organization called the Songs of Love Foundation. We knew this nonprofit organization that creates personalized songs for chronically and terminally ill children would be perfect for Aspen. Known as the "medicine of music," each song is one of a kind and never duplicated.

We immediately sent for more information and found out that the parents must contact the foundation and submit a profile sheet that lists their child's hobbies and interests. The child is then matched to a composer, who writes the music and lyrics.

Aspen's mom was enthusiastic when we told her about the foundation. We explained there was no cost if a parent requested the song; friends or relatives could sponsor songs though, as we did, through a donation.

Within a month, Aspen finally received her very own professionally recorded cassette. Soon after, her mother called me. "She plays the tape over and over again. She loves it!" Then she put Aspen on the phone. She squealed with delight, "Thank you!" as I listened to the tape blaring in the background. "Let me tell you about a girl I know, she's four years old, her name is Aspen . . ."

Whenever Aspen had to return to the hospital, she brought her tape along and played it for the hospital's doctors, nurses—anyone who would listen. The song brought smiles and laughter from the whole nursing station as some of them sang and hummed the tune right along with Aspen. "Her mommy and her daddy love her so, she's the sweetest little girl you could ever know . . ."

Almost two years after this nightmare diagnosis, spunky Aspen and her family continue to deal with treatment, knowing they are getting closer and closer toward recovery each and every day. Sure enough, her hair has grown back, just as her mother promised. When my husband and I saw her recently, she was celebrating her sixth birthday, and her parents told us about the best present ever: Aspen no longer needed chemotherapy.

This girl with blond curls still plays her very own Song of Love and she, her parents, family and friends are looking forward to the day when the "medicine of music" will be the only medicine she and others like her will ever need.

Mary Hjerleid

[EDITORS' NOTE: The *Songs of Love Foundation* has recorded over 1,400 songs for children in more than 100 hospitals nationwide since it began in 1996. Over 250 songwriters, singers and instrumentalists all across the country donate their time creating unique lyrics and melodies, each highlighting the child's personality. For more information, or to make a contribution, you can contact the Songs of Love Foundation at (800) 960-SONG or www.songsoflove.org]

Mother Teresa's One Heart Full of Love

Only in heaven will we see how much we owe to the poor for helping us to love God better because of them.

Mother Teresa

We have a home in Australia where, as you know, many aborigines live in terrible conditions. When we first arrived there to help these people, we came upon an elderly man who lived in the worst of conditions. I went and tried to start up a conversation with him. I said to him, "Please let me clean your house and make up your bed."

"I am fine like this," he replied.

I said, "You will be better off with a clean house."

Finally, he agreed. When I entered his house, which bore little resemblance to a home, I noticed a lamp. It was a beautiful lamp, but it was covered with filth and dust. I asked him, "Do you ever light that lamp?"

He asked, "For whom? No one ever comes to my house. I spend days without ever seeing a human face. I have no need to light the lamp." Then I asked him if he would be willing to light the lamp if the sisters came to see him regularly. He answered, "Of course!"

The sisters made it their habit to visit him every evening. The old man began to light the lamp for them and to keep it clean. He began to keep his house clean, too. He lived for two more years.

Once he gave the sisters a message for me: "Tell my friend that the light that she lit in my life is still shining." It was a very small thing, but in that dark, a light was lit and continued to shine.

Give the love we have all received to those around you. Give until it hurts, because real love hurts. That is why you must love until it hurts.

You must love with your time, your hands and your hearts. You need to share all that you have. Some time ago, we had great difficulty getting sugar in Calcutta. One day, a small Hindu boy, not more than four years old, and his parents came and brought me a cup of sugar. The little boy said, "I did not eat sugar for three days. Give my sugar to your children." That little boy loved to the point of sacrificing.

On another occasion, a gentleman came to our house and said, "There is a Hindu family that has eight children. They haven't eaten anything for a long time." I instantly took some rice that we were going to use for supper and went with the gentleman to seek out that family. I could see the specter of hunger drawn on the faces of the little children when we found the family. They looked like human skeletons. In spite of their need, the mother had the courage and compassion to divide the rice that I had brought into two portions. Then she went out.

When she came back I asked her, "Where did you go? What have you done?" She said, "They are hungry also."

"Who are they?" I asked. It seems a Moslem family with the same number of children lived across the street. She knew that they were hungry, too. What struck me was that she knew, and because she knew, she gave until it hurt. That is something beautiful. That is love in action! That woman shared with great sacrifice.

I did not bring them more rice that night, because I wanted them to experience the joy of loving and sharing. You should have seen the faces of those little children! They barely understood what their mother had done, yet, their eyes shined with a smile. When I arrived again, they looked starved and sad. But what their mother did was teach them what real love was all about.

Mother Teresa

The Church Lady

When a person is down in the world, an ounce of help is better than a pound of preaching.
                    Edward George Bulwer-Lytton

Caring for my ailing mother proved quite difficult. I lived 1,700 miles away. My young family also needed attention, so I could only manage to visit her just a week to ten days every month.

Mom's respiratory condition worsened. Oxygen, special medication and a lot of bed rest became her fare of the day, while fatigue, frustration and financial difficulties loomed in my life. Yet, I promised myself I'd try to do what was necessary for as long as it took.

"I can't go shopping."

"I can't visit my neighbors."

"I can't even get to church."

Mom's complaints were unavoidable and valid. Being housebound and isolated from all the activities she so enjoyed caused her to sink rapidly into a state of depression. In a short span of time, it was obvious her mental health deteriorated to the point of worry.

On one visit, I asked, "How are you managing when I'm not here?"

She replied, "Oh, I don't need much these days. But when I do, Gen, the church lady, as you used to call her, comes by and takes care of me."

"What does she do for you?"

"She tidies up, brings me treats, shops for my groceries, makes me a cup of tea and keeps me up-to-date on the latest gossip."

Smiling, I said, "She sounds like quite a friend and a natural caregiver."

Mom's face beamed. "Not only to me but to anyone who needs a helping hand. Look at all she's done for the church over the years. Not only does she cook a few meals for the clergy, she dresses the altar with ceremonial linens and flowers, and keeps the statues and the pews spotless. She washes, waxes and polishes every inch, from floor to ceiling. When you were just a little girl, you always wanted to help her."

I remembered the times I was allowed to go along and do a few small chores.

On another visit, just before Mom was hospitalized, Gen arrived at my mother's door with two home-cooked meals.

"I knew you were coming, and I had a little extra," she said. "Thought you two girls might enjoy not having to cook tonight."

Gen stayed and visited with me after Mom turned in for the night. I got the lowdown on whose children were engaged, getting married, having babies, plus recent deaths and all the new activities at the church. I so appreciated her generosity and company. I thanked her profusely for caring for Mom.

She smiled. "It's my pleasure," she said. "Besides, living right upstairs makes it as easy as can be."

"Mom can be stubborn; I'm surprised she agreed to letting you help her."

"We've been friends a long time, so once we worked out a few problems, everything fell into place. Now it's routine."

My stomach tightened. I asked, "What kind of problems?"

"I guess it started the day the washing machine overflowed," she explained. "I knew she didn't follow directions. And since she doesn't have much laundry, I asked if I could wash a few things of my own in her machine using a special low-suds cleaning product. Catherine was delighted. Now it's a regular routine." Gen added, "We've never had another flood."

"Was there any damage to the house?"

Gen shook her head.

My relief only lasted a few seconds when I saw her brow furrow. "Something else?" I asked.

There was a slight pause.

"Well, there was the afternoon I stopped in for tea." She closed her eyes and made the sign of the cross. "The minute I walked in, I smelled gas. Seems Catherine went to make a cup of tea, couldn't light the burner on the stove and walked away, forgetting to turn the knob back to its off position."

I gasped at the thought of an explosion.

"I opened the windows, aired out the apartment then told her I got a new supply of imported teas from England and hoped she'd help me enjoy them. I promised her I'd come every afternoon. Catherine was thrilled. Now, she waits for me to make the tea. Says I have a special touch." Gen smiled. "And, I've never smelled gas since."

I said a silent prayer.

Gen leaned in close and patted my hand. "Did you know she's not fond of the Meals on Wheels selections?" Before I could answer, she continued. "Catherine took it upon herself to sleep through the delivery time. I told her I loved their food and made a deal to swap it for some of my dishes. We switch all the time now, and she's not losing any more weight."

How I had missed these potential danger signs baffled me. I pointed to Mom's medication containers on the kitchen counter. "Your idea, too?"

A quick nod was followed with, "I convinced her that a different color pillbox for each day makes taking medicine a little more fun. Once we matched a day with a special color, there were no more mistakes."

The more I heard, the more I realized this "church lady" was more than a caregiver; she was an angel. "You're a special person. You've given Mom more than friendship and physical care; you've managed to help her keep her dignity when she needs it most. How can I thank you for your kindness? Can I pay you for your time?"

Shaking her head Gen answered, "Just keep me in your prayers and keep coming as often as you can. I don't think Catherine has much time left."

I promised I would on both accounts and hugged her wholeheartedly. "I worry about her all the time."

"There's no need to worry," Gen told me before she left to go upstairs to her apartment. "I'm here for her, just a few steps away."

Gen was indeed an expert in her field. She washed away my worries and heartaches with her presence and generosity. She waxed my spirit with her unselfish ministry. She polished my faith, hope and charity with her exemplary life.

Helen Colella

The Heaven-Sent Encourager

A good man's prayers will from the deepest dungeon climb heaven's height, and bring a blessing down.

Joanna Baillie

Summers in the mile-high Rocky Mountain state of Colorado can be quite hot, and on this scorching Saturday afternoon, I was driving home alone in my wheelchair-accessible van. As I skillfully carved my way along a curving country road, I congratulated myself on the high level of independence I had achieved—despite having been 80-percent paralyzed for almost thirty-five years.

At eighteen, I was working the summer between high school and college on the Massachusetts resort island of Martha's Vineyard. On a Fourth of July morning, I innocently dove from a pier during low tide and broke my neck at the C 5/6 level. The spinal cord injury caused lifelong motor and sensory paralysis below my chest, with limited arm use and no finger movement.

As a quadriplegic, I have lived a fulfilled lifestyle despite my dependence on motorized wheelchair mobility and daily help from the college-student caregivers whom I personally hire and coordinate. My graduate education has qualified me to serve my peers with disabilities as a university administrator, designer and marketer of accessible fitness equipment, author and future university professor. So while I remain mostly paralyzed, I routinely enjoy an independent and very active lifestyle during the daytime hours between my morning and evening aides.

The summer breeze of my open windows mixed with the jazz of a Denver radio station. The freedom I enjoyed today had required years of practice and also required that I occasionally nap so I can get through each demanding day.

Looking forward to a fifteen-minute rest, I drove into the parking lot of a rural church. To avoid being interrupted, I pulled into the lot's far corner and opened my side door toward a massive cornfield. Deciding to snooze in the sun, I began wheeling down the van's four-feet-long ramp.

Halfway down the ramp, I somehow lost my balance for a split second and fell forward. I was still sitting in the wheelchair, however, my body was bent at the waist and my head was now between my knees. Due to paralysis, I lacked both trunk and sufficient arm muscles for sitting back upright.

I was in serious trouble. If drivers on the distant road looked my way toward the other side of the van, they would quickly dismiss the appearance of a parked, empty vehicle. There was little sense in wasting precious breath or energy to yell for help, as I was facing an empty field. It was about two o'clock, and if no one rescued me during the remaining daylight, I estimated churchgoers would find me the following morning as they became curious after attending services.

As a reminder of the passing hours, the radio in my van

was still playing. During the first hour, as my body stretched in its contorted position, my head gradually slipped lower and lower. By four o'clock, my head was between my calves, and breathing was becoming very difficult. I felt my face and lips swelling, and I knew that to increase any slim chance of survival, I would need to turn down my metabolism and breathing.

Mind control was a trick I had learned during many hospital surgeries. Several times while connected to a pulse monitor, I found amazing correlations between purposeful, stressful thoughts and elevated pressure and pulse rates; and then, conversely, thinking calm thoughts and dramatically slowing down my system. Within this current crisis, I guessed I could only benefit from attempting a low extreme. I slowly and calmly went deep into the dark, quiet caverns of my mind and was quite successful in achieving a partial coma. My next memory was hearing the radio's six o'clock news.

While I had helped my chances of medical survival during those three or four hours, I had done nothing to increase my chances of being rescued. The sun over the field was getting lower, and in two hours, my empty van would disappear until the Sunday morning church bells called the faithful to find my body. I wondered for a few minutes what kinds of stories the community and press would create to explain the fatal situation they encountered.

I guess I was adjusting my mind-set for what now seemed inevitable. After over four hours of waning hope, I was preparing to die.

My wife and I were very close. Several times that afternoon I had attempted to send her clairvoyant messages. With all my mental strength, I repeatedly strained to transmit, "Peggy, I'm in serious trouble. Peggy, I'm dying, please rush, emergency, Boulder route." But now, several hours later, there was no sign of her or anyone else.

It was time to put my affairs in order. I expressed my love to Peggy and to God. I asked Him or Her for forgiveness. During the thirty-five years of living with my disability, I had often attempted to find a meaning or purpose for my life—to view the disability as an asset from which others and I could learn and benefit, instead of merely cursing it as a senseless liability to be endured. I expressed to God my hope that I had accomplished whatever my goals had been.

And with that thought, I expressed one final request. "God, *please*. I've endured and survived this situation as long as I believe I can. If I have completed my work in this lifetime, please help me to die soon and in the peaceful way I believe I have treated others. However, if my work for this lifetime is not through, I need a miracle. Please send someone to rescue me in these next ten or fifteen minutes, because I can't survive much longer."

With that all-out final plea, I surrendered myself to whatever would occur in the next few minutes and began to gaze absent-mindedly at the underside of the van behind me. I had been fighting to survive for over six hours. The eight o'clock news was announced on the radio, my lips had become so swollen they felt ready to pop, and my breathing was so difficult that I was limiting myself to eight or ten deep breaths per minute.

About ten minutes after my plea to God, I was sent a true miracle. My blank, mindless gaze under the van was suddenly broken by what I thought—but couldn't initially believe—was a pair of feet in sneakers! With a great surge of hope, I summoned all the air and strength remaining in my lungs and screamed, "Help, help me, please! I'm on the other side of the van!"

The feet stood motionless for a second then slowly walked around the van, stopping in front of me. The man stood still and slowly asked in a deep voice, "Are you okay?"

"Please, I need your help. Please lift my shoulders back so I can sit up."

As he did so with ease, I found myself face-to-face with a very large man whose facial expression indicated confusion. That look increased as I started crying and sobbing uncontrollably in gratitude and relief. "Thank you, thank you so much."

"Have you been here very long?" he asked slowly and in a caring tone.

His name was Frank, and from my professional experience, I guessed he had a developmental disability. He lived locally with a family and had a part-time job as a groundskeeper with the church.

"Frank, there is no doubt that you just saved my life. Thank you."

He smiled quietly. I suspected that if he informed his family of what happened, they might not believe him. I scribbled his address, and vowed I would immediately write him and his family a brief letter confirming the details, repeating my appreciation and providing my contact information.

I had to ask, "Frank, why did you walk to this remote corner of the church parking lot today so late in the afternoon?"

"I noticed your van parked next to a sprinkler head that's been broken for a long time—reminded me I should fix it. I've been putting off coming out here to look at it, but for some weird reason, I guess I felt like checking it this afternoon. I have no idea why I chose today."

He may have had no idea, but I did—to prove to me three things: miracles do happen; my disability has a purpose, it's not a random senseless tragedy; and caregivers are indeed among the most caring, loving and supportive people on earth—and some are heaven-sent!

Alfred H. "Skip" DeGraff

4

THE TRUE MEANING OF HEALTH CARE

*The highest reward for a person's toil is
not what they get for it, but what they
become by it.*

John Ruskin

Gone Fishing

As the voice of death whispers, "You must go from earth," let us hear the voice of Christ saying, "You are but coming to Me!"

Norman Macleod

When I entered her room, Mrs. Johnson was sitting in a chair by the window reading the Bible. Her thin frame bathed in the morning sunlight as she quietly thumbed through the worn pages. I stopped in the doorway and studied the elderly woman. The room was quiet and very peaceful.

I had only recently started my third year of medical school, and it was my first day on the urology service. Mrs. Johnson had end-stage ovarian cancer that had spread throughout her abdomen, obstructing her ureters and causing her kidney function to decline. I had spent two hours reviewing her chart, X-rays and old records. I also read all that I could find about ovarian carcinoma. For a moment, I felt very uncomfortable. Although I had a considerable amount of knowledge about her condition, I knew absolutely nothing about her as a person. She was dying, and I had been worrying about trying to impress my chief resident with my fund of knowledge. After taking a deep breath, I stepped into her room.

"Hello, Mrs. Johnson," I said while reaching for her bedside chart. "How are you doing this morning?" I asked.

"Sweetie, I'm doing just fine on this glorious day," she said, turning towards me with a warm smile on her face. "You look a little young to be wearing one of those white coats," she said, examining me over the bifocals perched on the end of her nose.

"Well, it's the only thing I could find to match these pants," I teased.

She chuckled softly as she closed the Bible on her lap. She turned her attention back toward the window and took a long, slow breath. "Sure is a glorious day," she said as she shook her head.

An unexpected calm came over me as I stood beside her. She seemed completely at ease as she basked in the morning sunshine that poured in through the window. I sat on the bed next to her chair and asked if she could spare a few minutes to discuss her medical condition.

For the next fifteen minutes, I talked with her about all aspects of her disease and how it related to her kidney failure. "Without functioning kidneys, toxins will build up in your bloodstream and will lead to your death. We can place stents in through your bladder, which will relieve the obstruction and save your kidneys from shutting down. It is a quick and painless procedure."

"My, my, my ... just look at this glorious day," she said.

"Mrs. Johnson, do you understand everything that we have talked about?" I asked, with a confused look on my face.

"Honey, I'm dying," she said, with no change in her expression.

"You don't have to die from renal failure," I interrupted.

She sat quietly looking at me. I felt uncomfortable in the silence. She turned back to the window and asked, "So dying from kidney failure would be worse than dying from cancer?" She already knew the answer. Suddenly, the notion of getting consent for the procedure seemed absolutely ridiculous. Who was I treating, the patient or myself? I was saving her from a more humane death, only to have her meet with a long and painful demise.

"Sweetie, the Lord takes care of all his children. He doesn't want me to suffer and neither do you," she said. She obviously sensed my sadness as I stared intently at the floor. "Look at me," she said. "It is okay to die. It is as much a part of life as being born. I have been on God's green earth for seventy-eight years and have loved every minute of it. Life is a gift. You take the good with the bad."

I didn't even try to hide my tears as she continued talking.

"I know this is difficult for you to understand, but I'm tired, very tired. God has a plan, and it is my time to go," she said. "You are a good doctor. Just listen to your patients, listen to your heart and do what is right."

I was numb. Why was this dying woman comforting me? She eased back in her chair and said, "Sure is a glorious day."

"Mrs. Johnson, what can I do for you?"

"Honey, why don't you go sign my release papers?"

"What are you going to do, Mrs. Johnson?"

She smiled and said, "I'm going fishing. I am going to pick up my grandchildren, and we are going to go down to the lake and catch some big ones."

I left and completed all of the necessary paperwork then returned to her room. We talked for a long time about her life and her experiences. I enjoyed getting to know her as a person. She was wonderful. She hugged me, and before I left she said, "Never forget what's important. No matter how busy you are, take the time to look around. In the end, the only things that really matter are the relationships you have with God and your loved ones."

I paused in the doorway as I left. She was staring out the window with a peaceful smile on her face.

"Sure is a glorious day," I said.

Adam Gold, M.D.

Project First Step

*M*ankind *owes to the child the best it has to give.*

United Nations Convention on the Rights of the Child

"The war here in Afghanistan has created many amputees, will you come to Kabul and help us?"

The answer was yes. Our team of four clinical specialists
at Hanger Prosthetics and Orthotics set off to spend ten
days in Kabul, Afghanistan, to treat as many amputees as
possible. Our goal was to fit forty patients, one limb per
day for each practitioner on the team.

We arrived to see the devastation of years of war that
had not only scarred the people but had also deeply
scarred the city of Kabul itself. We literally did not see a
single building that was not ravaged or damaged by mis-
siles, mortars or bullets. What was not damaged, however,
was the spirit of the Afghan people. Their collective will to
greet each day with a positive approach, a smile and a
wave to our group of foreign visitors was refreshing, and
it was a powerful reminder that attitude is not what happens, but rather how we react to what happens.

During the first few days, our clinic was overwhelmed

by military personnel missing legs and arms—some actually missing two or three limbs. Each soldier was excited and anxious to receive a new artificial limb, to stand tall once again as an active participant in the community.

After the third day, during a break in our hectic schedule, I noticed a young boy I guessed to be about twelve sitting on a curb across the street with a pair of crutches by his side. I could clearly see that one of his legs was amputated above what was once his knee. I crossed the street, and with the aid of an interpreter, I talked with the boy. He told me he had stepped on a land mine on the way home from school two years before. The blast killed his best friend and amputated his leg. He had been walking with the aid of crutches ever since. He heard about the clinic to get a new leg and had been waiting for two days to visit us. "But the rules are, I cannot enter the clinic for treatment until all the men have been treated first."

I returned to the clinic and convened an impromptu meeting with the team. We discussed the situation then asked for a meeting with our hosts. "Tomorrow we will be accepting only women and children amputees for the clinic."

This announcement was not well received. "We are soldiers! And we were here first! We demand that you treat us before the women and children!"

Our team stood firm to our commitment to help the people of Afghanistan, and to us that meant treating men, women and children equally. "We will not treat any more soldiers unless we treat an equal number of women and children," we said with false bravado.

We left the clinic that evening, unsure of what to expect the next morning. As we approached the clinic the next day, to our surprise and amazement there were over twenty-five women and children, all missing either a leg or an arm, sitting outside the entrance, waiting for us to arrive.

And smiling in the front of the line was the young boy I saw sitting on the curb the day before.

A few days later, it came time for him to stand and walk on his newly completed custom-made artificial limb. As I fitted the new leg, I realized that he did not have two shoes. The interpreter repeated the boy's explanation. "When I lost my leg, I lost my shoe."

Without hesitation, I untied my sneaker, pulled it off my foot and placed it on his prosthetic one. He looked up at me, smiling in disbelief—seemingly as excited about the new sneaker as he was the new leg!

I stood beside him in stocking feet and taught him how to walk again. The power of his spirit, his warmth and genuine gratitude overwhelmed me. Despite the devastation to his country and his fragile body, he stood tall and walked with pride on two feet in new sneakers. The interpreter translated, "Thank the people of America for my leg and new shoes. Tell them I will pray for them to have a good and long life."

Dale Berry

Strong Medicine

We are prone to judge success by the index of our salaries or the size of our automobiles rather than by the quality of our service and relationship to mankind.

Dr. Martin Luther King, Jr.

Our patient, a dark Haitian boy, appeared falsely rotund in this country of deprivation. Martin, the seven-year-old, hovered in the doorway wearing a clean but worn red jersey that hung from one shoulder. He clutched a white plastic bottle.

Ed placed a hand on the child's exposed shoulder and looked over him into the hospital room, where the boy's parents stood. Stray sunlight peered through the concrete-block windows. Edward tugged at the edges of his crisp, white coat, smiled at the boy's parents and said, "Your son, he is looking well."

The parents beamed, hugged their son enthusiastically and chattered in their native tongue. Edward's warm smile embraced them, and with a final pat to his small patient, he pivoted and rejoined our hospital rounds.

We were in Leogane, Haiti, on a medical mission for Physicians for Peace. I'd had my gastroenterology practice just three years when I jumped at the chance to come to Haiti with Edward. Our weeklong mission was to install a complete video endoscopy suite—the first in the country—into L'Hopital Ste. Croix. A hospital in Suffolk, Virginia, had donated the equipment. The U.S. Marines had delivered the gear by amphibious assault ship. Jacques, the hospital's chief of staff, was delighted with this visit of colleagues and the bounty of modern equipment, as well as the donated drug samples.

After we completed our rounds, I asked Ed about Martin. He told me that he'd met the boy the year before. At that point, Martin had been hospitalized for two months. "He had sunken eyes, was unable to eat and had wasted to fifty pounds with chronic diarrhea and rectal bleeding," Ed said. "His family had brought him to the hospital to die. They knew he would perish, because they were sure that a Petro Vodou curse had been placed on him by a black-magic Vodou priest."

I knew Vodou, which we refer to as voodoo, was the dominant religion in Haiti. The loa, or spirits which inhabit the body, may be Petro loa—angry and bitter—or Rada loa, kind and good. Martin's family believed that the Vodou priest had made Petro death curses on their son, and so he would die.

Ed had done a colonoscopy on Martin and found he had Crohn's disease in both his large and small intestines. Unable to absorb nutrients, the boy was starving regardless of whatever food his poor family might procure. A prescription of prednisone, the most effective management in this poor country, was started. Ed had then returned to Virginia.

Jacques had watched young Martin rapidly improve, having received correct diagnosis and treatment. However, the boy's family had attributed his improvement to the talisman of the pill bottle along with being in a holy place, the Episcopalian hospital. Eventually, his parents had moved into the boy's room, and all had been living at the hospital for over a year, finding safe harbor there from the Vodou. The boy carried the prednisone bottle with him at all times, for comfort and protection.

Our week in Haiti was hectic as we installed the suite and worked on so many improvements.

Shortly after our return stateside, Jacques contacted Ed with a follow-up. "After your last visit, when you said, 'Your son is looking well,' Martin and his family took the medicine and left the safety of the hospital. They said the Rada loa, the white magic, of the foreign wise man convinced them that their son was healed, that the crisis had passed!"

Sometimes, we in medicine forget the Rada loa we possess in our white coat, our voice, our touch. And our magic is without borders.

Patricia Raymond, M.D.

Earning Her Wings

At the end of her shift, Lois, a surgical and intensive care nurse for thirty years, was eager to go home to a hot bath and a novel. As she pulled out of the hospital parking lot, she saw the nearby ambulance station and felt an unexplainable urge to stop and greet the paramedics, most of whom she had worked with in the past as an EMT. The closer she got, the stronger she felt compelled to stop.

She had barely entered the building and greeted her friends when the phone rang. "There's been a two-car accident," the head paramedic said. "We're understaffed today and could sure use your experience, Lois. Will you come with us?"

Instinctively, she climbed into one of the ambulances. As a saffron sunset hung over the Rocky Mountains, Lois felt an unseen force urging her to help. The sirens shrieked, and they soon arrived at the accident site. While paramedics attended to an injured man in one car, Lois checked the vital signs of a woman sitting in the other vehicle. There was no blood or visible signs of injury, and the woman said nothing, but stared at Lois with vacant eyes.

Lois suspected a brain concussion but kept her

thoughts to herself. Hoping to comfort the woman, she said, "Looks like you're going to be fine, but just to be on the safe side, we'll take you to the hospital."

Mutely, the woman continued to stare at Lois, as if her eyes were about to pop out of their sockets.

The injured man was loaded into an ambulance that sped away, and the paramedics placed the woman onto a gurney and into a second ambulance. En route to the hospital, Lois held the patient's hands and comforted her with assurances that everything was going to be fine.

The following morning when Lois reported for duty, she discovered that the woman accident victim was a patient on her floor. After checking her chart, Lois was relieved to see she was well enough to be discharged.

She entered the room. "Hello, I'm Lois, your nurse."

The patient blinked her eyes and her face turned white. "Are you real or am I hallucinating?"

"Oh, I'm real, I assure you." Lois took her hand.

"A . . . are you sure you're not a . . . an angel?"

Lois smiled and attached the blood pressure cuff. "Nurses are often referred to as angels of mercy."

Her patient continued to stare at Lois and whispered, "I mean a real angel."

Lois raised her eyebrows. "A pair of wings would be handy, but, believe me, I'm just as human as you are."

The woman shook her head. "Last night, I was in an auto accident, and thought I might die. The sun was slipping behind the mountains when suddenly, an angel appeared in a halo of light. When she touched me, I felt a surge of love and knew God sent her to reassure me that I'd live." She clasped Lois' hands. "You look and sound exactly like her, except you don't have wings!"

Sally Kelly-Engeman

The Killing Streak

*By a divine instinct men's minds distrust ensu-
ing danger, as by proof we see the waters swell
before a boisterous storm.*

William Shakespeare

As a young paramedic working on Florida's gulf coast,
I had begun to develop the cynical attitude of my many
coworkers, believing that people were generally responsi-
ble for the trouble they got themselves into on a daily
basis. Although we tried to help, often the circumstances
of violence led to the loss of lives, lives we felt powerless
to save.

We countered this feeling of helplessness by joking
about the most morbid of human conditions. Humor
became our powerful protective mechanism. In general,
our crew was in a slump. Everyone we seemed to touch
was either dead or died shortly after their arrival to the
emergency room. We were "the Death Squad" or "the
Grim Reapers" to our colleagues, who were out delivering
babies or pulling children out of storm drains. At first it
was funny, and my partner and I took it all in stride, but

by the end of our second month of "Why don't you guys go to work for the coroner" jokes, the "killing streak" was getting old.

My partner, John, was a seasoned veteran of eleven years who had seen just about everything there was to see. He could tell stories that would make you laugh till you wet your pants, and some that would make you want to lose your lunch. He was an even-tempered soul with a frame that could fill most doorways. I admired his skill and his ability to calm even the most belligerent falling-down drunk.

As partners go, he was the best, and around the end of our second year together, I had begun to anticipate his movements and finish his sentences. I learned when to hold on as he drove our vehicle around a corner, and I learned to read the cadence of his voice as a situation turned from bad to *get the hell out of here*. I trusted his instincts and for whatever reason believed he could sense when something needed to be done. Whenever John said, "Let's hang around a while," I knew something was up. John, on the other hand, thought I was nuts and dismissed my belief in his street sense even though I had pointed out several instances when he had discovered something everyone else at a scene had missed.

The most profound example of his uncanny ability occurred the fourth month we were partnered together. We arrived on the scene of what appeared to be the natural or accidental death of a very elderly lady. From the looks of things, the dear soul was headed up the staircase and collapsed from any number of conditions plaguing ninety-something-year-old ladies. In a nutshell, she took a header down the steps, where she remained until our siren-wailing arrival, at which time she could be officially pronounced dead.

At the scene, John kept going to the table and picking

up the old woman's glasses—thick as coke bottles, giant cataract-compensating things, worn by just about every elderly woman who was now gathered in mourning on the front porch. "Let's hang around a minute," John said. Then he walked over to the detective, who was getting into his car, and told him the lady had been murdered! It took three days for word to reach the squad room that our dear little old lady was indeed murdered by her elderly next-door neighbor, who admitted strangling her when she refused his advances. "She would have needed her glasses to walk across the room," John reasoned. "I thought it was odd that they were on the table."

It was during our many tours as "angels of death" that we started to think about adding little skull-and-cross bones to our helmets. The grief of the families at every scene was starting to make us doubt our abilities. We drove faster, worked harder and prayed silently on our way to every call. The rest of our squad began to feel sorry for us and would offer to take our turn for, "Man down, CPR in progress," but John never wavered. We took our turn, and our patients died and we waited for our streak to be over.

Takeout always seemed to work best for us, because we have yet to sit down at a table and not get called out. Our food carefully stowed between us was all it took for the next call to come in. The Death Squad was on the move again, this time for an overturned dump truck on the highway. *Probably some speeding cowboy dumped his load that will tie up traffic till Monday afternoon,* I thought. But the view through our front window told a different story.

Before us lay a gigantic flatbed tractor trailer overturned on its side; a literal mountain of sand covered three lanes of the highway. "That's not a dump truck," whispered John as we leaped from our vehicle and ran towards the crowd of bellowing police officers, the remains of a compact car crumpled by the side of the road. The driver inside had suffered massive facial injuries and was unconscious, but still alive. John barked into his radio and summoned the life-flight helicopter to transport our victim to the trauma center. We frantically cut away the wreckage and lifted the broken woman onto a backboard. We supplied oxygen and intravenous fluids, and suctioned the blood from her mouth. We loaded her into the chopper and listened to the radio as they notified the hospital that she had suffered a cardiac arrest and that CPR was in progress. We had failed again. I wanted to go home, hide in a closet and cry for a week.

Then it happened. "Let's hang around a minute," said John.

"What?" I growled. "You want to help them move some sand?"

John walked over to the car and peered inside, and after a minute or so, he emerged holding a tiny shoe. "Where's the baby?" he asked.

"What baby? Whose baby?" I had no idea what he was talking about. Then I watched my partner take off running like I had never seen him run before, and like an idiot, I ran right behind him. We reached the top of the sand pile, and John started digging. "Find the kid!" he barked. "She came from the store up the road . . . diapers . . . milk . . . the shoe. Find the kid!"

We clawed through the sand like crazy people, yelling for others to help us. We were searching for a child who may very well have been at home safe and sound, a child whose mother would spend the next six months recovering from her injuries, including the loss of her beauty and the sight in her right eye. Then I heard my partner, a giant, doorframe-filling bear of a man with a heart of gold, scream with delight. "I found him!" Indeed he had. The him turned out to be a her, and at nine months old, she had been propelled through the windshield of her mother's car and landed in the biggest pile of sand I had ever seen, unharmed except for a small cut on her right foot, which surely would not have occurred had she been wearing her shoe. I cannot express the joy I felt.

Our streak was over; we were no longer angels of death. Although we continued to suffer our losses over the year that followed, the baby's shoe hanging from our rearview mirror reminded us that anything was possible if you just trust your instincts and listen to your heart.

Debbie Gallagher

Waiting for Mother

What do we live for, if it is not to make life less difficult for each other.

George Eliot

Mornings at the nursing home find Gretta's wheelchair stationed in front of the third-floor elevator, where she sits eyeing the arrivals. Outside, the August sun beats down on the slate roof. The third floor is the hottest. Every time I get off the elevator, Gretta is sitting, waiting, her hair plastered to her forehead. She is a small, neat-looking woman with curly hair and bright blue eyes. While many residents are pale, their color reflecting the slow circulation of the elderly, Gretta has pink cheeks and a lively expression. She wears pastel blouses and vel-vet slippers, that perch on the footrest of her wheelchair. As a member of the recreation department, I'm responsi-ble for engaging residents in meaningful activity, but I've had no luck with Gretta.

"Would you like to come to the activities room for our sing-along?" I ask.

"My mother's coming," she explains patiently. "If she

doesn't see me, she'll go home." She looks up at me. "Have you seen my mother?" Gretta is eighty-one. Her mother, according to her file, has been dead for thirty years.

Another particularly hot morning, I exit the elevator, and there she is as usual. I wipe my brow and say, "Gretta, let me take you to the television room, where it's cool." She shakes her head, determined to wait, though her blouse is damp with sweat.

When lunchtime arrives, a nurse wheels Gretta, under great protest, to the dining room. It's not long, though, before she wheels herself back to the elevator, as though pulled by magnetic force.

One day, Billy, a long-term resident with a face like Popeye's, decides to take matters into her own hands. Billy, who'd been no stranger to the bottle in her former life, rules the third floor. Even the nurses avoid confronting her well-known short fuse. Billy plants her five-feet-tall self in front of Gretta's wheelchair, deliberately blocking the view of the elevator doors. "Look, Gretta, you've got to knock it off. You're always in the way, day after day."

Gretta becomes agitated, shifting her weight from side to side, trying to see around Billy. "My mother's coming. I'm waiting for her."

Billy leans on her cane and bends down until she is inches from Gretta's startled face. "Your mother is dead. She's not coming to see you."

Gretta attempts to maneuver around Billy, explaining, "My mother's coming any minute."

With that, Billy pushes Gretta's wheelchair back with the tip of her cane, "Look, I hate to tell you this, but your mother's up in heaven." She jerks her thumb upward, adding, "With my mother."

Gretta blinks. "You mean . . . my mother's dead?"

Billy nods. "She's dead all right."

Gretta appears more shocked than saddened. "But . . . when did it happen?"

"A long time ago," Billy says, patting her shoulder. "Let's not talk about it anymore, okay?"

Later, while riding in the elevator with Billy, I tell her that for years the social workers have tried to get Gretta to accept her mother's death, and I'm impressed that Billy has done it with a direct confrontation.

Billy shrugs. "We've all lost our families. We have to accept it." When the elevator reaches the lobby, she pauses. "Besides, I was tired of that dame talking about her mother all the time."

Gretta no longer sits outside the third-floor elevators. According to the nurses on her floor, she stays in her room, staring out the window. When I go to see her, she grabs my sleeve and looks up at me. "Did you hear? My mother is dead."

The days pass. Summer winds down, and I don't see much of Gretta. One afternoon, while I'm on the third floor going from room to room serving ice cream, I'm shocked to discover Gretta lying in bed. The shades are pulled, and in the gloom I can detect the transformation. Her once-curly hair is dull and limp. Her cheeks sag, like deflated balloons. When I offer her ice cream, she shakes her head and looks away.

Billy is walking by Gretta's room and peeks in. "She babies herself," she declares dismissively.

When I express my concern to the social worker, she reminds me that the residents are not children and shouldn't be patronized. They should be encouraged to accept reality. They deserve the truth, she says, because, "The truth will set them free." She concludes by telling me not to worry, because, "Gretta is processing her sorrow and will emerge all the stronger."

I'm not so sure. Two days later when I invite Gretta to a

worship service, she raises her head from her pillow and says, "I'm too tired."

A housekeeper who's mopping the floor follows me outside to the hall and says, "She won't be around much longer."

"What do you mean?"

"I've been working here twenty years. I see it all the time. They give up and take to their rooms."

I glance back at Gretta's tiny form in the bed. There's no denying the huge change in her.

"She's given up," the housekeeper says, moving down the hall.

Labor Day brings a long weekend. Back at work, I exit the third-floor elevator and see a small, compact figure in a yellow blouse stationed to the right of the elevator door.

"Gretta! You look terrific!"

Her eyes are bright and her dimples flash when she smiles.

"Would you like to play cribbage later?" I ask, clasping her warm hand.

She gives me a patient smile. "You're nice to ask dear, but I'm expecting my mother any minute." Her gaze returns to the elevator. "Did you see her? Have you seen my mother?"

As long as she has breath, Gretta will wait. Fortunately, her sojourn into reality had been brief. For Gretta, the truth did not set her free.

"Haven't seen her yet, Gretta," I say. "But I'll watch for her."

Sharon Love Cook

No Response

Honesty is the best policy.

Benjamin Franklin

It was the third day my husband, Joe, had been in the intensive care unit following his fifth surgery for the removal of most of his remaining small intestine. The surgery took many more hours than expected. Joe was older and weaker, and he wasn't responding.

As I sat beside his bed, two nurses tried repeatedly to get him to cough, open his eyes, move a finger—anything to let them know he could hear them. He didn't respond. I sat praying to God to please help Joe respond—any sign that he might survive.

Finally, one of the nurses turned to me and suggested that perhaps if she knew something personal about our family, she could try to stimulate his response with that knowledge. She said, "Maybe you, as his daughter, could help us with such information." I smiled and said, "I'll be happy to give you personal information, and thank you for the compliment, but I'm his wife of forty-three years, not his daughter, and we're about the same age." The nurse looked at me and said, "The entire staff thought you were his daughter and had even commented how wonderful they thought it was that his daughter was with him all the time."

As they were expressing how I looked so young, a little cough came from my husband, and we all turned to stare at him. He didn't open his eyes, but loud and clear he said, "She dyes her hair!"

Donna Parisi

Good Night, Harry

Behold I send an angel before you to keep you in the way and to bring you into the place which I have prepared for you.

Exodus 23:20

My name is Harry. When I was forty-two, I was dynamic and distinguished, independent in life as I worked or traveled. Travel was my passion. By the time I was forty-five, I looked sixty. And now, at age forty-seven, I look ninety.

What robbed me of vitality, dignity and very life is AIDS and several of its henchmen—the worst of which is an aggressive cancer-like disease named Kaposi's sarcoma.

My travels are now limited to being rolled on my side and back to the other side while lying in bed in an inpatient hospice. I have come here to die and will oblige fate by doing so.

Kind, gentle hands care for me, but unfortunately, their kindness cannot stop the pain of wooden-hard legs rotting from within from the sarcoma. Being turned is now a major agony, even with the narcotics I'm given.

Often, I am uncertain of who is caring for me, even

though through the medicinal haze, the voices are familiar and sometimes I can connect them fleetingly to a name of a friend or a nurse, or an aide. Two weeks ago, I joked with them all. Now, I would trade my life for a moment of laughter and relief.

"Harry. Harry. How are you tonight?"

I recognize the voice as that of a woman who works the evening shift, although I could not have told you until a second ago if it was day or night. Her name comes and goes with an ebb and surge of pain.

I try to respond to her question, but all I can manage is a low sound. I am not sure if it is the greeting I meant to say or a low moan. Even though it is of my creation, I do not recognize the sound.

I know she is going to pat me on my shoulder, like always. And she does. And I smile what must be an internal smile.

I can hear the stretching of latex as she gloves her hands and the low click of the pump that pushes steady but now not-so-small doses of morphine into my welcoming veins. I can feel the pressure of her fingers as she checks the IV site in my right arm, and all the while she talks to me softly.

Suddenly, what attention I can muster is filled with the image of fruit, the smell of fruit. It must be her scented shampoo, because they discourage perfume here. The smell of berries is subtle, distant, yet pleasing, comforting.

There is a pause. I know she is clasping the head of the stethoscope in her hand to warm it. I know this because she always does this. She is both methodical and kind. It comforts me, and I begin to drift.

Then, an almost shocking damp coolness is against my face. I turn my head away because of the surprise of the sensation. I should have remembered. She always gently wipes my face with a cool washcloth. How could I forget something that feels so good?

The changing of the bandages on my legs is the opposite. It sends pain shooting up my calves, thighs and throughout my body. No amount of morphine helps. No amount of gentleness helps. It is always agonizing. I am sure it is horrible for her, too, because there are times when I can smell the rot of flesh from my legs. Still, she performs this mutually horrible task not because she is paid to, but because she cares for those in her charge.

I can hear the sounds of instruments being placed in a tray, plastic bags opened and tied shut, and all the while she continues to talk softly. I am not lucid enough to understand all that she says, but the words and her tone comfort me as the intense pain from my legs subsides slightly.

There is another snap of latex and the flow of running water as she washes her hands across the room. And then, once again, a calm, quiet reassuring voice comes to me above the dullness of my senses.

"Good night, Harry." I feel a pat on the shoulder and the softest of kisses on my forehead. I try to discern which side of life and death derived that kiss. There is an angel out there. I know.

as told to Daniel James Reust

Brothers

Greater love hath no man than this, that a man lay down his life for his friends.

John 15:13

The air temperature had already soared to ninety degrees; the humidity equaled that number. It was to be a blistering day in Southeast Asia. Last night's thunderstorm was making the mud stick to us like glue. By evening, the mud would dry, and the whirling chopper blades would throw up gigantic red-dust rooster tails. At times, it reminded me of angel wings, the dust was so thick.

I was a U.S. Navy Corpsman in the Hunter Angel 7 Helicopter Squadron. I looked out for my men. I took care of them, talked with them and consoled them. They called me "Doc." It was an honor.

We had been flying seven to eight missions a day for the past month. Most of the missions were air reconnaissance, where we took photographs to locate any signs of the Viet Cong infiltrating into the northern highlands of Laos. Our mission was different today, however. We were to locate a U.S. Marine Reconnaissance team (Recon) on the ground about 25 kilometers inside Laos. The North Vietnamese had spotted them, and a fierce firefight had ensued. There were casualties. One killed, two wounded. Angel-7 was quickly airborne. We were approximately forty-five minutes away. They would have to hold out until we got there. We were their only link to survival.

About fifteen miles out from the raging firefight, we dropped to 800 feet, then to treetop level. I could almost grab a fist full of leaves as we raced by at ninety miles per hour. I zipped up my flak vest, and locked and loaded my automatic rifle. Saying a quick prayer, I blessed myself, though I'm not a Catholic. I always did that. The adrenaline surged through my body; my nauseous stomach churned. Our flight-crew engineer, only twenty-four years old, crammed a whole pack of Beechnut gum into his mouth. Dennis, our back-up gunner, had a baseball-size chew of tobacco in his mouth. He was locked, loaded and ready.

Clang! Zip! Clang! Clang! Bullets ripped through the skin of the chopper. The door gunner sprayed the ground with deadly gunfire. Our pilot put the helicopter into a rolling zigzag maneuver. Our lieutenant shouted, "Everyone okay back there?" We all turned to look at each other. Then I saw my buddy Dennis, still in his jump seat, bent over, head down, his flight suit covered with blood. I quickly crawled to him across the deck, yelling his name, but he never moved, he never answered. He'd taken several rounds. I choked really hard and held him. Shaking, I released his safety belt and pulled him to the back, and I covered his face with his flak jacket.

At treetop level, coming in fast, we spotted the Recon team—they'd popped red smoke to mark their location. Hovering three feet off the ground, we saw guys making a break for the chopper. Our gunner started laying down cover. The Viet Cong fired back. Bullets hit the chopper, zipping in one side and out the other, shrapnel flying all over the place inside.

I leaped from the bird, landing in the cushion of grass. Two Recon guys were trying to carry a badly wounded man. I got up and ran to them, and placed my shoulder under the belly of the wounded guy. "Let's go!"

We got to the chopper, and the gunner helped drag the wounded guy in. I put my hand on the butts of the other guys and pushed them in. That was three. There were still five more. I looked in the direction of the two guys at the edge of the grass. One was standing, trying to help the other one to his feet. He'd been hit. I ran to them, keeping low while the gunner continued to fire from the chopper. I saw the terrified look on the guy trying to help his brother, who was covered in blood. We both got hold of an arm and dragged him back to the chopper. Two more men in. There were still three more, but where were they?

Just then, they came racing out of the trees like running backs headed for the goal line. Gunfire seemed to be chasing them, some of it coming my way. I got to them, helped them to the chopper, pushing them in while the gunner pulled.

I was about to climb aboard the chopper when, ka-thump! My ears rang. A round had struck my helmet. I could hardly hear. I was disoriented. An arm reached down for me, everything seemingly in slow motion. I reached for the arm, and it pulled me up. I got my right leg up on the deck as I felt the chopper lift off the ground. I struggled to get the other leg in. The arm held on like a death grip, pulling me up. The helicopter banked left, and I rolled onto the deck of the chopper, clasping the arm that had hold of me. We were safe. Angel-7 was airborne and headed home.

I turned my attention to see who was wounded worse. The rest of the crew and Recon guys helped me take care of the worst cases. We were brothers helping each other. I focused on the most severely injured guy. His chest and legs were soaked in glistening blood, coming mostly from a two-inch hole under his left armpit that went through to his back. I grabbed large compress dressings from my bag, pushed them against the holes and wrapped the ties around his shoulder and chest several times real tight and tied it in a knot. As I pushed morphine into his arm, he tried to reach into his shirt pocket, staring at me all the time. I reached into his pocket and pulled out a little brass-shielded Bible. I placed it in his right hand and closed his fingers around it. Shaking, he reached for me and tried to speak. I looked into his teary eyes, and he had the "thousand-yard stare." Knowing there was nothing more I could do for him, I cradled him in my arms. I choked hard, trying not to cry. I knew the life was flowing from him. I told him it was okay, it would be all right, he was going to make it. But he knew. He squeezed my hand and I held his tight. With his blood on my hands, I marked his head with the sign of the cross. I put my head next to his and prayed, "God, please tell me I did my best; tell me I did everything right." He couldn't have been but nineteen. I held him while he slipped from the bounds of the earth into the hands of God.

The lieutenant pointed to my helmet lying there with a chunk blown out of the back. I picked it up and saw blood on the inside. I touched the back of my head, and it was wet. Fresh blood. The lieutenant bandaged the wound at the base of my skull then wrapped the ties around my head.

The chopper touched down near the field hospital to the waiting corpsmen nurses and doctors. The non-wounded jumped out and helped with the wounded. I was still holding my patient in my lap. I reached down and closed his eyes. A doctor and corpsman climbed in and said, "Okay, Doc. We can take him now."

A brother was at my side, making sure the doctors checked me too. My head wound was minor, and later, after getting cleaned up and changed, I wanted to lie down and count my blessings. But instead, we all had to assemble for a debriefing.

Our gunner came over to sit by me. He patted me on the back. "You did your best," he said.

I tried to smile. "Thanks for pulling me in."

He looked at me. "Doc, I didn't pull you in. The kid with the Bible did."

Tom Williams

5

ACTS OF KINDNESS

Never doubt that a small group of thoughtful, committed citizens can change the world; indeed, it's the only thing that ever has.

Margaret Mead

The Little White Box

I don't think of the misery, but of the beauty that still remains.

Anne Frank

"What is it that Mrs. Mathers keeps talking on about?" I asked the nurse at the front desk of the nursing home where I had been working for about a week.

"I don't know. I just don't know. She has been here for two weeks. The family knows she won't live for another month, so they chose to place her here. She constantly goes on and on about some darn little white plastic box," the nurse replied.

"A box?"

"Just get her dressed for bed, and forget about her ramblings," she instructed.

"Yes, ma'am," I said as I walked away.

Every day I went to work, Mrs. Mathers chattered on and on about that little white box. She constantly lay in bed with her hands partially covering her face. When I moved her hands to wash them, I saw tears rolling down her cheeks.

"Before I die. My little white box. Please," she'd say.

"Mrs. Mathers. I don't know what you mean." I'd tell her.

Everyday, it was the same routine. No matter what I would say to her, I just could not understand what she was talking about. Several times over the next week, the doctor was called to attend her. I stood outside her room to see if the doctor would pull her through. After he left, I went in and wiped her forehead, and made sure she was comfortable.

"My house. My little white box. Please," she said over and over.

Finally, one afternoon at 3:30, when I was about to get off work, I walked up to the desk, pulled out Mrs. Mathers' chart and wrote down her last known address. I drove the five miles or so until I located the house number I had written down on my pad. When I arrived, I saw there was an estate sale going on, with cars and people everywhere.

"You're going to have to get a number if you are going to bid," said one of the men as I walked up.

"I'm not going to bid," I replied.

I walked around inside the house for about ten minutes, looking at what all had been tagged for sale. As I entered the dining room, I saw a gentleman wrapping various items and stuffing them into cardboard boxes. Sitting on the edge of the table was a little white plastic box.

"Excuse me. By any chance did you buy this little white box?" I asked him.

"I bought everything in this room."

"Could I look inside this little box?"

"Sure. There's nothing in there of any value," he told me.

Slowly, I opened the box and I looked inside. "Oh, dear God!" I said to myself. "Can I have this box?" I asked the man.

"Not worth nothin' to me," he said.

I ran out of the house as fast as I could, and I headed

back to the nursing home. When I arrived, I walked into Mrs. Mathers' room. "Mrs. Mathers, it's me, Roger. Look what I got."

Slowly, she opened her eyes then started to shake as she reached out and took the little white box from my hand. "Water," she said.

I walked over to the sink and I got her a cup of water, then I just stood there.

"Thank you, dear," she said softly.

"You are very welcome." I patted her hand then stood watching her as she removed the contents of the box. I nodded so she would know that I finally understood that she was a fine lady. Then, like a gentleman, I bowed my head and then left her room.

When I returned to work the next day, I learned that Mrs. Mathers had passed away during the night. In all my years of working in nursing homes, although there were many deaths, I only attended two funerals. One was Mrs. Mathers'.

I stood by the casket for more than an hour as many people filed past.

I could not count the times I heard her friends say, "Jane looks at least twenty years younger with her dentures in."

Roger Dean Kiser, Sr.

"I love Grandma. The only thing false that's ever come out of her mouth are her teeth."

On the Line

Strength is born in the deep silence of long-suffering hearts, not amidst joy.

Felicia Hemans

Multiple sclerosis wasn't her disease of choice. But by age fifty-six, Pat had discovered there weren't all that many choices in life. Some things simply happen, and you try to adjust. However, she'd lived with MS for twenty-three years, and it was getting worse.

Like a determined army, the disease marched onward, conquering her body a fraction at a time. It seized her dexterity, it crippled her range of motion, it weakened her coordination. The disease had stripped her of both strength and dignity.

Her kids were grown and on their own—their dad had deserted them ages ago—and she felt lonely, housebound, useless. Good for nothing anymore, unless you counted talking on the phone. At least that was something she could still do. She loved making contact with the "outside."

Day after day Pat sat, confined to her wheelchair, with the television remote her best friend. In fact, earlier that afternoon she caught the tail end of a local news story. She'd increased the volume so she didn't miss a word.

"... And with the rise in single parenting, the number of latchkey children in this community is higher than ever."

Pat couldn't get her mind off the issue of all those kids right here in her hometown, alone and with no one to care for them after school. In spite of everything, she always had felt fortunate to be home for her kids, present at the crossroads in their lives. Present to ask about their day and keep track of homework, friends and activities. And she'd had lots of time to listen. She was good at listening.

That's when it occurred to her. *What if . . . ?*

Using the weight of her arm to power her near-useless hand, Pat pushed the speed dial on her telephone. She had a great plan. If only she could get some of her house-bound support-group friends to agree. . . .

She spent the entire evening on the phone talking, not listening. By the time the home-care nurse arrived to ready her for bed, Pat wore a satisfied smile. She was tired but pleased. Tomorrow, she would set her plan in motion by calling an elementary-school principal she knew.

Pat phoned early. "Suzanne, I have the greatest idea. Could Lincoln Elementary use a Phone Pals Platoon for latchkey children?"

"What exactly do you have in mind?"

Nearly tripping over her words, Pat outlined the project, pairing latchkey kids to a phone pal. Someone they could call each day at a set time. Someone to answer homework questions, to remind them about their scout projects, to ask about their day. Someone to listen to them. Someone like Pat and her disabled friends.

"I love the idea. How soon can we start?" Pat smiled at Suzanne's eager response.

In no time at all, Pat organized the network of phone

pals, pairing eager invalids with equally excited students. And each weekday afternoon, at exactly 3:45, she placed her own special call and waited for the bubbly second grader to answer.

"Hi, Pat! Guess what? I got a one hundred on my spelling test! And Katie and I aren't mad at Jessica anymore...."

Pat grinned into the phone, settling deeper into her wheelchair to listen. After all, listening was her strength.

Carol McAdoo Rehme

The Package

The heart of the giver makes the gift dear and precious.

Martin Luther

Sharon was asleep when the package arrived. Though I was eager to discover what was inside the huge box, I didn't wake her. As her emphysema progressed, she seemed better able to sleep in the daytime than at night.

As a nurse and Sharon's mother, I assumed responsibility for much of her care, but her grown daughter, sons and family members frequently filled in for me, so it seemed unlikely that any of them would mail her a package. If they had a gift, they'd bring it along when they came to help.

Sharon had lots of friends in town. She'd raised her children here and had been involved in church and community activities. Recently however, as disease increasingly ravaged her body, visits from her friends had decreased. I wondered if one of her friends, unable to handle a personal visit, had sent the package. I studied the address. It wasn't local.

As I folded the clothes for Sharon, I tried to recall who she might have known way off in Kentucky. She'd spent her whole life in our small Colorado hometown, and we'd been so close through the years of her illness that I couldn't imagine she'd be receiving a present from someone I didn't know. I stacked the clean clothes on top of the mysterious box and carried it to Sharon's bedroom.

It was almost time for her medication. I put the pills on a tray along with a pink peace rose from the garden. Even though I'd spent many years in sickrooms, I always found them stifling. I opened the windows to let in some fresh air, air that Sharon couldn't enjoy because she was on oxygen full time now. I knew how much she must hate being almost totally confined to her bedroom.

I set the tray on the table by the bed we'd rented from the hospital supply center. Sharon could control its movement up and down, and that allowed her to go online on her computer independently.

While researching her illness, Sharon had discovered a chat room called "Smoke No More." She visited it every evening, e-mailing messages of hope and encouragement to people who were trying to give up smoking or who were suffering from smoking-related illnesses. "Some of the people in the group," she told me, "are lots worse off than I am. At least I can see out the window, Mom," she said.

And how she loved to look out at the night sky. Often, if I was there in the evening, we'd sit together in the quiet, peaceful stillness. "I think this must be what heaven is like," she said once.

Now, looking at her pale face and frail body, I knew that her time with us on earth was almost over. I bent down and kissed her gently on the cheek. "Sharon, honey, I have your medicine, and guess what? There's a package for you. It's a big one. Do you want to open it now or wait till this evening?"

Sharon grinned. "I bet you've been dying of curiosity. Go ahead and open it, Mom."

I read Sharon the return label as I eagerly pulled off the tape. She recognized the name immediately as one of her e-mail buddies. "But what ever could she have sent me?" I handed her the card. She read out loud,

> *Dear Sharon,*
> *At a time when you must need lots of care yourself, you've become the caregiver to all of us here at the chat room. You are a bright light to me as I struggle with my own illness. I feel stronger because of your prayers and your cheerful messages. I know you rarely get out, so I hope this will bring the outside world closer to you.*

Weakly, Sharon pulled the tissue paper from the box then gasped, "A telescope!"

That gift did indeed bring the heavens closer to Sharon. She gazed at the stars every single night until her death.

When we put the announcement of her passing online, she received more than 200 final messages from her chat-room friends.

"Thanks for your strength when I had none."

"Thanks for the hope."

"Thank the heavens, *you* cared for *me*."

Shirley Javernick as told to Ellen Javernick

I Can't Do a Thing

Wilma poured the puréed mixture of chicken and vegetables into a bowl then touched a spoonful to her lips, testing the temperature for her sister, Adah.

Adah had lived with Wilma and her husband for several years before her paralysis began. It first appeared as only a slight slowing of Adah's movements when she lifted a fork to her mouth. Then the day came when she couldn't push herself up from the table. The next morning she fell as she got out of bed.

Wilma made a doctor's appointment immediately, and a wearying round to specialists began. Finally, they received the dreaded diagnosis. Adah had super-progressive nuclear palsy—a mean cousin to Parkinson's disease that would gradually stiffen her muscles and paralyze her.

The next couple of years passed far too quickly, each month bringing more debilitation, until Adah's condition forced her to a walker, then a wheelchair and finally to bed. Adah's nieces and nephews remembered how they used to have trouble keeping up with this active woman when she escorted them to town. They missed her lessons in family history given as she mended their blue jeans or embroidered pillowcases for their weddings. Now her hands lay twisted and still upon the quilt covering her frail body. The change was so painful for many of the relatives, they stopped coming by, choosing instead to send another card that Wilma taped to the wall above Adah's railed bed.

Wilma, only two years younger and not in the best of health herself, took care of Adah—bathing her, turning her, feeding her, and trying to rub the achy pain out of a tired body that only vaguely resembled the woman her sister had once been.

One day had been particularly difficult when Adah managed to whisper apologetically, "I can't do a thing." Wilma patted her arm, fighting back tears as she said a silent prayer: *Lord, give me something encouraging to say.*

The answer came in a sudden brainstorm. "Adah, you can still pray," Wilma said. "Goodness knows the family needs plenty of that. Thea and the children left this morning for a long drive. Will you pray for them?"

Adah smiled and whispered, "I will."

During the next several weeks, each time Wilma received word of a particular need, she passed it along to her sister. When a neighbor mentioned his brother was facing a series of complicated medical tests, Wilma assured him of her prayers. Then she added, "And I'll tell Adah, too. She'll pray the whole time he's in the hospital."

A few days later the elated neighbor called. The doctors had decided his brother's problem could be controlled with medication. Surgery wouldn't be necessary after all.

When one of the men at church lost his job because the small company where he'd worked for twelve years closed, Wilma told Adah. The man found work the next month.

Gradually, folks began to hear about Adah's constant prayers and started calling with requests. Sometimes a worried mother called about an ill child; sometimes a child called about an ailing pet. Once a gruff husband called, clearing his throat several times before finally saying that well, yes, he, uh, had heard that Adah was a praying woman. Would she, uh, pray for his marriage?

Sometimes Adah's family wondered aloud how those prayers affected Adah herself. They couldn't help but notice that even in the midst of her pain, she possessed a graciousness and peace not expected from one so bound to a disease-captured body. Perhaps her concentration on others pulled her thoughts away from her own situation. Perhaps her constant prayerfulness wrapped her in God's grace.

Day after day the requests came, and day after day Adah whispered her prayers. The time came, though, when her voice faded totally. When she didn't whisper her usual morning greeting, Wilma pulled the bed rail down to comfort her sister with a hug. Then she said, "Adah, even if you pray only in your mind, the Lord hears you." Adah nodded.

Then one morning as Wilma relayed yet another prayer request, Adah only stared at her, unable to nod her acknowledgment. Wilma silently prayed for her sister's suffering, then patted her on the arm. "That's okay, Adah, honey. You just blink your eyes to answer me; one blink will mean yes, two blinks will mean no. Now, do you understand that Josie called to ask you to pray about moving her widowed mother?"

Adah blinked once. Yes, she understood.

That was the beginning of Adah's third and final year, still praying for others, until God released her.

Today, relatives are grateful that she is free after years of painful paralysis, yet they miss her still. They know Adah's prayers lifted their pain—and Adah straight to heaven.

Sandra Picklesimer Aldrich

Long-Distance Vitamins

Sweetest melodies are those that are by distance made more sweet.

William Wordsworth

We arrived at the hospital to find Dad exhausted and weak, but his smile was as sure as ever. It was another bout of pneumonia. My husband and I stayed with him for the weekend but had to return to our jobs by Monday morning. Local relatives would see that Dad got home from the hospital and they would look in on him regularly and prepare his meals. They would make sure he got his daily medicine and take him to his doctor appointments. But I longed to be able to let him know that we cared too, even when we weren't with him.

Then I remembered a family tradition I initiated when our children were small. When leaving their grandparents' home after a visit, each child would hide a love note about the house for their grandfather or grandmother to find after we were gone. They hid notes in the cereal box, to be poured into their bowls the next morning. They'd tuck a note under a hairbrush, in a deck of cards, next to the

phone or even in the microwave. For days after our departure, their grandparents would smile as they discovered
these reminders of our love.

So as I tidied Dad's kitchen and made up a bed for him
downstairs in the living room, I began writing notes.
Some were practical. "Dad, I froze the casserole that was
in the fridge so it wouldn't spoil." Some expressed my
love. "Dad, I hope you sleep well in your new bed." Most
notes were downstairs, where he would be confined for
several weeks until he regained strength, but one note I
hid upstairs under his pillow. "Dad, if you have found this
note, you must be feeling better. We are so glad!"

While others cared for Dad's day-to-day needs, we, of
course, would stay in touch by phone. But our notes were
a tangible reminder of our love and concern for him during this recovery period. Just like his medicines boosted
him physically, these "emotional vitamins" would boost
his spiritual health.

Several weeks later, in one of our regular phone calls, I
asked Dad how he was doing. He said, "I'll tell you how I'm
doing. I just found your note under my upstairs pillow!"

Emily Chase

Food for Thought

*I have often thought what a melancholy world
this would be without children; and what an
inhuman world without the aged.*

Samuel Coleridge

Heart failure had robbed her of her husband, and now macular degeneration was stealing her eyesight and osteoporosis was plundering her body.

I worried about my elderly neighbor's loneliness and her diet. Lack of appetite and motivation kept Gwen from cooking. More than a quiet street separated the two of us. Her life had been derailed, while mine was a locomotive on a fast track as I raised a house full of kids and maintained a demanding time schedule to match. So I turned to Koy, our little redheaded caboose, for help.

"Do you think you can carry these muffins over to Mrs. Potter's?"

"I fink I can," he nodded.

With me watching from our front door and Gwen waiting at hers, three-year-old Koy cautiously crossed the street, carrying the plate of fragrant goodies. And so began their long relationship.

"I fink Grandma Potter needs me," he would say. Or, "Don't you fink Grandma Potter wants some of those cookies?" And, "I fink Grandma Potter likes cupcakes." Then off he would go, thoughtfully bearing a plate of this or a sandwich bag of that, and always taking time to settle in for a nice little talk. Well, Koy talked; Gwen listened. A lonely last child; a lonesome lost widow.

Those regular visits continued through the years, sometimes at her invitation and other times at his instigation. As his age, sensitivity and caregiving expertise grew, Koy did more than take food. He ran her errands, did light chores and drove her to doctor appointments. On prom night, he and his date even dashed through the rain to model their finery before an admiring Grandma Potter.

Finally, as we stood arm-in-arm in the street waving Koy off to college, Gwen turned to me.

"I'm certainly going to miss that young man and his visits. You know, when he was little, he rarely came empty-handed."

I nodded agreement, remembering all the baking I used to do.

"But, when you didn't send something, our little Koy must have raided the pantry." She winked. "No matter what, he always took good care of me."

"What do you mean?"

"Over he would come, his pocket filled with raisins, pretzels, popcorn or even Cheerios. Whatever he could scavenge."

I laughed in motherly embarrassment. "Oh, good grief." I could just imagine grubby little boy hands and fists full of crumbs. "What did you do?"

"Why, I got out a serving plate," she smiled at the memory. "I watched as he proudly piled his offerings on the kitchen table. Then . . . well . . . then the two of us sat down and ate them, pocket lint and all."

Carol McAdoo Rehme

Time Flies

God sends children for another purpose than to merely keep the race—to enlarge our hearts and to make us unselfish and full of kindly sympathies and affections.

Mary Howitt

Back in the 1960s, with six children ranging from toddler to teen, my parents' lives were already full. The house overflowed with lively voices. Dick needed his work shirt ironed. Virginia wanted her dolly. Walter needed help with his biology homework. I couldn't find my gym shoes. Tom and Ray waited for a bedtime story. There never seemed to be a quiet moment.

In the midst of these demands, Grandma Jessie moved in, with her deteriorating health, increasing confusion and never-ending fears.

During storms, Grandma panicked. "Mercy, look at the violence outside. I just know the roof is going to go!" Mom would quickly drop what she was doing to gently sooth Grandma's fears. "It's a good, strong roof, Mother. You know God will take care of us." Eventually, Grandma relaxed, at least for a little while.

At night, Grandma was afraid to go to sleep. "It's only nine o'clock, but if I go to bed now, I'll wake up in the night and won't be able to get back to sleep. Oh, mercy, what will I do?"

"Jessie, what was it like when you were a little girl?" Mom would ask to reroute Grandma's thoughts.

Days and nights overflowed with caregiving responsibilities. Mom dealt with Grandma all day long. After work, Dad joined the struggle.

Even as teenagers, my two brothers and I could see the toll that constant caregiving took on our parents. As their anniversary approached, we agreed it was time for action. After school one day, we huddled in the crisp air on the front steps and talked.

"Okay, I've been thinking," I said. "Mom likes to bowl, but Dad doesn't. Dad likes to fish, but it's December. Why don't we just send them to the movies?"

"Sounds all right, but are there any good movies around?" Walter wanted to know.

"Well, I can answer that," Dick exclaimed, and he ran inside to find the morning paper. Sinking back down onto the cold, concrete steps, he opened the paper and perused it. "Look. *Brigadoon* is playing downtown. That will work."

Walter agreed, "Okay. But how in the world are we going to get all the way into downtown Baltimore to pick up tickets without Mom and Dad finding out?"

"Simple," Dick said. "I'll bike over and get them at the local box office."

Soon, the tickets were bought, and we were ready.

The big day arrived. It was hard to contain our excitement. Mom and Dad would be so surprised! Everyone was gathered in the dining room for breakfast. I could hear the crackle of bacon even before the scent reached me.

I set the table and joined Mother in the kitchen.

"Hurry, Mom," I encouraged. I grabbed a big bowl of grits in one hand and a platter of eggs in the other.

Mom followed with a basket of steaming biscuits.

After the prayer, none of us touched our food. Dad and Mom looked around. "Is there a problem?" Mom asked. "Why aren't you eating?"

Dick began his succinct speech. "Mom, Dad, you're going out tonight for your anniversary. Here's two tickets for a movie date." He handed Dad a plain business envelope. "It starts at eight."

"How . . . my goodness, how did you do this?" Mother was amazed.

Then reality hit. "Oh, but, kids, we couldn't possibly go off and leave you with your grandmother. You can handle the younger children just fine. But taking care of Grandma Jessie would be way too hard."

Dad agreed. "Goodness knows your mother deserves a night out, but you know how Grandma is. And it's worse after dark."

Maybe it was knowing that we had spent our hard-earned dollars on nonrefundable tickets. Maybe it was our conviction that we could handle the situation. Whatever it was, Mom and Dad reluctantly agreed to give our plan a try.

So at seven that night, they walked out the door. Soon, we heard the diminishing roar of the car engine.

Our challenge began in earnest. It was simple enough to say we could handle anything. Now we were about to see if we actually could!

Our strategy was to "divide and conquer." While I doled out bedtime snacks to the little ones, Dick patiently listened to Grandmother's stories for the sixtieth time. Then Walter took over, calming Grandma Jessie's nighttime fears, while Dick made sure three little sets of teeth got brushed. While Walter read a bedtime story, I helped Grandmother look for the papers she imagined she had lost.

By nine o'clock, the younger children were settled in their beds and drifting off to sleep. But there was nothing "settled" about Grandma Jessie. Just as my parents predicted, she couldn't relax or rest.

"Oh my, are Bill and Frances going to be all right? What if they have an accident?" Grandma Jessie paced the floor. Pacing from her bedroom, through the living room, dining room and kitchen, and into her bedroom again, she walked in an endless circular pattern.

I soothed Grandma as best I could, while Walter and Dick snuck off down the hall and cooked up a plan.

"Dorothy, go sit with Grandma Jessie in her room for a while," Walter came and whispered in my ear. "Keep her there till we call you, okay?"

I took Grandma's hand. "Hey, Grandma, would you show me your crocheted teacup and saucer. How does the cup stand up like that?" I coaxed. Obligingly, Grandma led me into her room.

Within minutes, Dick beckoned me into the hallway. "Hurry, now, let me have your wristwatch." Quickly, he spun the hands on the small dial.

Time flew that night, as 9:15 became 11:15 in a matter of seconds. I looked around. Every clock had "magically" changed.

Grandma was soon wandering the house again, but we were ready for her. "Grandma, it's way past time for bed. Mother and Dad will be upset to come home and find us all still up," I reasoned.

She quietly studied the kitchen clock, then the living room clock, then my watch. "Oh, my, it's late!" she declared, and she shuffled off to bed.

Now we suddenly realized the three of us would have to turn out the lights and retire, too. We wouldn't have to be asleep, but we'd have to be as quiet as if we were!

The only other sound that night was the ringing of the

telephone. I hurried to silence the bell. At the other end of the line, I heard Dad's strong voice. "It's intermission. How's your Grandmother? We can come on home now if you need us."

"Oh no, Dad," I whispered. "Everything's fine. We've all gone to bed. It's so late," I teased, quickly recounting our strategy.

"That's using your heads," Dad laughed. "I should've known you kids would figure out something. Your mother will be delighted."

I returned to my room. There was plenty of time to think before sleep overtook me. Come morning, things would still be the same. Children would fuss. Laundry would get dirty. Grandma would become distraught.

But for one night, my parents had a chance to be a newly-wed couple again.

Dorothy Palmer Young

The Magic of Making a Difference

To cultivate kindness is a valuable part of the business of life.

Samuel Johnson

We were all looking forward to Easter. Charlie had run to get last-minute candy for the Easter baskets. Finishing breakfast, both of our children were running and laughing through the living room. Suddenly, Ken, our eight-year-old, burst into the den, where I was on the phone.

"Steph is acting really funny," he said.

"Yes, I know. I hear you laughing."

"No," he insisted, "There's something wrong."

I hung up the phone and walked quickly into the bedroom where five-year-old Stephanie was lying on the floor, unconscious, with a small amount of foam in the corners of her mouth. Unable to wake her, I told Ken to call 911 and I, nurse-mom, quickly assessed her condition. Though breathing with a steady pulse, her color was gray.

The ambulance arrived and took her to Children's Hospital. Shortly after entering the emergency room, she had a seizure. Within minutes, she stopped breathing. As the staff feverishly worked on her, my husband, Charlie, arrived. We stood together, looking through the emergency room windows, not believing what was happening.

The doctor pulled us aside and told us he had no explanation for Stephanie's condition but was very concerned because her status had changed so quickly. After routine questions regarding overall health status, history and access to poisons, they transported Stephanie for a CAT scan. We were left to pray. In a state of shock, I could not believe how rapidly our lives had been turned upside down. An hour ago, we were eagerly looking forward to Easter, and now our world was crumbling around us.

With no remarkable results from the CAT scan, Stephanie was taken to the intensive care unit, where she was placed on a ventilator, in a coma. They called in expert after expert. Each ran tests and then let us know they didn't know what was happening. While I hoped and prayed for answers, I was also relieved as they ruled out one serious explanation at a time. I knew that in spite of the uncertainties, no diagnosis was good news.

We took turns at her bedside, making sure that someone was there at all times. After six days, there was no improvement. The doctors informed us that they believed she had viral encephalitis, and there was little they could do except provide supportive care. They also cautioned us that children with encephalitis often do not make a full recovery. If she did get better, we should brace ourselves for a child with severe disabilities. We were very discouraged yet hopeful for a miracle.

Later that evening, Stephanie began to move her feet and hands. By the following morning, she was breathing on her own, and the nurses detached the respirator. As I was washing her face, she suddenly put her arm around my neck and said my name. I thought I was dreaming and just stood there and stared.

From that day on, Stephanie showed steady improvement. With great courage, she approached her recovery with energy and humor. She never complained or asked "Why me?" She simply would ask, "What's next?"

We met with a series of rehabilitation specialists, who outlined a program for her to regain her strength and her skills. After a day at physical therapy, where many of the kids were coughing and sneezing, we decided it would be better to rehabilitate her at home. Both Charlie and I took a leave from work, and my mother came to help. We helped Stephanie re-learn how to walk, feed herself, ride her bike and read. We stayed focused on small improvements and watched slow, steady progress.

After six months of daily care, we decided to take a break and go to Disney World. Planning the trip gave Stephanie a new focus and seemed to accelerate her progress. After careful coordination with her doctor, we were off for a week of fun and relaxation.

From the moment she entered the Magic Kingdom in a stroller, she was fascinated by a rocket-ship ride on top of a building. The faster the ride went around, the higher the rockets flew. She begged to take a spin, but the line was long, and in the heat, we knew we'd have to pace ourselves. Instead, we went on the Teacups. What a mistake! It seems like someone was always getting sick on the Teacups. Then we tried It's A Small World After All. We didn't know that once you heard that tune, you could never get it out of your head.

All Stephanie wanted was to ride that rocket ship, but we knew she couldn't tolerate waiting up to an hour in such heat. Finally, on the last day, right about closing, we saw that the line had all but disappeared. We ran over to the gate only to have a smiling attendant pull the chain across saying, "That's all for today. You come back and see Mickey tomorrow."

With tears in my eyes, I found myself explaining about our year—how Stephanie had been so sick, in a coma and had spent months working every day at recovery. I practically yelled, "You have to let her on this ride! This is the only one she really wanted to do."

The young attendant grinned, pulled the chain open and motioned us onto the platform. As the sun set and beautiful colors streaked across the sky, Stephanie and I climbed onboard the rockets. We were the only people on the ride, as throngs of visitors streamed out of the park. As the rocket began to go faster and faster, and climb higher in the sky, Stephanie laughed and screamed with joy.

At that instant, I knew she would be okay and our family would continue to recover together.

Just as the ride slowed, the attendant came on the loudspeaker, "That ride was from Mickey. Now, here is an extra ride for Stephanie from me." And he gave us an extra ride.

Now, if you were to ask happy, healthy Stephanie today what is the best thing that ever happened to her, she would say, "That extra ride at Disney World, because that one was just for me."

A small gesture from a stranger who magically made a difference in our lives.

Barbara Bartlein

Fostering Memories

Kate was six years old when we first became her "holiday people." She lived in a children's home in our South African city, where she had been since the age of two. Her mother was an infrequent visitor whom Kate barely remembered, and no one knew the whereabouts of her father.

The children were allowed outings two Sundays a month. My husband and I didn't have children of our own, and we felt that sharing a couple of Sundays with Kate would not be much of a sacrifice if we could bring some pleasure into her life.

Kate was a thoughtful, sensible and well-behaved child with a ready giggle. Soon, we planned every alternate Sunday with her in mind. We found ourselves at places we'd never previously visited—mini-town, the fun fair, the bird park—and doing things we'd never done, like riding model trains and ponies. Sharing in her enjoyment brought us an enormous amount of pleasure.

We would arrive at the home at nine in the morning to find a cluster of excited girls waiting on the veranda for their parents, or "holiday people." Soon, there were only a handful of "leftovers" to wave a wistful good-bye. There was never jealousy from those left behind, who willingly shared their best clothes with the girls going out. Sometimes, we would add a couple of leftovers to our threesome.

At the end of the day, when it was time for home, we gave Kate pocket money to buy sweets. She took great care to be sure everything was shareable, and she took into account the likes and dislikes of the other girls. Lollipops could not be shared; packets and tubes of sweets could.

When we arrived back at the home, she hugged us and gave cheery good-bye kisses, then off she went to share her carefully selected goodies.

On one occasion, after we had given Kate her money, she went skipping ahead of us to the shop. We saw her stop and talk to a beggar. Then she turned and slowly walked back to us, admitting she had given all her money to the beggar.

"But what about your sweets?" we asked.

"That's all right, it doesn't matter," she assured us.

On holidays and special weekends, she was allowed to stay over with us. At first, we wondered how to keep her entertained. I asked if she would like to help with the chores of everyday family life. We did the dusting and washing-up together, hung out the washing and bathed the dogs. Then we swam, took the dogs for a walk or played games.

We had an old cash register that she used for playing shop. "Have you got a jar or tin?" she asked, placing the jar on top of the cash register.

"What is it for?"

"For people to give donations to the poor."

We obviously had a lot to learn from Kate.

We tried to cram as much as we could into the time she had with us, and at bedtime, she was often tired but "not sleepy." Yet, within half an hour, her eyes closed and we carried her to bed. Sometimes, we would find hidden under her pillow presents for us fashioned from scraps of paper and material, and touching thank-you cards.

Over the next six or seven years, we tried to enrich her life by taking her to as many places and doing as much as we could—the aquarium, feeding pigeons in the town square, a children's Christmas party, shopping for new clothes, a niece's wedding, ballet lessons, visits to restaurants, learning to ride a bicycle, the botanical gardens. When we ran out of ideas, we asked parents where they took their children for a treat. That's when we discovered the historical village, the model-yacht pond, the mini-zoo, and a rowing boat on the river.

When she entered her teenage years she moved to another home and we gradually lost touch. Ten years went by.

One day, there was a knock on the door. A young man in his twenties stood there with an air of apprehensive excitement. "Are you the couple who were Kate's 'holiday people?'"

His name was Peter. Kate was in a nearby maternity home after giving birth to their first child. He hadn't told her he was coming to look for us, but hoped we would come and see her and the baby. She would be so excited.

I invited him in, anxious to catch up on all the news.

"Kate often spoke about her times with you." He looked around. "Is that the same dining table that Kate sat under to dust the legs? Is that the kitchen stool she sat on to help with the washing-up? Are these the same cats and dogs?" He knew all their names.

I showed him "Kate's bedroom" and the swimming pool where she had learned to swim. I even found the old photograph album. He pored over the photos, exclaiming, "Kate told me about that! I remember her talking about this. She's going to be so excited to see you."

The following afternoon, I set off for the maternity home armed with gifts. Kate and I immediately hugged and wiped away the tears. Then I had to see the baby, a daughter who looked just like Kate. Was this how a grandmother felt?

And then began the 'remember-whens.' Kate rattled on, "Remember when I was little and helped you to dust the legs of the dining table, because I was small enough to fit underneath? Remember when Uncle Neil used to play tricks on me? Remember how we used to wash the dishes together? Remember how we bathed the dogs? Remember how you taught me to swim and to read Roman numerals? Remember how the cat slept on my bed?"

I recalled all the special places and events we had so diligently planned. "Remember the aquarium, the children's Christmas party, shopping for new clothes, the ballet lesson, riding model trains and touring the botanical gardens?"

Kate sat pensively. "Yes, those were all nice, but my fondest and most vivid memories, the ones I really treasure . . ." she kissed her baby, ". . . are the ones of everyday family life."

Janet Nicholson

The Eraser

Kindness effects more than severity.

Aesop

My life as a boy was filled with violence, blood and hiding places. My siblings and I were shuffled back and forth between our violent-alcoholic parents and a terribly abusive orphanage.

We lived in a small Saskatchewan town with my parents during these rough periods, and school was just a blur of new teachers, taunting faces and lonely lunches.

I carried the abuse inside me like a brick. I felt like I had so many bad secrets I wasn't supposed to tell anyone, and I was so scared to let them slip that I stopped talking. I was also in perpetual mourning for my brothers and sisters. We had made many promises to each other while hiding under the bed, crying while real monsters roared and no heroes came to the rescue. We promised that no matter what, we would always be together. Well, this was easier whispered from a terrified child than done. We were inevitably split up and thrown to the mercy of the convent again.

You could say I was barely surviving, at best, when I met a very special lady. With all that was going on with my mother and the nuns at the convent, I had never had any positive contact with women in my life. That's why I was filled with dread when she asked me to stay after school.

Her name was Mrs. Shannon, and she was my second-grade teacher. I spent the afternoon filled with anguish as the clock ticked the seconds by. What new torture was I in for now? What ever had I done? I remembered taking half an empty milk carton and a carrot off another child's desk at lunch and eating them. I was so desperate for milk and real food that I couldn't help myself. Maybe that's what I was to be detained for. At the end of the day, the final bell found me numb with fear. I sat at my desk while the kids bustled by me with taunts of "You're really gonna get it now" and "What kind of flowers do you want at your funeral?"

The classroom soon emptied, and it was just the two of us. She smiled and said that I wasn't in any trouble, that she just needed some help cleaning up. I was only slightly relieved as we started tidying the classroom up. While we worked, she talked to me about everything.

Somehow, she seemed to know that I was afraid to talk, so she talked for both of us. She told me what it was like on her family farm and of all the animals there. She talked about school and how she became a teacher. I heard tales of family and friends that I secretly longed for.

She kept me after school every day, and I looked forward to these sessions with this kind woman. Once, she gave me a sparkly eraser, and I kept it in my pocket for weeks, fingering it with a smile on my face.

She encouraged me to read, and she showed me that not all adults are monsters. She told me I could be someone, and if I tried I could do whatever I wanted. She gave me hope.

I would like to say that was the start of a new life for me, but it wasn't. I was soon moved back to the convent, and I lost touch with Mrs. Shannon. Eventually, the department of social services moved me back to stay with my father, as he and my mother had finally divorced. This proved to be a bad mistake. He soon began to drink and get violent. It all escalated, until one day he took his own life in a fit of depression.

I kicked around after that, moving aimlessly through life, until one day my sister called and said she found some things in the attic. I looked in the boxes of old toys and in one I found the sparkly eraser. I started to cry for this woman and the gift of kindness she had given me as a child.

I changed my life that day. I stopped drinking and turned my life around completely. Now, I'm married and have an eight-year-old daughter. I owe it to a lady who instinctively knew I needed a friend, not a teacher—a lady who gave me my greatest gifts as a child—kindness, hope and a sparkly eraser.

John Gaudet

May Day

*F*air-handed *spring unbosoms every grace.*

James Thomson

Time. Oh, God, there's just too much of it in here.

Yet, Brenda could remember when she seemed never to have enough time. Of course, that was before, when she used to bustle through the full days and nights of motherhood and normalcy. The comparison of then and now suddenly gave new meaning to the phrase "Once upon a time!"

And I'm sick and tired of being on a schedule.

Schedule, not routine. Routine was different. Routine meant fixing breakfast in the morning. Routine meant giving her husband a good-bye kiss along with his sack lunch each day. Routine meant doing laundry every Monday. A schedule, on the other hand, was something you stuck with because you had to. Like being bathed each morning at ten. Being turned three times each shift to prevent bedsores. Or even being diapered—as regular as clockwork—every time you were, well, regular.

Brenda groaned inwardly at her clever play on words,

something she'd always been good at. *Something I am still good at . . . maybe the only thing I'm still good at. In fact, God, if you'll recall, people used to admire me for my quick wit and quirky humor.*

And she still had it. Only, no one knew but her. Even now, like this, she was something more than IV feedings, more than a nurse's duty, more than a wasted body. Did anyone remember that? Did God?

Are you listening, God? Or can't you hear me think over the hum of this respirator?

Why, Brenda could hardly hear herself think. The rhythmic hiss and underlying drone of the oxygen muffled each and every sound. It insulated her. Irritated her. Isolated her.

I despise being so helpless.

That's what the advanced stages of multiple sclerosis did. It was a demon that stripped her of both dignity and choice. Like a thief in the night, multiple sclerosis sneaked in to rob her of one treasure after another: sensation, dexterity, range of motion, coordination, strength. Now, at fifty-three, she found herself as helpless as a baby—worse, even. At least an infant had a voice to vocalize its needs.

I miss so much.

Brenda could remember (after all, she had lots and lots of time to remember) her favorite activity: traipsing the woods after a fresh rain. She recalled how it made the soil cocoa rich, and how the breeze was as crisp and clean as a new dollar bill. She loved how the rain left everything smelling as sweet as a freshly bathed baby.

I feel so deserted. So alone. I'm not certain You're even there anymore. Are you, God? Are you there?

In the waning evening light, Brenda let her gaze slide around her room at Front Range Manor. She focused on the wall-to-wall photos tacked up by good-hearted, well-meaning friends and family. Sometimes, like today, the pictures were bullet-sharp reminders of a life she didn't have, couldn't have, wouldn't have.

Plump tears bounced their way down her cheeks, and she was too helpless even to wipe them away. She closed her eyes.

"Brenda," hesitantly.

"Brenda," louder.

"Brenda, are you awake?"

Brenda tediously twisted her mouth into a guttural answer.

"Today is the first of May, Brenda. May Day, and I wanted to share it with you. Here, smell."

Even with her eyes closed, Brenda recognized the springtime scent of lilacs tickling her nose. Umm, lilacs. They even *smelled* purple, bringing back pleasant memories of her Grandma Bessie. Yes, little Grandma Bessie, smelling like talcum powder, always dressed in shades of violet.

"And feel this. It's from the park across the street. The blue jay's loss, but our gain," the bell-like voice tinkled.

Powder soft, a feather stroked—delicately, deliberately—across her forehead. It dallied down her cheek and onto her chin. Meandering over folds in her neck and into nooks behind her earlobes, the downy quill discovered a new path and traced it lazily up the other side of her face. Then, a playful swipe to her nose, like dotting an "i," and the feather was gone.

"Oh, and Brenda, what would spring be without its sounds!"

Magically, the chirping of birds filled and flooded both her ears and her room. The music was light and airy. The simple melody flowed from engaging to majestic, and on to joyous. She could almost see the birds climbing, dipping and winging their way across the sky. Twittering, trilling, thrilling her with sweetness and filling her with the goodness of life.

So, this is what it feels like to be administered to by an angel. By someone who knows me. The inner me. Thank you, God.

A smile stole across Brenda's face, crinkling the corners of her closed eyes, tweaking the edges of her mouth and sneaking onto her parted lips.

Brenda didn't see the new volunteer slip out of her room. Brenda didn't hear the door whisper shut. The cassette player still warbled. The oxygen pulsed on, but the lilacs lingered.

Carol McAdoo Rehme

In Over Their Heads

By ninety-six years of age, Marie had outlived two husbands and both her children. But she still lived in her rural home, thanks to her support crew—thanks to her friends.

Marie relied on them all. Each helper had an assignment. One brought the mail every day; another picked up her groceries. This one did her laundry; that one chauffeured her to the beauty shop. Someone else drove her to church and the rare doctor appointment.

But she had an especially close relationship with Jean. Almost half her age—and nearly half her size—petite Jean was a bubbling bundle of energy.

Jean brought over racy romance novels; Marie recited improper limericks. The two shared a feisty history of heart-to-heart confidences and irreverent jokes, touching stories and outlandish lies—and Christmas.

And it was Jean who was "sitting" with Marie that night after medication for an infection left her aged friend shaky, disoriented and confused.

"I believe I'd like to soak in a bath," Marie suggested.

"Are you sure you feel up to it?" Jean worried that Marie was weaker than she thought.

But Marie insisted. So after helping her elderly friend

from bed to bathroom, Jean sat outside the door to keep her company and to give her privacy. After a time, she heard the water draining.

"Do you need some help, Marie?"

"No, I'll pop right out. You just wait."

She waited—and waited. "Marie?"

"I can't do it. I can't get out. My knees won't work."

Jean stood in the doorway to assess the situation. There sat Marie, folded in the bottom of the deep, claw-foot tub. Ancient, wrinkled and naked as a jaybird. Her once-buxom friend's solid frame had dwindled in recent years until she was nothing more than bones and lots of sagging skin. But she was still considerably larger than Jean.

"Uh, Marie, I think I'd better call the fire department. They've rescued other people in similar situations."

"No, you *won't* call the fire department." Marie was horrified. "I *know* those people. They're . . . men! Why, I'd be the talk of the entire community." She looked down at her accordioned body. "Besides, I need a good ironing."

They both began to laugh. Still grinning, Jean climbed into the high-sided tub, shoes and all.

She edged behind Marie, put her arms around the water-slick woman and lifted. Up came a lot of loose, corrugated flesh—but Marie stayed put. Jean tried again. The same thing happened. Tears of hilarity weakened them both as she strained even harder. But only Marie's skin cooperated.

Exasperated, Marie finally ordered, "Jeannie, just throw my tits over the side and maybe the rest will follow!"

Marie leaned forward, Jean's adrenaline kicked in for one final heave, and they were soon on dry ground. Giggling like girls, the two of them dried off, dressed for bed and added a new story to their repertoire—a "steamy" one.

Carol McAdoo Rehme

Lost & Found

Kindness is the golden chain by which society is bound together.

Goethe

What caught my eye was that she wasn't carrying a purse.

It was just before dinnertime. I was driving my son Bryan, then ten years old, home from his piano lesson. As I turned left at a busy intersection, I spotted her walking carefully on unsteady feet over a rocky path at the side of the road. What was she doing there with traffic whizzing by? Where was she going? She looked to be in her late seventies or early eighties. She was dressed neatly in a blue flowered cotton dress and white cardigan. But where was her purse? Something made me pull off the road.

"Wait in the car," I said to Bryan as I undid my seat belt. I darted across the road. She was even more fragile-looking up close.

Everything about her was gentle: her white hair, her trusting smile.

"Hello," she said warmly.

"Can I help you?" I asked.

"Oh, no, dear, I'm just fine," she assured me. "I'm on my way to work." Her voice was strong. She sounded clear, definite. Maybe she was okay. Maybe I had intruded. But something told me otherwise.

"Where do you work?"

"St. Joseph's Hospital. I'm a nurse on the maternity ward." *St. Joseph's?* That couldn't be. I knew that hospital. My dad had been a surgeon and head of the medical staff there before his death in 1983. It was in the heart of Philadelphia, at least twenty miles away. There was no public transportation in the vicinity, and she certainly couldn't get there on foot. Something was very wrong.

She politely tried to excuse herself, explaining that she could not be late for her shift. The babies needed their baths. But when I went to take her arm to steady her on the path, I saw she was holding a nickel and two pennies in her hand. We both stared at the coins. "Car fare," she whispered when our eyes met.

That was it. She was coming home with me.

"It's getting dark," I said. "Why don't you come to my house and we'll have a cup of tea. I'll call the hospital and tell them not to worry." To my relief, she agreed and let me guide her to my car.

"My name is Linda," I said, fastening her seat belt. "What's yours?"

Her sudden look of panic made it all clear. She was old, she was lost and now I was sure my new friend was one of the estimated 2.4 million Americans with Alzheimer's disease who often put themselves in jeopardy by wandering away from their home or place of residence.

"This is my son Bryan," I said to put her at ease. "Bryan, say hello to my new friend. She's a nurse in the hospital where Pop-Pop used to work."

As I drove, we chatted about her years as a nurse, a

subject that brought her pleasure. Her face glowed as she recalled the moms and babies she had cared for. But her conversation was sprinkled with outdated terms, trolley car, icebox, maternity ward. When was the last time anyone had called it that?

At home I served her tea in my living room and turned the television on with the sound off to catch the local news. Perhaps she had been reported missing and her picture would flash on the screen. I'd have to call the police eventually, but I didn't want to do that just yet. Sipping her tea and playing with my son Christian, then three, she seemed to feel safe.

Seeking clues to her identity, I began asking her about her past, a subject she seemed comfortable discussing. Where had she gone to school? Where had she lived while working as a nurse? Had she married? But none of her answers was helpful.

Then, a framed photograph on a table next to the couch caught her attention. It was a picture of my dad with other family members. A look of delighted recognition crossed her face.

"Do you know him?" I asked, trying to hide my surprise. Then I remembered. *Of course. St. Joseph's Hospital.*

"Oh yes," she said. "Dr. Cherken is always so nice and appreciative of the nurses. He never forgets to say thank you."

"That sounds like him," I said. "He was my father."

"So you're his daughter," she said. "Lucky girl."

Then it happened. "I have a daughter, too," she said, smiling.

"A daughter? Where does she live?"

"Near here. Her husband's a dentist."

Finally, some information I could use. I asked her to join me in the kitchen while I used the phone. "How about some dinner?"

"I'd love some soup."

As it simmered, I began calling every dentist in the area. Half an hour later I found the right one. "You have the doctor's mother-in-law?" a receptionist asked. She put the dentist on the line.

When he arrived at my home a little later, he told me the rest of my friend's story. She had Alzheimer's and lived in a nursing home a few miles from where I had found her. Her daughter, the dentist's wife, had visited daily until she died of cancer a few weeks before. Her death had left my friend even more disoriented. Apparently, she was searching for her daughter when I picked her up.

I held my friend's hand as I walked her to the car, and we hugged good-bye. Her son-in-law thanked me repeatedly for finding her, but I knew it wasn't me he should thank. Today, when I think of my friend, I remember the way her face lit up when she saw the picture of my father, and I know it was "that nice Dr. Cherken" who tapped me on the shoulder as I was driving home that evening and made me turn my head.

LindaCarol Cherken

[EDITORS' NOTE: *If a loved one has Alzheimer's, consider enrolling him or her in the Alzheimer's Association's Safe Return program, a national registry that facilitates the return of those who wander. To learn more, call (888) 572-8566 or go to* www. alz.org/SafeReturn]

"Sure, I'd love to take a trip down memory lane,
s'long as I can get a ride home."

Reprinted by permission of Jonny Hawkins

6

OVERCOMING OBSTACLES

*M*ake *it a rule, and pray to God to help you
to keep it, never, if possible, to lie down at
night without being able to say, "I have
made one human being at least a little
wiser, or a little happier, or at least a little
better this day."*

Charles Kingsley

I Will Always Be Here for You

A *life spent worthily should be measured by deeds, not years.*

Richard Sheridan

When I was laid off from my fifteen-year career as a television executive, my then eighty-three-year-old father packed up my seventy-eight-year-old mother, still frail from a heart attack a decade earlier, and drove from San Francisco to Los Angeles just to give me moral support. "Don't worry, sweetheart. We'll always be here for you."

A few months later, days before I was scheduled to endure risky spinal surgery, my doorbell rang unexpectedly. I couldn't believe it. There they were: My barely-able-to-stand elderly parents, proudly standing behind a wheelchair they had hauled four hundred miles for me to use after my surgery. Dad said, "We love you so much. Don't you worry, honey, we'll always be here for you."

But soon after, my life changed forever when I received the call that my mother was dying. I hobbled from my recovery bed and flew home to discover that she was not dying from her damaged heart, but from an infection caused by her own waste. I was horrified to learn that my father had not been able to keep her clean, nor had he thought to take her to the doctor. She weighed eighty-two pounds when I arrived, and my heart ached with overwhelming sorrow that I had not been able to be there sooner.

For eleven years, I had begged my father to allow a caregiver to help him with Mom, but he adamantly insisted on taking care of her himself. Every caregiver I had hired to help him lasted about three days, and then I'd get the familiar call. "Jacqueline, I just *can't* work with your father. He screams and yells and stands over me and won't let me do anything!"

Growing up, my father had always been 90 percent wonderful, but that 10 percent raging temper was a real doozy. He had never turned his temper on me before, but then again, I'd never gone against his wishes, either. Now I knew I had to step in and risk his wrath to save my mother's life, as well as his, having no idea that in the process it would nearly cost me my own.

I spent the first three months feeding my mother every bite of her meals and nursing her back to relative "health" in a convalescent home, while my father screamed, yelled and repeatedly threw me out of the house for trying to help him and for making changes he didn't want. I was stunned to see him get so upset over the simplest things. Even running the dishwasher could cause a raging tizzy. I cried rivers, devastated to have my once-adoring father turn verbally and even physically abusive toward me.

I took him to his doctors, and I was astonished that he could act completely normal when he needed to. I couldn't believe it when one doctor looked at me like *I* was the crazy one. I found out much later he'd told her that all I wanted was his money.

Weeks turned into months, and then nearly a year passed as I became trapped in my parents' home trying to solve the endless crises. My father refused to see anymore doctors, and I couldn't hog tie and drag him to one, but I thought about it. When I finally got some medication to calm him, he flushed it down the toilet. Forty caregivers came and went (some were there for an hour), as he called them nasty names—raging, spitting and spewing, and literally throwing them out of the house.

It was such a catch-22: I couldn't leave my mother alone with him, because she'd surely die from his inability to care for her. I couldn't get him to accept a caregiver, and even when I did, no one would put up with him for very long. I couldn't place her in a nursing home, because he'd just take her out. I couldn't put him in a home, because he didn't qualify. They both refused any mention of an assisted-living situation, and legally I couldn't force them. I was trapped in an unbearable tragedy.

Then, the worst day of my life: My father attacked and choked me with his bare hands for adding HBO to his cable television package, even though he had previously requested it. I was barely able to get away from him and frantically dialed 911 for the first time in my life. The police came and took him to a psychiatric hospital for observation, but he was completely competent as far as they could see, and they released him. Unbelievably, similar incidents occurred, not once, but four more times.

One day, a friend casually mentioned that she'd heard that the Alzheimer's Association provided referrals to local services and dementia specialists. I blew off that idea, as I was positive that my father didn't have Alzheimer's—he was still able to be *so* crafty and manipulative. Maybe my mother had Alzheimer's—she'd ask the same question over and over, and often said things that were untrue. Finally, at my wit's end and ready to try anything, I made the call that saved our lives. They referred us to a compassionate geriatric dementia specialist, who convinced my father of how much he could help him and Mother. After performing a battery of tests and exams, the doctor uncovered stage-one Alzheimer's and vascular dementia in *both* of my parents. I was in total shock.

Finally, with the right combination of medications and optimal nutrition, my parents began to improve dramatically. Once their brain chemistries were balanced, I started behavior-modification techniques on my obstinate father. I noticed that when I rewarded his good behavior with tons of affection, attention and raving words of praise, he tended to be a lot nicer.

Next, convincing him to go to adult day care was an absolute nightmare. But once he realized that Mom was going without him, he decided he'd better go too. Who'd have guessed it would completely change their lives, as well as my own. They finally had some place to go, friends to see and fun things to do. The pressure on me to entertain them was drastically reduced, as was my stress level. We could still spend quality time in the evenings and on the weekends.

Finally, there was one more important need to be met—mine.

I was as stubborn as my father, as I really didn't want to go to a caregiver's support group to hear other people's problems. But soon, solutions started presenting themselves while I listened to others who were coping with caregiving. I learned how to shift my perspective from the heartbreak of watching my parents' decline to focusing on the life they had left. I learned to cherish the good days and just let go of the bad.

Finally, after a year of caring for my parents without a day off, the last piece of elder-care puzzle came together when I hired the "Amazing Ariana"—the *only* caregiver who was ever capable of managing my father. He actually accepted and respected her.

As I packed my bags to go back home to pick up the pieces of my shattered life, Dad shuffled into my room. With a tear in his eye, he kissed and hugged me. As I sat cuddled in his arms, I realized the horror and heartache had all been worth it when he said, "Thank you, honey. We love you so." He kissed my cheek. "And we don't worry—we know you'll always be here for us."

Jacqueline Marcell

The Last Blooms

Flowers are God's thoughts of beauty taking for to gladden mortal gaze.

William Wilberforce

A family emergency precipitated my move back to my hometown. I hadn't even had time to renew my high school friendships when I received a call from my hospice-volunteer coordinator. "I hope you've had time to get settled. I have a lady who desperately needs your help."

I was stunned to learn that the lady was Ginny. We'd been the best of friends all through high school and college, but, except for brief notes on occasional Christmas cards, we'd lost touch over the years.

We were both in tears from the moment I walked through her front door. Our first days together were flooded with the constant chatter of "remember when" flashbacks. We used to say we were closer than sisters, and we found out we still were.

But she wouldn't discuss her illness.

Her life had been an artistic one, boasting many talents, but gardening had been Ginny's main love. She was reputed to have the most imaginative garden in town.

"Working with plants and flowers is when I feel closest to God," she admitted. "Each bloom represents a message of love from Him. It's very powerful. I miss it so."

During my daily visits, I'd catch Ginny staring out the window. The landscape in its winter sleep looked bleak, with any hope of spring many months away. Crocus and tulips, already planted, would never bloom in time. From Ginny's faraway gaze, I knew she was mentally seeing her perfect garden as it once was: rare flowers meticulously planted in raised beds and winding brick paths edged with breathtaking colors. She confided, "Flowers feed my spirit."

According to her doctor, Ginny had less than three months to live. As her hospice volunteer and friend, I wanted so to help her deal with, yet distract her from, her impending death. So I began making phone calls, contacting old friends and becoming reacquainted with Ginny's life.

On the morning my plan went into action, our conversation had been as dull and lifeless as the dreary winter day. Then a beautiful box was delivered, wrapped in extraordinary paper that shone like a burst of sunshine. I took it in to her, feigning ignorance. "Sweetheart, this just arrived. It looks interesting and valuable. Wonder what it is?"

Ginny struggled with renewed energy to sit up. Her eyes glowed as she manipulated the gold foil seal on the front of the box. "It's from Gus, my old friend, the German-nursery man. Because of him, I won the Most Beautiful Garden award in the city contest." With a giggle, she continued. "I'll just have to force myself to open it right away. That Gus is an absolute expert, and his timing on when to plant is always perfect."

She eagerly opened the box and went completely quiet

as she read the card. I could see the rough edges of bulbs inside the box.

"What are they?" I asked innocently.

With a rush of tears, she held the card out for me to read.

Ginny, plant these daffodils immediately, and I promise you they will bloom in time. In admiration, Gus.

I remembered my initial conversation with Gus. "Bulbs will be the perfect answer. They can be forced to bloom. Nothing else can beat the clock."

"Oh, let's hurry and plant these today," she said. "I have the perfect container in the loveliest color of bluish white. It was my grandmother's."

I had just finished planting the bulbs into the antique bowl when the doorbell rang. Ginny's friends had followed Gus's instructions to the letter. As each visitor arrived bearing her gift, the bedroom slowly filled with a variety of lovely vases and urns; each one labeled, perfect for the bulbs it contained, many of them already showing fresh growth and promise. The miracle of nature would allow her to watch the bulbs sprout fragile green as they warmed to the light and then slowly reveal their individual beauty in a burst of blooms! The spring blossoms would share their charm, bringing their fragrance and color back into Ginny's darkened world. By the look on her face, I knew she felt as treasured as her gifts.

In a burst of enthusiasm, she cried, "Oh, I can't wait until they bloom!"

As she settled into her pillows, gazing around the room she whispered, "These last blooms—they will be my most beautiful garden ever—and I'll feel closer than ever to God."

Ruth Hancock

The Red Geranium

Do not be afraid, only believe.

Mark 5:36

The stairs from our bedroom led into Mama's pantry. The first sound my sisters and I heard every morning was Mama preparing breakfast. Throughout the day when we wanted to find her, she was always there, and while she worked we would sit on the stairs and tell her our secrets or problems. Sometimes we just sat there eating fresh-baked bread and listened to her singing. Mama never had time to sit; there was butter to churn, bread to bake, pies, cakes, cookies and donuts to be stirred, and bowls of food to prepare. She never complained, though, she just talked a lot about God. Our pantry held secrets, too, as treasures for special holidays were stored out of sight. Even though we searched, we never could find her hiding place.

Bob, our oldest brother, helped my father, uncle and the other farmers with their work. Nancy liked helping Mama in her pantry. Mina was the tomboy, running through the fields, taking the men water while they worked, jumping in the hay wagons for rides or escaping to Grandmother's when Mama had a chore for her to do. In her spare time, Mina planted flowers.

The summer of 1952 started out as any other summer in our quiet Canadian countryside. In the evenings, the children spent hours romping in the newly mown haystacks, playing hide and seek behind the already stacked bales and daydreaming about the fair at the end of the summer. Mina planted her first red geranium, a gift from the pastor's wife.

But as the lazy days of summer passed, a great concern fell over our pantry sanctuary. Words like paralysis, iron lungs and polio became part of our conversations, and we wondered to Mama how we would even know if we came down with the dreaded disease. Mama wondered if she dared send her children to the fair. There would be so many people, and it may increase the danger of contracting the germs. But Daddy insisted that Mina and Nancy must go; they had worked so hard during the summer picking and selling blueberries to earn money to go.

The days after the fair were filled with excitement over all they had seen and done, and Mina was at Mama's side, doing the only job she ever liked in the pantry, chopping tomatoes and onions for homemade chow. At times, the talk wasn't so cheerful—a young boy in a nearby community had died of polio and another was paralyzed. On one such evening Mina said, "Mama, I don't feel so well." In the pantry, there was a cure for everything. "Take two aspirin and go to bed, dear, you will be better in the morning." It always worked. But the next morning, as the sounds of breakfast came into our room, Mina struggled downstairs. Her head tilted backwards, her fingers were swollen, an arm and leg could barely move. Screams came from Mama's pantry. "Alfred, Mina has polio! Get someone to take us to the hospital immediately!"

Phones and cars were few and far between on our country roads. Daddy ran to the nearest phone and called a friend, who came without hesitation. Mina was very carefully laid in the backseat of the car with her head on Mama's lap. At the hospital, the doctor performed a spinal tap. Emergency vehicles were not available, so he gave the spinal fluid to Daddy, and the same car that rushed Mina to the doctor now rushed to the lab in a city hospital fifty miles away. Mama stayed with Mina and prayed. When the tests were completed, the results were given to Daddy, who brought them back to the doctor. Mina had polio. Again she was placed in the backseat of the same car and taken to the Moncton City Hospital. A polio specialist was waiting at the door, and Mina was rushed down a corridor into a room marked ISOLATION. An iron lung was placed at her door in case it was needed to breathe for her. Mama and Daddy could only stand outside the room and peer in through a small window at their daughter who was fighting for her life.

Long days followed. Neighbors drove Daddy to the hospital with letters from Mama, which he read to Mina through the window. Mama spent sleepless nights walking the floor at home, praying to God to heal her daughter. During the day, she kept up with her chores and watered Mina's flowers, taking special care of the red geranium that seemed to stop living when Mina became ill. Everyday, radio reports gave the number of casualties of the polio outbreak—the number of those who would return home crippled, the number of those who would be paralyzed, those who would return home with the aid of an iron lung and, yes, even the number of deaths. But Mama's faith never wavered. She knew the power of prayer. Her daughter would be coming home.

Much to the doctor's surprise, Mina began to recover. The iron lung was removed from her door. The specialist praised Mama for her alertness and the doctor's immediate attention. Mina could go home. Daddy wrapped Mina in blankets and carried her fragile body to the upstairs bedroom. Mama was busy in her pantry making rice pudding, Mina's favorite.

The days that followed were not easy. Mina had lost the use of her legs, and her aches and pains were constant. Friends and family were afraid to visit. When the sun was hot, Mama and Daddy carried Mina outside and sat her on a chair, so she could feel the warm sun and wind on her face. Sometimes they would hear her crying and would go outside to find her lying on the ground after a failed attempt to walk. In the afternoons, she would lie on the couch close to the pantry and watch as Mama made her bowls of rice pudding. And Mama told her stories of how she watered her plants while she was away; how her red geranium had almost died and then one day it began to grow beautifully again. Mama told her it was her sign from God that she would come home.

When Christmas was near, Mama ordered three pairs of skates: one pair for Bob, one pair for Nancy and one pair for her daughter who could not walk. She instructed Dad to prepare a sled. The Christmas holidays came with clear, cold skating weather. Bob and Nancy searched for the perfect patch of ice to try their new skates. Gone all one morning, they came in for dinner and told Mama to get Mina ready. They put skates on her and bundled her in the sled, then Bob and Nancy pulled her to the skating patch. With one on each side, they stood Mina up and carried her around the ice, her skates gliding over the surface. The next day, they did the same thing, then day after day, over and over again . . . until she was able to stand on her own. Soon, Mina needed only to hold their hands, and then, finally, the day came when she could skate the ice patch on her own.

When winter passed, Mina walked into school. Everyone said it was a miracle and praised Mama for buying the skates. But Mama raised her eyes to heaven, smiled and praised God, for she had seen the miracle many months before in the red geranium.

Darlene Lawson

God Answers Prayers

Mike was only fourteen years old when he had his accident.

His family operated a small farm in our rural area of Alabama. Mike was working with friends hauling and loading hay into his father's barn. It was a beautiful fall day. The gentle breeze was just strong enough to make the southern temperatures comfortable. The sky was crystal clear and full of white fluffy clouds. Mike and his friends had just stacked a load of hay in the barn and were on their way back to the field when this gorgeous day turned into a nightmare.

Teenagers have a way of making the toughest work into horseplay if given a chance, and that day's work was no exception. Two boys were in the cab and two boys, including Mike, were on the back of the truck. Each boy had ice water to drink on his way back to the hot field. At the very moment the one in the front decided to throw his water out the window, Mike decided it was too windy to sit on the truck bed and stood up. The cold ice water blew back into the face of the driver, and he swerved off the road. The jerking motion threw Mike off the back and onto the pavement. He landed on his head, unconscious.

From that point forward, the events seemed like a horrible dream for everyone—the ambulance coming, the trip to the hospital, the flight to a larger intensive care unit and all the machines keeping him alive seemed like it was happening to someone else. It couldn't be going on in our family; Mike was so young and so strong. One instant couldn't be taking his life away. But it was.

The days turned into weeks, and the weeks turned into months. Aunt Mildred prayed each day that the Lord would restore her child and let her bring him home. She longed to hear Mike's voice again and prayed for another chance to ask him to be quiet.

In times like these, many people are tempted to ask God for reasons behind His choice, but Aunt Mildred never doubted God and His judgment. She just prayed that if it were His decision that Mike would be with her family again. If not, take care of him until they met again.

She visited him when allowed and held his hand. She talked to him like she always did before, because the doctors said it was possible he could hear. She told Mike to pray to God. She never gave up hope. She had never given up on one of her children before, and she refused to begin now that things got tough. She would be by his side until he was well.

After weeks in the hospital, the doctors advised removing his machines. There was nothing more they could do, and it was now up to him to breathe on his own. Everyone stood in a prayer circle around his bed as they disconnected the respirator. Mike breathed! Soon, he was transported to a hospital closer to home to make things easier on the family.

Months passed with little change in his condition. Knowing he would be nothing more than bedridden, the doctors suggested Aunt Mildred put Mike in a nursing home. Aunt Mildred said he'd go nowhere but home with her, and he did.

She spent countless hours praying and taking care of Mike every day. His care consumed her, and she missed spending time with her other children. But Mike needed her now, and she wasn't going to let him down. Almost a year after his accident, through God's healing hands, along with other measures recommended by the doctors, Mike regained consciousness and even took his first step! Aunt Mildred cried, but she knew God's job wasn't finished. She wanted to hear Mike speak again. She continued to pray beside him.

One afternoon, she called her daughter to wish her a happy birthday. Mike was sitting at the table, as he always did while she was in the kitchen. A different expression came over his face as she began to sing to her daughter. He smiled in a way that he hadn't in a very long time and seemed to understand what she was actually saying and to whom. Mike lifted his hand toward the phone and Aunt Mildred quickly placed it to his ear. His sister spoke to him and then, what the doctors said would never happen, did: "Hap . . . py Bir . . . day," he echoed.

The house soon filled with relatives, and Mike repeated this phrase to everyone who entered. Now, Aunt Mildred prays in thanksgiving to the Lord for listening and restoring her son.

Today, Mike is married and lives with his wife and family without the help of any assistants. He is not 100 percent back to his former ability, but he functions well in the world and even drives.

Now *he* prays in thanksgiving to God for his devoted mother and for answering *his* prayers as he shares in her golden years.

Denise Peebles

"Mom talks to God about us so
we'll be prayer conditioned."

Reprinted by permission of Jonny Hawkins

New Tasks and New Titles

We trust that somehow, good will be the final goal of ill.

Alfred Lord Tennyson

My eyes pop open as if they're spring-loaded. Darkness still crouches behind closed blinds. I turn my head just enough to see the bedside clock. Pick any number between midnight and three in the morning—it'll never be enough to classify as a good night's sleep. I lie there listening with envy to my husband Kay's deep, even breathing.

"Just turn off your mind," he often suggests. If only it had a switch. Turning on my side, with a clear view of the clock's digital face, I watch the red squares and angles rearrange themselves in their painfully slow, electronic dance toward daylight. The monotony produces a hypnotic state that sets in around dawn, uncannily synchronized with my bright-eyed, well-rested, disciplined husband's awakening.

Though he can't leap tall buildings, he can and does defy the laws of physics as he silently lifts his 6'5" 240-pound frame off the bed so as not to disturb me. He pads barefoot to the dark closet, slipping legs into jeans and arms into sleeves with just the slightest whisper of skin against fabric. Shoes and socks in hand, he tiptoes to the family room to finish dressing and watch the news. Within minutes, he brings a glass of chocolate-flavored milk and sets it on my bedside table. The soft *tink* on the marble top reminds me to take my morning medications. I'm left to snooze as Kay goes about his day.

As painful, deforming and debilitating rheumatoid arthritis has taken over my body, new tasks, new titles and new challenges have taken over his life. With hands the size of baseball mitts, he can in one minute wield a hammer or wheelbarrow, and the next carefully cradle a tender joint.

Finally, I'm awake and ready for my bath. First, Kay cleans an open wound on my hip with alcohol, packs it with gauze and covers it with a sheet of waterproof, adhesive film. After lowering me into the tub and adjusting the water's temperature, he adds the perfumed bubbles and leaves me to splash about.

Kay waits in anticipation for me to finish, because his newest title is that of "Heavy-Equipment Operator." We recently installed a lift over the tub. He fastens a sturdy snap hook into the ceiling track. The white unit is shaped like the skull of an animal left on the prairie to die, it's bones bleaching in the sun. We've named it Angus. Once I'm wrapped in a fabric sling with six straps looped over Angus's "horns," with a push of a button, I'm airborne. A scene from *Free Willy* comes to mind.

A mound of frothy mousse in hand, my resident "Beautician" coats the thinning strands of my hair. "I shampoo it clean, then you make me glop it with this stuff," he teases.

"It needs the body. The label says it will 'volumize' what little hair I have left."

Stirring about with a comb, he coaxes the short curls into submission.

As "Captain of Pantyhose Patrol," he's tops. I need never worry about saggy socks, he pulls them on with such gusto! Always astonished at the elasticity built into each one, he playfully sees just how high they'll stretch. If it weren't for that tight center seam, I'd be trussed to my neck like a sausage! He watches for rough hands and fingernails, frets over a snag and despairs when he spots a run.

He's equally as proficient as "Boss of the Zipper, Bra and Button Brigade." I risk some touchy-feely horseplay with this one, but I chance it. Let's see now, is he an all-around male lady-in-waiting? Woman's valet? Female's male attendant? Whatever, he's good.

Kay has perfected his Cinderella role of cooking, cleaning, shopping and doing laundry. He delivers cookies and fresh bread to neighbors. That used to be my role. He shares recipes and garden produce, cooks for funerals and church suppers, and loves a table surrounded by contented, smiling guests. Occasionally, a load of laundry emerges slightly tinted. The last culprit ... dark-blue pajamas.

Eating is a necessity, cleaning is not. "Spotted window panes reduce sun fading," I tell him. As he dusts, Kay muses that God is in the details. "If that's true," I say, "tell Him while He's in there, please vacuum the corners and clean the refrigerator!"

As Nurse Nightingale through my countless surgeries, he has mastered the language of medicine. For weeks, nimble fingers manipulated IVs, aware of the difference between a triple lumen and a Groshang line. He inserted saline, antibiotics, saline then heparin in the prescribed order. The crisis passed, but the infection lingers, leaving him the task of changing my hip bandages twice a day for the last ten years. Because I've frequently been assigned ancient nurses as bony as sparrows and nearing retirement, I welcome his size and strength.

Kay serves me day after day without complaining, always assuring me I'm beautiful and that he loves me. And yet, he has his own distressing health problems. Besides sporadic arthritis, a familiar tremor in his neck and hands slowly worsens. His writing is jagged and jumbled. His teeth clink against his glass. Unruly fingers rattle silverware against china and fling veggies about.

Because these new tasks, titles and challenges have taken a toll on Kay's life, I pray there's a grand reward for him in heaven. I hope it's *me, healthy.*

Mary Kerr Danielson

An Early Mourning

I wonder many times that ever a child of God should have a sad heart, considering what the Lord is preparing for him.

Samuel Rutherford

The phone rang at seven in the morning, awakening me from a sound sleep. *This had better be good,* I thought. After all, it was Saturday, and my children were sleeping in for a change.

"Hello, this is Peggy," said the voice on the other end of the line. "We need your help with a four-year-old boy. How soon can you get here?"

"I'll be out the door in fifteen minutes," I assured her. After jotting down the address, I hung up the telephone and prepared to leave. Dealing with bereaved children was but one of my tasks as a hospice social worker—a task for which I was summoned far more often than I wished.

I splashed icy water on my face, trying to wake up. There would be no time for that leisurely cup of coffee while the kids played at my feet. I ran a brush through my hair, trying to look as presentable as one could sans shower. I threw on some clothes and tiptoed into the bed-room of my two slumbering cherubs. I kissed them lightly on the cheeks, mouthing the words, "I love you." I grabbed my daughter's plush white-kitten puppet and stashed it in my bag, knowing I would probably need it.

I headed for the car, pulling my coat together and clutching my bag as the winter wind howled around me. I maneuvered the icy, snow-covered roads in Michigan's rural upper peninsula, thankful it was too early for many other travelers to be out. Arriving at the home, I grabbed my staff-identification badge from my rearview mirror and attached it to my shirt. I headed toward the house with my bag, shivering in the December chill, waiting for someone to let me in.

Peggy, the nurse, greeted me at the door and pointed to the middle of room. "He's over there," she said. "We can't get him to come out from under the bed."

I glanced in the direction of the living room. The twin-kling Christmas lights were a stark contrast to the hospi-tal bed in the center of the room. I approached the bed, bowing my head to the boy's deceased grandmother. I had never met this woman, yet I knew one thing: She was deeply loved by this family and by the little boy who sought refuge under her bed, refusing to budge.

I crouched down, peeked under the bed and told him my name. No response. I asked him if it would be okay if he and I talked for a while. No answer. I told him I knew he might be sad or scared or angry, or all three. Intense blue eyes met mine. He looked away, saying nothing.

I dug inside my bag and pulled out my daughter's pup-pet, and slipped it on my hand. "I brought a friend," I said, praying this would work. "This is Cuddles." Cuddles joined him under the bed, and the two of them spent a few minutes getting acquainted. Then Cuddles introduced me again and told the little boy that I could help kids who were feeling scared, angry or sad. Cuddles told him that he sometimes had those feelings, too, and shared with the little boy how he coped. Cuddles listed all the things that I had in my bag: paper, crayons, bubbles and clay, and that when he was ready, he could come out and play with them.

Slowly, the little boy emerged, all the while eyeing me. "Would you like to see what's in my bag?" He nodded. "Follow me." In the other room, he drew pictures and pounded clay.

"It will all be okay," he told me. "I asked Santa to bring my grandma some medicine."

"Santa would have done anything he could have to help your grandma," I soothed. "The doctors found lots of medicines to keep her out of pain, but they didn't have medicine that could make her all better." We talked about all of the kinds of things that doctors could fix and that they can usually make things better, but not this time.

"But did they try the grape kind of medicine?" he pleaded. "I just know that will work." I sat down beside him, and told him in words he could understand how his grandmother's body had stopped working—how she could no longer feel pain, cold or hot. That she no longer needed to breathe or eat. He stared straight ahead in silence.

"Can I talk to Cuddles again?"

"Sure. You may speak with him as long as you'd like."

The two of them talked a long time, then the little boy asked me, "Can I keep Cuddles?"

"I know Cuddles would love to stay with you, but he has lots of other kids who need his help."

He hugged Cuddles one more time then helped me pack him in my bag.

I headed home, certain everyone was awake by now. I walked through the door and into the hustle and bustle of another day. My exuberant children ran to hug me, never guessing I needed those hugs more than they did.

"Daddy made us pancakes," exclaimed Jimmy, my oldest.

"I hope you saved some for me," I said.

My daughter, Gabrielle, saw Cuddles in my bag. "Did my Cuddles have to go help someone again?"

"Yes," I told her as I tousled her golden locks.

"Did he help a lot?"

"He sure did."

She smiled.

"You left real early in the morning," Jimmy said.

"I know," I responded, thinking of another little boy who had had an early mourning of his own.

Wendy Young

7

INSIGHTS
AND LESSONS

*Good timber does not grow with ease.
The stronger the wind the stronger the
trees.*

J. Willard Marriott

Learning from a Teenager

The sacred books of the ancient Persians say: If you would be holy instruct your children, because all the good acts they perform will be imputed to you.

Montesquieu

Instead of hanging out at the mall with her friends, fifteen-year-old Carly spent most of her spare time taking care of her dad.

Andy had been a strong, healthy, physically fit man who excelled at sports and loved outdoor activities. But one day he noticed his right hand was numb, and he dropped his cup of coffee. Over the next few months, several similar incidents happened to the point he could no longer ignore the strange and alarming symptoms. After months of exhaustive tests, a neurologist confirmed the terrible news that thirty-eight-year-old Andy had ALS, or Lou Gehrig's disease. When he learned this incurable illness would result in progressive neurological deterioration of his body, Andy tried to conceal it from his family as long as possible. He was separated from his wife, and his three teenage children lived with him. Despite his efforts, it soon became impossible to hide his illness, and the effect on his youngest child, Carly, was the most profound.

He soon lost the ability to use a knife and fork. Carly would quietly lean over to cut his meat. She couldn't wait to come home from school to see him. At first, her friends were intrigued by the close relationship she enjoyed with her father. They patiently waited while she attended to him before she went with them to the mall or the movies. Little by little, though, Carly started declining invitations from friends. Doing homework, helping out with the household chores, and helping her dad button his shirts and tie his shoes took most of her spare time.

Andy was acutely aware that Carly needed to live a normal teenager's life and not be his private duty nurse. Her older brother and sister were more typical teenagers, and although they loved their father, they were less involved in his care. An old childhood friend of Andy's worked for the local Visiting Nurses Association as a home health aide. She made the referral to initiate home-care services. I became Andy's visiting nurse. Over the next several months, I arranged for a physical therapist, an occupational therapist, a speech therapist and daily home health-aide services. In spite of our best efforts, including a course of experimental drug therapy, Andy's disease progressed. He became weaker and weaker each passing month.

Home-care services only provided help six to eight hours per day and none at night, so Carly continued to devote all of her spare time to her father's care. As professional caregivers, we were expected to teach the family members all aspects of care, but Carly had already learned how to dress her father, assist him in the bathroom, prepare his easy-to-chew foods and feed him. We frequently deferred to her to show us an easier method of dressing him.

When I advised that it was time to get a hospital bed for ease of transfers in and out, Andy insisted on having a double bed so that his children could sleep next to him after they had helped turn and reposition him every two hours at night. The professional caregivers conferenced and decided it was inappropriate to have his teenage children sleeping in his bed with him. Carly taught us by her admirable behavior that closeness and warmth with her dad were more important than our stuffy rules. My persistent recommendations to hire private caregivers for nighttime duty also fell on Carly's deaf ears. She was only a freshman in high school. Lack of sleep and leisure time was taking its toll on her physically and academically, but her perceptive guidance counselor informed all of her teachers of the extraordinary conditions Carly faced at home.

All of us professionals worked diligently to keep Andy at maximum safety and function. However, nobody was as perceptive to Andy's subtle changes and deteriorations as Carly. When his speech became slurred, Carly understood him best. When he started to choke and have difficulty swallowing, a feeding tube was surgically implanted in his stomach. We taught Carly to prepare and instill the feedings into the tube. She taught us how to do it in the way he tolerated it best. When his lungs became weak and congested, we taught her to use the complicated portable suction machine. She taught us that she could learn anything needed to care for her father.

I had a lump in my throat watching this fragile, 98-pound girl hoist her 155-pound father out of his wheelchair and into bed day after day after day. I wondered where she got her strength. "From my dad," she answered.

Finally, the day came when it was impossible for Andy to remain at home. Carly had spent most of the night suctioning the mucus and giving him his oxygen treatments. He could no longer breathe unassisted, so he was hospitalized and agreed to go on a ventilator for a short time, just until his family could accept the fact that he was dying. Carly had to be forced to go to school, but as soon as her last class ended, she hustled to her father's hospital bedside to sit with him, along with her brother and sister.

Andy went into a coma on the last day of his life, and his devoted daughter told him one last time how much she loved him. But she did not need to say the words; her love and dedication had been proven countless times. As experienced professionals, we had taught her the techniques needed to care for her dad, yet, a fifteen-year-old taught all of us a poignant lesson in love, caregiving and devotion.

Alice Facente

Emily's House

Emily was four years old when she started coming to my home for day care. She was bright, talkative and had beautiful red hair, which she loved to have done up in pigtails. Sometimes her mother got up too late to fix her hair, so Emily brought fistfuls of ponytail holders and hair clips for me to use. This often turned into our "talking time," as Emily called it. I could usually tell we were going to have a talking time by the troubled look in her eyes.

"How is everything at Emily's house," I would ask as I brushed her hair.

"Not good," she'd answer.

"Do you want to tell me about it?"

With that, Emily would tell me about her parents' latest fight. Her grandmother lived with them and "drinks whiskey," as Emily put it, causing loud and coarse behavior before she eventually passed out. Emily skirted around her until she heard her snoring.

There were usually three or four fights a week—some quite volatile, some milder—but there was never much peace at Emily's house.

My mind kept searching for ways to help her. I knew it

helped to have someone to talk to, but I wanted to somehow empower her to go after a better life one day.

One morning, Emily told me about the screaming match her parents had the night before and how she had been so scared, she ran into her room and hid in the closet.

"Emily?" I asked. "Can you control what the adults do in your house?"

"No," she answered.

"It's *their* house and *they* make the decisions about what happens there, don't they?"

She nodded her head in agreement.

"Did you know that some day you are going to have your own house, Emily?"

"I am? What kind of a house?"

"That will be for you to decide," I said. "Between now and then, you can be planning it. We can start a list of what you want in your house and what you don't want," I said, taking a sheet of paper out of the desk. "Would you like to do that?"

Her eyes lit up. "I get to decide everything?"

"It will be *your* house," I said.

The next morning, I was braiding her pigtails, and Emily asked me if I wanted to hear what her grandmother said sometimes after she drank whiskey. I shrugged and told her if she needed to tell me, it would be all right. There came cascading out of Emily's mouth words that no child should hear. She stood there staring at me, waiting for a response.

"Wow, Emily, are you going to allow those words in your house?"

"No way," she said.

We wrote *no bad words* on her list.

"Write down *no whiskey*," she added. "I'm never going to have whiskey in my house, either."

I cheered inside for her. "Good thinking," I said.

We were weaving bright-yellow ribbons into her hair a few days later, when I thought of something else Emily would one day have in her house.

"Emily, let's talk about who you will let live in your house. When you're older and going out on dates, what if the man gets mad and yells all of the time. Will you ever marry him and let him live in your house?"

"No," she answered firmly.

"So, as you're dating a man, if you see that he drinks too much, or yells too much or does anything that you don't like, you can decide to stop dating him right away, can't you?"

"I'll never date anyone mean or let them live in my house."

Bravo! I shouted to myself. "I'm proud of you for being so smart," I said to Emily.

One Monday, she came in and was so excited because she had gone to a sleepover at her friend Jenny's house. She told me everything they had eaten, the videos they watched and the games they played.

"I really like Jenny's house," she said.

"It sounds like you had a great time," I said. "Were there things in Jenny's house that you would like in yours?"

She nodded yes, and we wrote on her list—*eating dinner together with no yelling; holding hands and praying.*

"I think you are very smart to watch how other people live and then decide what you want in your home."

"I know what you're doing," she said.

"You do?"

"Yes, you're trying to help me and be my friend."

"You're right." I swallowed back tears.

One day after my husband left for work Emily asked, "How come Chuck hugs you?"

"Don't you hug at your house?"

She looked down and shook her head no. I regretted asking the question.

"We hug because we love each other," I said. "Is that something you want to put on your list?"

"I might need to practice," she replied.

"Oh, it's easy," I said, reaching out and hugging her.

When Chuck got home, she walked over to him, stood with her hands down at her side and leaned slightly against him. He looked at me, questioning.

"Emily is practicing hugging for when she gets her own house," I said, motioning for him to hug her.

He reached down and gave her a bear hug. She didn't say anything, but each morning, she stood nearby waiting for her good-bye hug as Chuck left for work. When he came home, she watched while he hugged me and waited for her turn.

She liked to hear Chuck laugh, so she thought up funny stories or jokes while he was gone and would tell him when he came home. Always, she was rewarded with a belly laugh and a pat on her head.

"Write jokes and laughing on my list," she said.

Emily's situation at home didn't get any better, but something inside of her did. In the year and a half that she was with me, I can't count the number of times we talked about *her* house, always pulling out the list to add things she did or didn't want. We also talked about her going to college, going to church, having a job and what it would be like when she had children. We covered it all.

A short while before she left my day care, she asked me where Chuck and I were going to live when we got old. I told her I wasn't sure.

"Well, if you and Chuck need a place to live . . . you can come and live in my house. It'll be great."

Sharon Armstrong

Broken Vow

*An acre of performance is worth a whole world
of promise.*

James Howell

I went right to the kitchen to prepare lunch without changing my church clothes, high heels and all. As I reached in the cupboard for plates, I teetered off balance as Rusty came up to me with a push. Down I went, plates and all.

When our family sat around the table for lunch, Rusty became agitated and pushed the table across the room. This was happening more and more lately. Our precious son was hydrocephalic, autistic and now a teenager. I couldn't handle him anymore; it took two of us to change his diaper, because he was bigger than me. Plus, his increasing aggressiveness was making his younger brother, Stephen, feel understandably resentful.

In my heart, I wanted to ignore it, but my intellect said we had to move on to another phase in our lives and Rusty's. I had vowed to take care of him forever, to do what was best for him. Yet, it was painfully apparent that it was time to look for a placement for Rusty. Thus began a two-year hunt for the perfect home.

Some were too expensive. Some were so quiet and controlled, we knew Rusty would not be happy there. Some were for non-ambulatory children, and Rusty was not eligible. It seemed he was either not handicapped enough or too active.

Christmas weekend, while visiting my mother-in-law in northeast Ohio, she mentioned a niece had told her of a home in a nearby town. When I called, the director, Mrs. S., said we were welcome to visit but to beware that the home was a mess from Christmas fun.

As we entered, we heard children laughing. Toys were strewn all over the living room. A Christmas tree stood decorated with homemade ornaments, some not recognizable but cherished nonetheless because of the hands that made them.

When she took us on a tour, the director continually called the children *her kids*. She reached out and stroked the child in bed who could not see or speak because of a brain injury. The little boy responded with a smile. She mentioned that she had adopted two of her special kids rather than see them institutionalized.

Then Mrs. S. took Rusty onto her lap as she told us more about the home. He did not accept strangers freely, and to see him sit there content, chewing on his tennis shoe, as always, was foreign to us. We knew then there was something exceptional about this woman. She explained that she didn't have an opening but would put us on the waiting list if we were interested. This would be the third list we were on, and it seemed futile to even sign Rusty's name. Yet, the simplicity and love we saw expressed was exactly what we were looking for.

We drove the two hundred miles home praying that we could place Rusty there. One week later, we received the call. Mrs. S. had an opening, and she requested that we bring Rusty the following weekend. "That's not enough time," I begged. "I need more time."

"Mrs. Houseman, it won't be any easier two weeks from now. Please try."

I had just taken Rusty for a physical and gotten him caught up on his immunizations, so I had no excuse. The only thing left was packing his clothes.

I packed for a while then sat and cried. I'm sure Rusty was confused, for I would grab him, sob into his shirt and kiss him then go back to the packing. This went on for several days. I struggled with being a failure as a mother. Guilt lay heavily on my shoulders. *I vowed to take care of him forever, to do what was best for him. This is my baby, am I abandoning him, breaking my vow? But how can I take care of him, Lord?*

The answer I wanted didn't come, and the day arrived when we pulled into the parking lot of Rusty's new home.

I wanted to unpack his clothes and get him settled there, but Mrs. S. said she would do it. This was her way for her and Rusty to get acquainted.

I was sure Rusty would be upset when we prepared to leave. Mentioning the words "bye" or "car" always sent him running to the door. But that didn't happen. Instead, as we waved to him, he took Mrs. S's hand, walked down the hallway with a little strut and a giggle that said, "See you later, Mom, I'm home now."

I was crushed.

My husband and Stephen seemed to take it in stride that Rusty was gone. I, on the other hand, alternated between guilt and relief. I enjoyed shopping and not hurrying home to see what mischief Rusty was up to. I loved sitting in a bubble bath for half an hour without someone banging on the door reporting that Rusty was into something. But then the walls of the quiet pressed in. I missed his running from room to room. I missed his giggle.

Mrs. S. had told us it was best not to visit for six weeks. I called every week, expecting the worst. Every week she told me all the good things Rusty was doing. How he was going to bed without getting up during the night and wandering. How he let the younger children crawl all over him in play. How they both enjoyed his sitting in a chair in the kitchen, watching her. Within weeks, Rusty was eating regular food instead of his usual Fruit Loops and white bread. The home trainer had him doing simple commands. They were even talking about his attending school off the premises. *This is amazing,* I thought. *My baby is doing things I had never been able to teach him. He was surely where he was supposed to be.*

Rusty was eventually toilet-trained, had a vocabulary of fifty-five words and had gained some independence.

Now when I gaze upon his cherished bowling trophy and bronze Special Olympic medal, I realize I didn't break my vow after all.

Beverly Houseman

The Miracle of Forgiveness

The narrow soul knows not the god-like glory of forgiving.

Nicholas Rowe

It was one of those hot, sweltering July days in Tennessee. I was going about my routine of laundry and housework, after putting on a pot of coffee, anticipating the usual Saturday morning visit from Dad.

Every morning, with the exception of Sundays, Dad drove from his house in town to my brother's farm, where he did daily chores. He had always loved farming, and staying active after his retirement was important to him. A few years earlier, I bought some property from my brother and built a house on his farm. It had become a Saturday ritual for Dad to stop by for a visit after finishing his chores.

Usually, Dad and I just sat and chatted about the latest family news while we sipped coffee. Sometimes he would give a little fatherly advice. I looked forward to our weekly visits. They had become a welcome source of comfort after my very painful divorce almost five years earlier.

Mom and Dad were so wonderful during that difficult time. I don't know how I would have made it without the support of my entire family, who prayed for me and loved me unconditionally through all of my dark days. They stood by me even when I was wrong. I had been unable to forgive my dad for several years. I blamed him for everything that went wrong in my life. I reasoned that if he hadn't been so strict, so overbearing, so distant, so volatile, I would have turned out to be a better person. Maybe I would have made better choices as an adult if he had just taken the time to show me that he loved me. Maybe I would not have wanted to get married and leave home at such a young age.

After the divorce, I spent a lot of time with Mom and Dad. They were so different than I had remembered them twenty years earlier. They didn't judge me—they just loved me. I came to realize that my dad was only human, just like I was. I understood that he did the best he could as I was growing up, based on what he knew at the time. I also came to know that as an adult, I could no longer blame anyone but myself for the bad choices I made. Once I accepted all of that, the miracle of forgiveness occurred. Privately, I forgave my dad, and eventually, myself for making so many poor choices. I didn't have to make those mistakes anymore. I was able to move on with a new resolve in life.

As I looked out the kitchen window at my brother's cornfield, I breathed a prayer of thanks for all my family and special thanks for my fiancé, Dan. Our wedding was only a month away. I wondered what I had done to deserve so many blessings—a wonderful family, a fiancé who was everything I had ever dreamed of in a mate, a new house of my own. I loved my new life. Somehow, I didn't feel worthy, but God blessed me anyway.

With all these thoughts swirling in my head, my concentration was suddenly broken by the sound of a car door slamming in the driveway. Dad called out to me. I could tell there was something wrong by the sound of his voice. When I opened the garage door, there he was, staggering and breathless. His face was flushed and his eyes seemed unable to focus. He managed to say, "Something's not right. . . . I'm not right. . . ."

The doctors at the hospital in Nashville confirmed he was having a stroke. He underwent surgery to clean out a main artery in his neck to prevent another, possibly fatal, one. For the first several days, he required twenty-four hour attention. When the nurses told him not to get out of bed, he could not remember their instructions. His inclination to be active kicked in, and he repeatedly tried to get out of bed when the nurse left the room. It was like trying to put a jack-in-the-box back in the box. Each member of our family took shifts staying with Dad the entire time he was in the hospital to make sure he didn't fall and hurt himself.

During one of my shifts, I slept in a recliner next to his bed. He had to get up to go to the bathroom at least six times during the night. As I was helping him get back into bed for about the fourth time, he stopped and looked up at me with a helpless look in his eyes and said, "I'm so sorry you have to do this. I'm sorry for a lot of things." He stared into my eyes, as if to penetrate the message.

At that moment, I realized Dad didn't know I had forgiven him. My own father was uncertain about where he stood with me.

I said, "Dad, it's an honor and a privilege to take care of you." As I said those words, it seemed like it was someone else I knew who was so angry with him just a few years before.

Dad looked up heavenward and whispered, "Thank you, Jesus."

Then I knew that he had been praying for this miracle of forgiveness for years.

On my wedding day, tears streamed down my face when I saw Dad walk in the door of the church with his cane. God had granted us another miracle. At eighty-two, Dad was a survivor of the Great Depression, World War II, rheumatic fever, open-heart surgery, a stroke—and of raising me.

It was my turn to whisper, "Thank you, Jesus."

Karen Davis Lees

This Space

The very commonplaces of life are components of its eternal mystery.

Gertrude Atherton

It was a very warm Colorado morning, bright with a vivid blue sky. I arrived at the hospice center, wondering if this was going to be the day that Mary Jane, my best friend and speaking partner for over twenty-five years, would choose to leave.

She had been fighting colon cancer for seven years. After two remissions, the long road of countless operations, procedures and chemotherapy had brought us to this third and final round. Mary Jane was just fifty years old.

For so long, we had lived with cancer. We had feared it, treated it and cried over it. We bought wigs to cover it. We discussed the sadness around it, lessons learned from it, and the legacy of pictures and written messages Mary Jane could leave behind to help her son and husband heal from it.

As I walked past the front desk, I noticed a lemon meringue pie on the counter. When I entered Mary Jane's room, I casually mentioned seeing it. She immediately perked up.

"Lemon meringue is my favorite. My mom made the fluffiest, golden brown meringue in all of Oklahoma. Whenever she baked her pie, people came running. Will you get me a piece?"

As I headed to get a slice, Mary Jane and I both knew what lay ahead. With advanced colon cancer, even the smallest morsel of food wreaked havoc. Still, as I carefully propped her up and lifted a tiny bite of pie to her lips, she smiled and said, "Look how the filling wiggles!"

I gave Mary Jane just enough for her to taste the essence of lemon. The nibble of pie stayed with her only seconds before her ravaged body rejected it. Yet, in a weak but ever-so-clear voice, she said, "Gee, thanks. That was great."

I put the fork down on the plate. "After everything you've been through, how could you possibly say *that* was great?"

She rested her head back, "I've been thinking," she said, "how we've got to focus on the space between events."

I wiped her chin. "What do you mean by 'space between events?'"

"It's all the moments leading up to and directly after an event—the minutes and hours that define how we respond to it."

She caught my puzzled look and continued. "The space between events is where you find a feeling of peace watching snow-capped mountains as you travel to and from a hospital or office each day. It's the excitement that comes from watching your team before they actually score. It's the warm memory of home sparked by the smell of lemons as you lift a forkful of pie to your lips." She squeezed my hand. "The space between events is where most of life is lived ... and it is in this space, my friend, that you and all caregivers must also focus."

Pamela J. Gordon

What Mrs. Karcinski Taught Me

Open my eyes that I may see wonderful things.

Psalms 119:18 (NIV)

The shadows were getting long, and I hadn't even been to the grocery store yet. Supper wasn't started, and here I was on the other side of town.

I was happy enough to serve on the board of the Multiple Sclerosis Society. We provided a good service and, besides, generated a lot of good publicity for the cause, especially with our annual fund-raising telethon. Since I was the token registered nurse, the board often asked my advice regarding patient services.

Our budget was limited and we had several patients needing wheelchairs, so we advertised for used ones. I wasn't prepared for the response. Every day this week I had picked up one more wheelchair in our family minivan.

Parked in front of Mrs. Karcinski's house, I made a snap judgment of her home: small, neat, but austere. Yes, compared to her neighbors, her place was really plain. The grass was clipped short, but there were no shrubs or flowerbeds. Well, to each her own taste. *I'll just pick up the chair and scoot on home,* I thought.

After knocking twice on the front door, I began to think I had been stood up. But then, I heard the shuffling of feet. My impatience wasn't really her fault—I had children at home and a husband who would also be home soon, tired and hungry. I prided myself on my efficiency, making lists and marking every item complete, most days. This might not be one of those days.

The door opened slowly, and a short, plump figure appeared. "Yes?" she asked.

In a business-like tone, I both introduced myself and told her why I had come. "Well, come in, come in. I'm so glad you can use Paul's wheelchair."

I walked into the small living room, which I noticed was furnished with a minimum amount of furniture. There were no knickknacks, no doilies and no pictures on the wall. And the light was off.

I followed Mrs. Karcinski back to an equally dark and sparse kitchen, only half listening to her cheerful patter.

"I was so afraid I might miss you, because I go to the Community Center on Tuesdays and Thursdays."

I made the appropriate monosyllabic remarks.

"We spend our time doing things for the less fortunate, you know. I've been going over every week since I lost Paul."

Although she kept on talking to me, she never really looked at me—only a quick glance my way—which I found disconcerting.

Through her continual chatter, I learned that Paul had suffered from brittle diabetes, which took his toes, his feet, his legs and, finally, his life. She shuffled to a door that opened into a dark garage. I didn't follow her into the gloom, and she quickly returned pushing the wheelchair. It was an older model but looked sturdy. "I hope it's clean enough," she began, continuing her friendly monologue yet still not making eye contact.

"I was so blessed all those years, to have good health so I could take care of Paul at home. My diabetes wasn't nearly as bad as Paul's."

Suddenly, God opened my eyes, my heart and my head full of nursing knowledge.

This dear little woman, who spent her days helping the "less fortunate" at the Community Center had nursed an invalid husband until his death. I remembered then, no flowerbeds, no whatnots or pictures, the darkened house. How could I not guess? She was blind from diabetes.

Just as I was thinking all that, she seemed to read my mind. "I'll bet it's getting kind of dark in here. Let me turn on a light for you."

As she shuffled over to the light switch to turn on the dimmest of bulbs, I could plainly see the prosthesis on her right lower leg.

I managed to speak. "We have several who need a wheelchair and can't afford to buy one. Paul's wheelchair will be very much appreciated by someone."

Her already pleasant face lit up the dark room. "I just wish there was something more I could do."

I stuck out my hand to shake hers, but of course she didn't see. "Well, thanks again." It didn't seem enough. "Uh, could I give you a hug?"

She eagerly reached out, sort of in my direction, and I embraced her.

That night, supper got cooked and all my errands marked off my list, but I had accomplished—and learned—a lot more that day, thanks to Mrs. Karcinski.

Vera Huddleston

Wisdom Within the Walls

*Tell me a fact and I will learn. Tell me a truth
and I will believe. But tell me a story and it will
live in my heart forever.*

Indian Proverb

One of my earliest memories as a little boy was hearing
my late grandfather say, "If you help dig someone out of
their troubles, you'll always find a place to bury your
own." He was a simple man, the salt of the earth, and he
possessed wisdom unknown to most. He spent his last
moments on earth in a health-care facility for terminally
ill cancer patients. I was nearly sixteen when I began visiting him. Through my youthful, exploring eyes, I quickly
discovered he was not the only person there to possess
such precious knowledge. There was much wisdom
within the walls.

Within this home there was a peace of which most
people can only dream. Removed from the rat race of
society, the tranquil surroundings were absolutely
breathtaking. Hundreds of green plants filled the rooms,
while a handful of birds chirped in harmony. The sun's

rays engulfed the interior of the building, and the same sweet melody seemed to play over and over on some hidden stereo. Sometimes while my grandfather snored, I listened carefully. There were always the muffled sounds of laughter.

Although torment loomed over each bed and death lurked behind every corner, I discovered a silent bliss. Each patient had reached the end of life's path, and most were finished with the denial, the negotiating with God, the anger. There was no battling the inevitable. Instead, the snickers of a friendly card game could be overheard or the whispers of some treasured conversations detected. Peering into the patients' eyes was like gazing into a history book. For those who dared to open the cover, lengthy discussions revealed years of hard lessons and the wisdom achieved. The teachers were old, they were sick and tired, but they had more to offer than anyone I'd ever met.

One frail woman told how each winter she strapped on ice skates and commuted across the river to work every morning. Her brother, during the Great Depression, kept his family alive on a staple of potatoes.

One of the quieter men boasted of the fortune he made during Prohibition, while another recalled the Great New England Hurricane of 1938. As if he could still see it, his eyes widened. "Many homes were wiped out back then, but the folks in the north end came together like nothin' I ain't ever seen since!"

Most could even remember exactly where they were when the Titanic sank or when Elvis Presley gyrated his hips for the first time.

From bed to bed, there were endless stories from both world wars. The graphic and brutal details of combat caused me several sleepless nights. Awestruck, I also learned that the families who remained on the home front suffered terribly in their own silent ways.

Some spoke of the day-to-day life—trolleys that ran from one side of the city to the next and the boys who thought nothing of stealing a free ride; steamboats that paddled down the river and horses that transported those with land legs; the value of the dollar and all one could buy then; of men peddling their goods in the streets—blocks of ice, vegetables, everything. "Shoot, you could get your scissors sharpened, buy a new set of flatware or a Sunday hat without ever leaving your doorstep!"

All meals were cooked at home, and children never dared disrespect an adult. They all agreed radio programs left more to the imagination than televisions do.

I marveled at the raspy whispers about Lizzie Borden and her infamous axe. I asked, "Do you think she did it?" Looking past their grins and into their eyes, it was almost as if they knew the truth and weren't talking. Then again, it was as if they knew the truth about everything.

After three months, I considered each one of them a genius. Grandfather was right. Anytime I was in search of answers, I needed only to visit a haven for elderly souls.

It was a cold March morning when my grandfather decided he had endured enough pain. Before his departure, I visited him then made my rounds. As if they knew they would not set eyes on me again, many of the patients thanked me for my time and compassion. It seemed silly. If I'd done anything for them, I had already been paid back tenfold. Though there was no exchange of money, the gifts I received each visit were worth a fortune. If time was all I needed to give, then it was the best investment I'd ever made.

Steve Manchester

Grandma's Quarters

He who gives all, though but little, gives much;
because God looks not to the quantity of the gift,
but to the quality of the givers.

Francis Quarles

It was October 1962, and we had just experienced in the Northwest what would later be called the Columbus Day Storm. A severe ice storm with pounding winds damaged homes and trees alike. The area was a mess. The wind was finally silent, but the air temperature was still freezing. We had no power, which meant no heat, and our house was ice cold with its bare-wood floors.

I huddled in my new cotton nightgown next to my brothers and sisters while we waited for Dad to light a fire in the fireplace. He added extra wood to help the house heat quickly. As he walked away from the hearth, we all ran to find our place standing directly in front of the crackling fire to get warm as quickly as possible.

I had just finished warming my front side, stretching out my hands to feel how hot the fire had become, then turned to warm by backside. Standing there in comfort, I relaxed for the first time on that cold morning. Shutting my eyes, basking in contentment by the fire, I was abruptly brought back to reality. In only a second, a spark flying from the fireplace caught my nightgown. Flames instantly ignited the cotton, and the smell of my burning flesh singed the air.

At the hospital, my mom was told I had third-degree burns and extensive deep-tissue damage on the backside of my left leg. After months of treatment and daily bandage changes that were the most painful thing I had ever endured, the doctor grafted skin off my bottom to my left leg. Due to the severity and depth of the burn, he predicted, "Melodie will likely have a stiff leg after her skin graft heals. At the very best, she'll walk with a limp." My mother cried.

Oh, the agony of healing. Any movement brought tremendous pain, and walking was out of the question. My pain threshold could not bear it. I lay on the couch day after day, trying not to disturb my throbbing leg. Any movement was torture, so I became an expert at laying still.

My grandma lived in town and drove daily to our house in the country to visit me, then back every night, never missing a day. My grandmother was poor—based on government classification of income, she was actually extremely poor, I later learned. Yet, she afforded the gas to come to be with me every day.

Grandma never accepted the thought of me walking with a limp or a stiff leg. She was diligent in her faith and encouraged me daily, coaxing me to move it. I loved her so much that I wanted to please her. I would move my leg with tears in my eyes, barely handling the pain. Day after day she came. Then came a day when the pain was too great to bear, even to please Grandma. I didn't want to try to walk anymore, period. It just hurt too much. I just stopped trying.

One day after my long siege of "No, I am not going to try anymore," Grandma came to the house with oodles of quarters. I don't mean a few. I don't mean a handful. I mean a bunch of quarters that filled up her lap. A quarter in 1962 was a lot of money to a child. Penny candy existed back then. She wore a housedress, or what she called a "moo-moo," and placed all those shiny quarters right there on her lap next to me. Lying on the couch, I could see them. I had never seen that amount of money, never. It excited me.

She said, "If you stand up, I will give you a quarter." I wanted a quarter, so, disregarding the pain, I stood up. Grandma smiled so big and placed a shiny new quarter in the palm of my hand. I quickly sat down, the pain throbbing in my leg. She looked right into my eyes and said, "There's more where that came from. Do it again, honey, stand up."

I did it again, and she repeated the reward—another shiny quarter in my hand. This went on for months, day after day. Grandma was faithful and so determined I would not have a stiff leg and would walk without a limp. One day, I asked her, "What if you run out of quarters, Grandma?"

She said, "Don't worry about Grandma running out of quarters, honey. I got all the quarters in the world for you."

I missed the entire third grade. It had been almost a full year since the fire. When I went back to school, I sauntered in the door, walking perfectly. No stiff leg. No limp. The doctor said, "In all my years of treating burns, I have never seen a leg heal so completely."

There was an extra bonus—only a minor surface scar, instead of the common deeper skin-graft type. Again, the doctor was amazed. He had me come back many times to the hospital to show my leg and demonstrate its agility to other doctors.

It wasn't until after my Grandma died and I was much older that I realized the gift she had given me. My mother said, "Your grandmother could not bear the thought of you limping or walking with a stiff leg. She willed that leg well, and God heard her."

"And she willed me to walk," I said. Then I had to ask, "Where did Grandma get all those quarters, Mom?"

My mother replied, "I suppose she went without."

In all the years, I had never considered that. Only then did I realize the selfless act of love my grandma had given me so joyfully. Her daily gifts to me were actually her sacrifice and her faith all rolled up inside those silver coins.

Melodie Lynn Tilander

"Two quarters make fifty cents, Kevin, not a halftime."

Saying Good-Bye to a Village

There is no calamity which right words will not begin to redress.

Ralph Waldo Emerson

I wonder how liable I'll be if he drowns, I thought, as I boosted Mr. Denny into the front seat and heaved his wheelchair into the back of my van. Mr. Denny wanted to go fishing. He was a quiet and kind man who had me hooked.

We stopped at the Bait Shop for minnows. Being a city girl and proud of it, I'd never heard of minnows. When they scooped those babies out of that tank, I felt my skin crawling. "Oh, please, Lord, don't let Mr. Denny make me touch these!"

People often think of hospice work as quiet, depressing and no fun. I looked at it as my all-time favorite job. My heart sang as I thought of making the last months, weeks or days of my patients' lives the best they could be. Mr. Denny was dying of colon cancer, and he wanted to fish. And even though I have the outdoor skills of an indoor goldfish, I would not deny his wish. Of course, I had been told not to take any patients anywhere in my car. We didn't have liability insurance for that kind of excursion. I had told him that the week before. The smile left his face and the wrinkles around his eyes grew deeper. I was heartbroken, because his heart was broken. I asked him to be patient and let me talk to my boss again and pray about it. "Okay," he replied, "but, don't pray long . . . I don't have long."

I knew then that we'd be going fishing—my worst nightmare, except maybe camping. My boss quietly suggested that what I did on my own time was my own business.

As I drove to his home that morning, I was smiling—scared to death, but smiling. I was getting off very lucky. He'd wanted to take his boat. "No way!" I'd told him. "I don't drive anything that doesn't have brakes!" His wife had planned to go with us, but when she greeted me at the door, she looked ten years older than she had the month before.

"Do you like to fish?" I asked. She smiled as she rolled her eyes. "No, honey . . . but, I don't think you're a fisher-woman either." She was so right about that. "Why don't you go get your hair done and go shopping, or just get some much-deserved rest?" I said.

It didn't take a second time to ask. Mr. Denny and I waved good-bye and headed off to get those slimy min-nows. Then, he gave me directions to his favorite "fishin' hole." I parked the van, got the wheelchair out and put him in it. When I turned around, I saw the trip to the creek was straight down a huge mountain-like incline. I thought for a minute. "Wait while I get my cell phone out of the car."

"For what?" he asked.

"So you can call 911 when I have my coronary getting you back up this hill!" After he stopped laughing, he showed me the winding trail we would take a little further down the road.

I didn't have to touch a minnow. He baited my hook and his. For hours, we talked. I, of course, didn't catch a thing. He caught many mini-fish and tossed them back into the water. He explained the thrill was in the catch. He didn't want to take them away from their habitat and families. We sat for a while in silence, breathing in the sunshine, the peace, the smell of fish. Then I asked, "Are you afraid to die?"

He admitted he was. "Not so much of leaving this world," he said, recasting his line, "because I feel fine with my Maker, but afraid of leaving everyone else." He reeled in his mini-fish. "How am I supposed to say good-bye to a whole village of people?"

"It might be easier if you leave nothing unsaid," I suggested. "Then it seems like less of a good-bye but more 'until we meet again.'"

Soon he grew tired, and I did too. I gathered all the gear and put it in his lap, then shoved his wheelchair up the longest, steepest incline I'd ever made. Maybe it was the wheezing of my lungs, or the grunts and moans that escaped from my lips, or maybe because this fat lady was sweating like a pig, but he could not quit laughing! When we finally made it to the top, it took me fifteen minutes to get my heart to beat regularly again. It was a grand day!

Mr. Denny died in his sleep about three weeks later. It wasn't the usual dying process most terminal patients experience. His wife woke up, and he was gone. I arrived to find him looking so peaceful lying there. No wrinkles, no gray color and maybe a hint of a smile on his face. As I prepared his body for the funeral home, his wife on one side of the bed and I on the other, a few tears threatened to drop from my eyes. Tears were dripping down her chin. I asked if she felt cheated because she didn't get to say good-bye.

"Oh, no," she smiled. "He has told me so much in the last couple of weeks. He never was a man of many words, but he kept telling me how much he loved me and appreciated me, what I've meant to him all these years. He told the kids how much he loved them, too . . . and his brothers and his friends. It's been a wonderful time."

Mr. Denny figured out how to say good-bye to his village.

Sue Henley

8

A MATTER OF PERSPECTIVE

*He who wishes to secure the good of others
has already secured his own.*

Confucius

Holding On to Hope

*For the present grief there is always a remedy;
however much thou sufferest hope, hope is the
greatest happiness of man.*

Leopold Schefer

Mom walks five paces behind us, a second-class citizen from a third-world country, her passport stamped "Alzheimer's disease." Her vacant eyes peer from beneath dementia's wax mask. Dad is on a mission, and I can barely keep up with him, despite his heart condition. We are off to see another distinguished, well-meaning doctor who will have little to offer Dad's failing bride of sixty years.

We march through the opulent, twelve-story granite outpatient building of The Cleveland Clinic, known locally as the "pink pyramid." The clinic is one of the world's premier centers of healing. However, no healing will occur here for my mother today, or any day. As a physician, I know that Mom's dementia is now untreatable. Dad also knows her dire prognosis but is incapable of surrendering hope. He clings to the belief that one day I will reach deep into my empty medical bag and deliver a miraculous cure at the last-possible moment.

Strangely color-coordinated with the building's pink walls, Mom is attired in a neon-pink, polyester pantsuit. The color epitomizes the personality of this firecracker-of-a-woman who raised me. Mom has always been *electric pink* in her flashes of laughter, anger, joy and flushed embarrassment. Now, the electricity is gone, as if she'd been unplugged. Although Dad continues to style her hair and dress her in forgotten fashions from kinder times, I only see a woman who I barely recognize—one who is all dressed up with no way to know. The gold ID bracelet that I gave her accents her outfit. It is engraved with her name, address, diagnosis and Dad's telephone number, in case she ever gets lost. Just as Mom clipped my gloves to my coat when I was a child, I try to find ways to keep her attached to us as she recedes back into her childhood.

With Mom trailing behind, Dad and I stride across the second-floor balcony, engrossed in trivial conversation about the upcoming baseball season—anything to distract us from reality. As we argue possible starting line-ups, I glance back and realize that Mom is gone. Poof! Vanished into a bank of wood-paneled elevators. A thousand questions swirl in my mind: Will Mom notice she's alone? Will she panic or get violent? Will she follow someone who looks like us? Or, will she sit in one of the many crowded waiting rooms and become a nearly invisible, human *Where's Waldo?*

The rasp of Dad's labored breathing snaps me back to reality. All color drains from his face, leaving only the etched pain of the past months. He seems to age in an instant. I know that his ailing heart must be fluttering like a wounded bird. He staggers, gripping the balcony rail with shaking hands. Although I want to stay with him, to hold him, I know I must first find Mom.

"I'll check the floors above!" I yell as I run toward the stairwell. Dad enlists the help of a uniformed guard and then positions himself so that he can watch both the bank of elevators and the doors below that exit onto the mean city streets.

I fly up the stairs two at a time. My brain begins to short-circuit, sparking random thoughts. Amidst flickers of guilt, I conjure my brother in my mind, a look of disbelief on his reddening face as he stutters, "My God! How in the world could you manage to lose our mother—and kill our father—in only one afternoon? What's wrong with you?"

Shaking my brother's expression from my imagination, I hit the third floor running. Here, labyrinths of hallways connect with multiple above-ground walkways that access the whole Cleveland Clinic complex of buildings, a city within a city. Panic strikes! Seeing no pink in the sea of color on this floor, I launch myself up the stairwell again.

Time slows. People, lost in their own diagnoses and destinations, move about me randomly. The din of daily chatter shrouds my silent crisis. My senses in overdrive, I smell disinfectant and sweat, but catch no hint of Mom's Chanel No. 5 perfume nor of the butterscotch candy that fuels her second childhood. As I climb to each floor, my thighs and calves begin to burn, and my panic mounts. People stare at me with apprehension, then anger and then fear, as if I were a child running with scissors. Wild-eyed and erratic, I'm fortunate not to be wrestled to the ground by the alarmed medical staff.

Staggering to the top floor, I see a befuddled woman dressed in pink at the entrance to the Center for Children. Standing next to her is an equally bewildered young couple trying fruitlessly to extract useful information from her. "Mom!" is the only word I can muster, but the sigh of relief from the couple confirms that this is the one word that they most want to hear.

A butterscotch candy cleanses Mom's palate and her memory of the day's debacle as I reunite her with a husband whom she doesn't know. The vision of my brother pops back into my head, and I hear myself tell him, "Well, the good news is that I got a nice workout today, Mom made two new friends and Dad's heart is stronger than I ever imagined."

Dad clings to me for strength, as his breathing slows and color returns, weeping softly, "Thank God! Thank God, I was afraid we'd lost her." Watching Mom fiddle with her ID bracelet and wipe invisible crumbs from her pink pants, I think, *Sorry, Dad, we already have.* I want to tell him that we worry about him, that his burden is too great and that it's time to put Mom in a nursing home. But we've had this conversation. I know that my concern will be rebuffed and his answer will be "It's *my* turn to take care of *her.*" So, I return his embrace, keeping my thoughts to myself.

Dad's impish grin, which has been my beacon for a lifetime, begins to glow softly again. He takes Mom by the hand, and we resume our quest for a cure. And in that moment, I realize that my black bag is not entirely empty. It still contains one last magic bullet. I reach in and rummage about and there it is. Hidden under medical jargon and discarded theories, I find what is indisputably *the* most potent curative known to medicine—powerful enough to keep the dead alive in concentration camps and keep the word "miracle" in the dictionary: *Hope.* I grab as much as I can hold.

J.A. Vanek

Gratitude

Gratitude is not only the memory but the homage
of the heart—rendered to God for his goodness.

Nathaniel Parker Willis

For the first time, my mother cannot really help prepare our Seder meal. She wanders around the kitchen, pausing at the counter, the stove, the table, as if to collect something lost.

"What are you doing?" she asks.

"Setting the table," I say.

"How many people are coming?"

"Ten," I say, so irritated that I spill a spoonful of cooking oil. An old football cheer floats into my mind, "First in ten, do it again." And again. Mom has already asked me these questions several times in the last ten minutes.

For the past couple of years, Mom's speech has been like an old record that skips. The simple anchors of life—the who, what, where and when of things—often elude her. Mom is older than most of my friend's mothers, having had a nursing career and many adventures before she settled down to marriage and children. Now, those years are showing.

"Did you remember the macaroons for dessert?" she asks, a fork in hand.

"Yes," I say, again. I crack an egg and have to scoop shell out of the bowl. I stir the matzo mixture and take a breath. I have trained myself to be brisk and efficient, but now, around my mother, I try to be slow and soft.

"How many people are coming?" she asks.

"Ten," I say, impatience pinching my throat. "Let's take a break and go for a walk."

I wipe my hands and look for the house keys. They are not on their usual hook in the cabinet. They are not in my purse or resting on the kitchen table. I feel a brief flutter of shame over the impatience I felt just this morning, when Mom misplaced her glasses case for the second time. Then I feel a stab of fear: Am I, too, losing my mind?

I spot the keys and double-check to make sure I have turned off the stove.

The redbuds are flowering, the dogwoods skirting baby-green lawns. My mother and I walk past a closed lemonade stand, three broken wicker lawn chairs set out on the curb and a blond floppy-haired girl skipping over a pink jump rope.

As we walk, my mother tells me the story of her father leaving the household. She tells me about sitting on the steps, age fourteen, waiting and waiting for her father to return. I let the familiar tale flow into me. I remember as much about my mother's childhood as I do my own.

We pass a woman strolling a sleeping baby, and Mom smiles.

"Did you get the macaroons?"

"Yes, I did." My voice is stern and prim, like a schoolteacher with a child who simply won't learn the lesson.

"Did I already ask you that? I'm sorry," Mom says.

"It's okay." Sadness fills me, not anger. "What's it like to not remember?" I say as an eager black spaniel rushes up to us.

"I start a thought," Mom says, bending to pat the dog, "and the end disappears. If I try too hard to catch it, that makes it worse. So I let go, and eventually I get the answer. Of course, by that time, something else is going on." Mom smiles and shakes her head. Her hair is silvery and curly, her hands like fine dried flowers, her stride deliberate.

All weekend I have watched her happily listen to the conversations around her, passionately asking a question, then moments later, with equal passion, asking the same question. I have listened to her stories, which have the comforting familiarity of a well-worn quilt. These stories, which interspersed my growing-up years, are now the major part of our conversations.

That evening, we celebrate Passover with a Seder service, which my father leads. In the past, my mother cooked the soup, created the special apple blend of harosis and arranged the ritual Seder plate. My mother filled the wine glasses and blessed the fruit of the vine. But this year, I am the one shaping the matzo balls and chopping the apples. I feel a stab of loneliness as I stand to say the Hebrew prayer over the wine.

As the service progresses, my father tells our guests about "Dayenu," a Hebrew word that means, "Even that would have been enough."

"It sounds like Die-aa-new," he says. "You repeat it after each of the sentences I'm going to read. It's a way of expressing gratitude." He began, "If God had divided the sea without leading us onto dry land."

"Dayenu," we all repeat.

"If God had taken care of us in the desert for forty years without feeding us manna."

"Dayenu."

And so we follow the journey of our ancestors, promising we will be satisfied—with whatever we get.

As I repeat my gratitude and pledge my satisfaction with life as it is, I think of my mother. I miss her remembering all the details of my life. I miss her knowing where the silverware drawer is. I miss telling her something I'm proud of and having her remember it. And yet, she is the living symbol of Dayenu, graciously accepting her failing mind and making the best of it.

"And now, it's time to eat," my father says.

My mother reaches over and pats my wrist. I see the patina of softness that burnishes her, the loving core that goes far beyond mundane daily detail. I see the woman who has loved me even during the years I wandered through my own difficult wilderness.

As we sip our sweet wine and break off a piece of unleavened bread, I create my own litany:

If my mother gets pleasure out of life,
Dayenu.
If she remembers who I am,
Dayenu.

"This is a lovely Seder," she says. "You did a beautiful job of putting all this together."

I press her hand, look into her smiling face and say, "Dayenu."

Deborah Shouse

Switching Roles

*I love these little people; and it is not a slight thing,
when they who are so fresh from God, love us.*
Charles Dickens

My mother suffered from dementia caused by frequent mini-strokes. I tried to find live-in help for her when it became apparent she could no longer be alone. But her paltry income combined with what little I could pay someone made it impossible to find consistent help. My husband worked away from home most of the time, so my two children, ages nine and six, spent about four nights a week at her home, while other caregivers came and went filling in when they could. It soon became apparent I needed to help her full time. I quit my job and moved my family into her home.

The hardest part were those unpredictable times when Mother no longer recognized us and thought we were strangers in her house. She even got confused about the home she had lived in for over thirty years thinking, after I prepared and served her a meal, that she was in a restaurant. She offered to pay for her dinner.

My children had spent lots of time with their grandma before this disease. She had taken care of them while I worked. She rocked them as infants and played with them as toddlers. They had loved being with her and she with them. She taught my daughter, Theresa, to knead and bake bread, and polish her nails. She taught my son, Ben, card games like Go Fish and Crazy Eights, and her all-time favorite, Rummy.

With this new living arrangement, I was concerned for my children making this adjustment, living with a very different grandma. Often, their sleep was interrupted in the middle of the night by Mother's frequent awakenings. She was very hard of hearing and refused to wear her hearing aides at night, so I had to shout. I was concerned that even though they understood the situation, they would feel I placed them second in priority. I worried that they would feel resentful of the attention I gave Mother and would become disgruntled by the disturbances and restrictions brought to their daily lives.

Then, one day I watched Ben taking time and patience re-teaching his grandma her favorite card game. "Rummy!" he squealed. "Grandma, you won!" He obviously let her win, taking delight in her triumph as much as she did. He stayed calm and loving when she forgot again how to play or zoned out during her turn. Many times after that, I saw love in his eyes and heard it in his voice when he sat down to play with her.

When we brought Mom home from the hospital after a touch-and-go bout with pneumonia, she required physical therapy to keep her arms and legs strong. I did some of the harder exercises with her and then Ben would take over. He helped her finish them and then made it into a game, playing indoor kickball to make sure she got her leg lifts done. "Score!" he yelled, raising his hands over his head.

I wondered how Theresa would deal with the fact that Grandma seemed to recognize Ben more than her. I worried her feelings would be hurt and she might withdraw from the Grandma she loved so dearly. Sometimes I watched her wipe away tears of rejection. Yet, one day I found her sitting at the table with Grandma's wrinkled, old hand resting in her palm. "What color do you want, Grandma?" she asked, then polished the old worn nails lovingly and gently. Other times, Theresa sat at the piano, playing songs she knew her grandmother might remember, songs they had sung together. My mother's feeble voice joined in, bringing a smile of joy to Theresa's face.

I thought I'd have to teach them how to handle this huge adjustment, but I learned from them instead. Not only does wisdom come from the mouths of babes, but it comes from their hands and hearts as well.

Julie Schneider

It's Late . . .

There is in all this cold and hollow world no fount of deep, strong, deathless love, save that within a mother's heart.

Felicia Hemans

My mother and I were arguing about my bedtime, and I was feeling a bit resentful. A teenager trying to spread my wings? No, though I had one, the youngest of our five kids. Mother had just recently celebrated her one-hundredth birthday. I was closing in on retirement age and spending much of my time caring for her and my father, who was also bedridden. Yet, here she was, barking orders from her hospice bed, itself a startling piece of furniture that loomed large in what had been our master bedroom.

"It's time for you to go to bed now. You need your rest," she directed.

"Mother, I'm an adult—I know when it's time for me to go to bed," I snapped. "Here is your water, and the bedtime pills are on the tray. I'm going to read a while, but I'll check on you before I go to bed."

Who's in charge here? I wondered. *She just can't seem to stop giving orders and directions. She also tells me what to eat, how to dress and drive, and that I'm working too hard—all this from her deathbed.*

I was clearly part of the "sandwich generation," caught between caring for my super-senior parents and our children. I learned the truth of this saying when my parents came to live with us. "The very, very old need so very, very little, but the little they do need, they need so very, very desperately."

Both teachers, Mom and Dad had retired in their sixties to garden, hunt and fish, and to volunteer in the community. At ages ninety and ninety-eight, they had enjoyed more than fifty years in their cozy home at the foothills of the Blue Ridge Mountains of North Carolina. With their retirement income, good neighbors and a caring church family, they had managed well.

Many years ago, my only brother and I agreed that "when the time came," he and his wife would move into the home place and care for our parents. But my brother died of a massive heart attack at age sixty-five. So when relatives, friends and church members began calling to express concern that my parents were "not doing so well on their own these days," my husband and I faced a crisis.

"You know how fiercely independent they are," he said. "They'll never agree to any plans we suggest. It's out of the question to expect them to adapt to assisted living or a nursing home."

Indeed, Mom had been a headstrong woman who often went against the flow. During the 1960s, she'd taught American history, in the South. One student, noted for his outspoken racial prejudice, was forced to read John Howard Griffin's *Black Like Me*. He went on to become a minister, a leader in civil rights and founder of the Faith and Politics Institute. He was just one example of the many lives Mom influenced.

We began with little hope of reining in such an independent spirit.

Any attempt to discuss moving to be near us included Mom saying, "I might consider it, if your dad dies first," and Dad saying, "I built this house with my own hands. The only way I'm leaving it is feet first!"

But a few years later, seemingly out of the blue, they called one Saturday morning and announced, "We're coming to live with you. You will be in charge of our move."

For once, I was happy for their orders. There would be no recriminations like "You made us come here. It's all your fault."

Our family got busy preparing for the great grandparents' move to Texas. David and I transformed our master bedroom into an elder suite. We refit the bathroom with a roll-in shower, raised commode, and side rails. We hauled out the wall-to-wall carpet and laid a new tile floor to make it easier to use walkers and wheelchairs. And because we knew they'd be sleeping on their own schedule, we hung special blackout drapes.

My mom's first response? "You shouldn't have done all this. It must have cost a fortune. You should make better use of your resources."

Now I heard her calling down the hall to me again, "Go to bed! It's late."

It was Christmastime, and I was overwhelmed with food, gifts, laundry, medications and getting hospice care for her. My oldest daughter had phoned amidst the chaos to say she was en route. "Be careful on the roads. They're slippery tonight," I warned. Now, out of the chaos of many other noises—the television, conversations, games, quarrels and general uproar—my eight-year-old granddaughter said to me, "Great-grandma wants you to come to her room and tell her good night. She says it's late and time for you to go to bed."

I groaned, knowing I'd have to drop everything and go.

Then my granddaughter added, "I think she loves you and wants to tuck you in bed, like she did when you were little."

A light came on in my mind and heart. "Be careful on the roads. They're slippery tonight."

"It's late. Go to bed."

It's all the same translation: "I love you, and you'll always be my little girl."

Maryella Vause

Through My Mother's Eyes

My daughter, do you have any idea of the fears that haunt me? One is that I'll no longer be needed. Another is that I'll become a burden. I break out in a cold sweat when I think about having a stroke or an accident when I'm alone. This worry is alleviated somewhat by wearing my Lifeline Help Button that connects me with a hospital emergency room, but what if I couldn't press that button?

I live in terror that I might have some kind of lingering illness. And this fear flows into another fear—such an illness could wipe out my savings, destroying my very last shred of independence.

Do you realize how much of my precious freedom I've lost? Consider, if you will, having to depend on someone to take you to church, the market, everywhere. Once I was master of my own transportation. I could go anywhere I wanted, anytime. In our society, the automobile is an arm of independence. For me, old age amputated that arm.

I know my elimination reports bore you at times, but at my age, when my body lets me know it is cooperating, I like to share the news. Another accomplishment in another seemingly insignificant day.

Octogenarians are proud of any accomplishments. And

one in which I take great pride is that I've conquered city living, and in my own apartment, to boot. When you moved me here years ago, it wasn't easy to leave the small town that had been my home for almost my entire life. But I adapted. Yet, sometimes the longing to be back in my hometown brings tears to my eyes.

But then, sundry things cause me to weep these days. Some of the tears you don't see, like when I remember the two husbands I've outlived. Or the tears I shed when staring at my one-sided flatness, where a few years ago there was a breast. When I contemplate the chance I might someday face the cancer monster again, extra tears well up.

More often than not, my emotions erupt with the hormonal spontaneity of a teenage girl. But at least emotions prove I still care, I still hurt, I still love. Emotions prove I'm alive, even though my life has taken some bizarre turns. One example is that I've lost my adult status. Yet, no matter how many motherly duties you may perform for me, I'll never be a complete child of yours in the same way you were mine.

Although I'm deeply grateful that I have you to help me, I cringe each time you're forced to take over another of my tasks, such as balancing my bank account. I'm angry that I can no longer do it myself. I could tear that bank statement to shreds when I remember all my excellent office skills during those many years I worked. Perhaps if you'll now try working an algebraic problem (since algebra was never your favorite subject), you'll understand how I feel.

It's not only the bank account. You've taken over Medicare and insurance forms. And now you must dispense my medicines, too. Over and over, day by day, I'm rendered more helpless. For every chore relinquished, old age claims another little chunk of me, making me fear the day I will be completely dependent.

Therefore, so long as I have a wee scrap of independence left, may I offer some loving advice to you, my daughter?

Don't fret when I eat a food not included in my medical diet. I know as well as you that it's wrong, but some pleasures are worth the sacrifice. To sneak a forbidden bite of a favorite food is just about the only adventure left in my life.

Try not to criticize me for what you see as clutter. While you choose to put things away, I find it convenient to leave them out, saving me steps and energy.

Show patience with my physical slowness. A quick step for you can be a slow, painful one for me. Pain is my Siamese twin.

Let me talk, if I choose, about the past. Compared to the limited future, it's often more comforting to remember what has gone on before, instead. And if in the process of reminiscing, I repeat myself, try to overlook it.

Everybody forgets sometimes, even you. Grant me the same human frailty.

Forgetfulness doesn't always mean senility.

Let me complain about the weather. Realize that for me there's no perfect climate control. My personal thermostat responds to allergies, thinning blood and aching joints.

Please don't push your way on me too much. Your way may not always be best for me. I'm not even sure efficiency is all that important anyway. A jumbled grocery list isn't the end of the world.

When people address you concerning my requests, bypassing me entirely, stand up for me. I still have a brain, as well as the ability to speak for myself.

I don't like to whine, but please spend as much time with me as you can. I love you, and I enjoy being with you. Contrary to what you might think, I'm aware of the toll all this responsibility has taken on you. It shows in your face. To take on the parental task of caring for an elderly child is to look in a mirror and see your own mortality. I can't help being a constant reminder of your future. And I know all the devilish challenges you'll face.

Now for my most important piece of advice, which is experience-borne. Strive to grow old with courage. I pray that in the future you may know more of the joys of old age than I and less of the trials. And may you always have someone like you, someone who cares.

Martha Larche Lusk

That's Enough

The voice of parents is the voice of gods, for to their children they are heaven's lieutenants.

William Shakespeare

Alzheimer's is smearing Mom's brain like Vaseline on a mirror. Distinctions of time, of place and of events blur. Sometimes I'm her daughter; more often I'm her friend, her sister and sometimes even her mother. Dad's vascular dementia, on the other hand, is like an old mirror of imperfect glass, its back chipping and peeling, leaving ever-growing black spots that reflect nothing, empty spaces that used to contain memories. Empty spaces into which words that could finish sentences, comprehend books, and even design and build a house that was accurate to plan within an eighth of an inch have been sucked like a black hole.

I'm always surprised when, while talking with Mom and Dad's friends, I become emotional. No, that's too soft a word; too easy. I cry. I try not to let them hear it in my voice, but I'm afraid they do. I love when they call, because it means they care, but even that caring is enough to cause a catch in my throat.

I can't tell them everything, these friends: Anne, Mary, Frank, Bernie, Betty, Elda. Most of these people have known Mom and Dad longer than I have, have shared experiences with them, were attendants at their wedding, served aboard ship with Dad in the Coast Guard in World War II, hall monitored with Mom in junior high school and planned to run away to Hollywood with her. All of these people have had their own tragedies—you don't live to your eighties without tragedy—and they don't need further evidence of their own mortality. I can't tell them Mom and Dad don't know them anymore, that they can't bathe themselves, can't use the telephone or the television, and sometimes not even the toilet. It won't help them, won't comfort them, for they can't change things any more than I can. Besides, I don't need to tell them the hard things. They know. And I cry because they know.

I never cry when I'm with Mom and Dad. When I'm with them, they're so glad to see me, and they smile and hug me, and Dad talks like Donald Duck to make me laugh, even though he's not quite sure who I am. The idea of crying never enters my heart. Instead, I talk to them. I tell them about my day, the kids, something the dogs did, my sister and her latest boyfriend, my brother's latest ski trip, my husband's latest genealogical find, my sister-in-law's latest foray into pottery. I tell jokes Dad used to tell, and he laughs, and I hug him when I catch the brief glimmer of self-recognition in his smiling blue eyes that have lost, for a time, their dullness. I use some of Mom's words and expressions to describe a person or a thing, and she knows—somehow she remembers that the phrase means something, something personal and special. And she laughs. She laughs a lot more now than she ever used to, and I'm so happy when I make her laugh that I hug her again and call her my sweetie.

I sing. Mom always liked it when I sang, so I sing. She loves it, and I love doing it. Sometimes I sing as I'm coming onto the floor to visit, and she hears me before she sees me. Any silly thing, even old nonsense songs she taught us as kids, or old standard songs Dad used to make up funny lyrics for: ". . . I had a dream, dear, you had one too. Yours was the best dream . . . because it was about me!" Then I dance into view, and Mom calls out my name as if it's the sweetest music she could make.

Dad dances with me—infrequently because of his bad hips and knees. He slides one foot around a little and keeps the other in one place, the same way he danced at my wedding a quarter of a century ago, when his hips and knees worked just fine, and the same way he danced at their fiftieth-anniversary party six years ago. While we dance, I tell him about both events as if they just happened, and I never once use the word "remember."

Mom likes to polka. All I have to do is pop a Frankie Yankovich CD in the boom box, and away we go, yee-hooing our way around the room like a pair of reckless, whirling dervishes. She went to Slovenia with Frankie Yankovich, I remind her. Eight years ago. She and Dad took my daughter, Allyn. We dance, Mom and I, and I tell her about my daughter ringing the bell in the church, on the island in Bled, on that trip. I tell her about the caves at Postojna, and the way the hotel maids arranged Allyn's blanket and teddy bear on her bed every night.

Dad hardly talks at all, but he loves to listen and to joke, and he never misses a chance for a pun. Like Shakespeare, he always treated the pun as the very highest form of humor. And Mom still treats his puns with a roll of her eyes, a slight shake of her head and her inimitable half-smile, half-grimace.

Mom talks and talks, sprinkling her always-impressive vocabulary, every word used properly, into improbable monologues to loved ones long gone. I go with her as if on a guided tour of Eden, and I'm whoever, wherever, whenever she needs me to be.

They never want me to leave, but I have to go. We hug and we kiss, and we exchange "I love yous" and "See you tomorrows." They walk me to the elevator, and we blow kisses and say good-byes long after the door closes.

I never cry when I'm with them nor when I leave them. I'm happy. I had today. I had the chance to make them smile, and I did. I had the chance to hug them, and I did. I had the chance to be with them knowing that we might not have tomorrow, but we had yesterday, and we had today, and that's enough.

Carole M. Howey

Crossings

This world is the land of the dying; the next is the land of the living.

Tyron Edwards

She was death's handmaiden.

And Sue took the job gladly. The hushed night hours lent a kinship to her caretaking. A dim lamp's glow haloed the bed, almost pulsing with the patient's measured breaths. Some saw this as a deathwatch. Sue saw it as a ritual journey, and she was merely there to attend to the boarding pass.

The thick soles of her worn, comfortable shoes padded across the room. Sue smoothed the bleached bed sheet, tucked in his thin blanket, and gently straightened the man's head to a more comfortable position. She plucked spent blossoms from a vase of daisies, tidied the hospital stand and scooted a vinyl chair closer to the bed. The oak frame groaned as she sank her ample weight into it.

The end wasn't always peaceful. Sometimes it arrived with distress, pain and fear, but, more often, the opposite was true. Either way, families wanted someone in attendance, and, for one reason or another, many couldn't be there themselves. For some, it was simply too painful. For others, they couldn't spare the time. And a few families lived too far away.

That's why Sue had replaced her cozy retirement slippers with her old nursing shoes—to tend the dying for the living. She felt comfortable volunteering to sit with terminally ill patients between the deep, holy hours of midnight and morning. She rarely slept well at home, anyway. And it felt good to be useful again, especially with a patient like this one.

She and Arnold Taylor went way back. Why, they had attended the same schools, the same church, the same potluck dinners and the same weddings and funerals in this small Iowa town. So it was only fitting that she attend his death, and Sue knew it wouldn't be long. She recognized the signs: his skin was mottled, his hands and feet discolored. And since tonight's shift began, she'd already seen a change in his breathing. The patient shifted slightly and moaned.

"It's okay, Arnie." Sue's strong, corded hand blanketed his, gently stroking the parchment skin. His eyes, as pale as a work shirt that had suffered too many washings, opened and stared beyond her.

"You've had a good life, Arnie, but there's an even better one waiting." She reached over to caress his grizzled cheek. "When you're ready, Arnie, just cross over. It's okay. When you're ready."

And then it happened.

She felt it at almost the same time as she witnessed it: his wide-eyed look of radiant joy, and his thin hands reaching toward a presence. Sue glanced hopefully at the foot of the bed, all the while knowing she wouldn't see anyone there. She never could.

Then it came, an almost tangible release, as soft as the

tiny last sigh that puffed from Arnie's smiling lips while his arms sank back to the bed. Expelling her own pent-up breath, Sue's trembling fingers brushed his eyelids closed.

Glancing at the clock, she noted the time then paused to feel once more the solemn sacredness in the moment. Fleeting yet perceptible. Hopeful and holy. She felt privileged to witness it.

With a farewell glance toward the bed, Sue pulled a list from her pocket. Names. Telephone numbers. Now there was an entire family to notify and console.

She was life's handmaiden.

Carol McAdoo Rehme

Send for Jane

*Judge thyself with the judgment of sincerity,
and thou wilt judge others with the judgment of
charity.*

John Mason

Before I die, send for Jane. Send for her when I can't get
into the tub anymore, and when I need someone to brush
my white hair, and spray Chanel No. 5 above the collar of
my flannel pajamas. When my breath is shallow and my
old words few, send for Jane.

I was Jane's supervisor before I left that job, but I still
look for her. Four days a week and every other weekend
I'd see her at the bus stop, her gray winter coat and yellow sweater as much a part of her uniform as her white
pants and oxfords. She's a home health aide. She cares for
those unable to leave their homes or accomplish their
own basic activities of living. Some are dying, some are
disabled, and some are heavily laden with frailties of old
age. Jane can change the bed linens with a patient still in
bed. She listens to advice about growing tomatoes, setting a proper Seder dinner, and adjusting a carburetor on

a 1927 Roadster. Jane brings the beauty of the season with spring wildflowers tucked behind her ear. She pulls back the curtain so a warm summer ray can reach an isolated face. I've seen her carry scarlet maple leaves to share the beauty of a last autumn. Once I watched her pack winter's first snowball into a plastic bag and carry it into a home. There she announced the season's arrival to a bed-bound man, and he told her of a long ago snowball fight that ended in his first kiss. She whistles while she mops and delivers a bedpan with a smile, as if to communicate it's a pleasure to scrub floors and wash their bottoms.

When Jane walks into homes for the first time, some don't see the gift she brings; they see only her sable skin. But she doesn't hate them for their ignorance. She smiles and says, "Learn something new every day. That's what my mama taught me, and that's what I teach my little girl."

Jane had married soon after high school, and the baby came just after her husband left. Because she was born under pressure, Jane named her baby girl Diamond. Her daughter was born with cystic fibrosis. At least once a year Jane takes a leave of absence from work because Diamond's lungs won't clear. Jane stays at the hospital, then carries on the treatments at home after discharge. For weeks and weeks she breathes each breath in unison with Diamond.

When Jane is absent, her patients torture the replacement aides, wanting them to have the essence of Jane. Though family, friends and caregivers often visit with good intentions, some are unable to hide their burden of obligation and duty, so they fail to bring the joy that Jane does. In a few weeks, after Diamond is again stable, Jane's back with a grin on her face and resilience in her step. She's always happy to go back to her patients who smile their biggest smiles when they see her. When she returns, she brings home-baked cookies or homemade soup in a used margarine container.

Sometimes only Jane and those she cares for understand and appreciate her skill and gifts. When she's asked what she does for a living, no one responds with envy or admiration. At the bank she notices the rude stares at her welfare checks, and at the supermarket she hears the sighs of disgust when patrons wait for the clerk to count out her food stamps. She knows the minivans, SUVs, and sedans that whiz by her bus stop aren't filled with respectful eyes.

I haven't seen Jane at her bus stop lately. Does she have a new schedule? Is Diamond sick again? I see others with old coats, or sweaters, and I see the white shoes. They remind me to pray that those who wear them will find grace and strength and honor. I still look for Jane.

Amy Jenkins

The Reason I'm Back

"No, don't die. Please, Lord, don't take her now. Not yet," I cried, as I bent over my near-lifeless elderly mother as she lay in intensive care. I felt the whole world crashing in on me. It was Friday, April 12, six in the evening— Dark Friday. I had just arrived in Cleveland. They must have been rushing Mom to the hospital at the same hour I was walking away from my dream job. This couldn't be happening. The mother I'd left behind to chase my dream was dying. The job I thought was going to make me rich and successful was gone. The one-two punch of that Friday drove me to the edge of insanity. Looking into my mind's mad abyss, a still, calm feeling came to rest on me. It said, *She won't be taken yet. There is a reason you are back.* I stayed by my mom's side for several more hours, desperately holding onto the quiet confidence that her time had not arrived.

As I drove away from the hospital to my home, my wife and our kids, I tried to reconcile what had happened that day. Just three short months ago, I was on top of the world. I had accepted a great job in another city. No one in our hometown would miss my family or me. We weren't special. My sisters, my mom, my in-laws would all do fine without us there. I would write, e-mail, call and, on occasion, drive back to visit.

However, underneath all the anticipation of a new job and new city, an invisible hound had tugged at my heart, begging me not to leave. Like a cruel owner, I kicked at my conscience, telling it to go away. Now, I was back. The tugs at my heart were replaced with despair. I wondered if this is how Jonah felt when circumstances and a whale forced him back to Nineveh. In my life, I always believed that things happen for a reason, but I could not understand why I was flung back home so suddenly.

Mom made a miraculous rally, just as the calm, still feeling said she would on that awful Friday. The doctors couldn't explain her recovery, but they warned us that Mom was weak. She was living on borrowed time. We all accepted that. Within a week, Mom left intensive care and the hospital, and she went back to the home she had shared with my eldest sister since Dad died twelve years before. Living together, Sis and Mom reinforced their mother-daughter relationship with the added epoxy of best friendship.

For the next two months, Mom was well enough to travel with a wheelchair and an oxygen bottle. I took advantage of my joblessness and became "one of the girls." My sister Marianne and I took Mom to malls, garage sales and long lunches. We reminisced about good times, old times and odd memories. We reinforced the love we had enjoyed and still shared with each other.

As I watched my sister perform the vast bulk of caregiving, I realized I was not providing any real care to our mom. I wanted to help but, as a man, I felt unnecessary. I couldn't deliver care as well as "Mare," and my mom preferred Marianne's gentle touch, anyway. I had no problem with this but still wondered why, if I couldn't assist with my mom's care, did providence bring me back home? I kept searching for the answer.

One day in July, Mom took the expected turn for the worse. We called for the ambulance, and the frantic rush to the hospital followed. Mom's deterioration was a terrible thing to watch. Everything began to fail—her heart, then kidneys, and she had a stroke. Watching Mom die was unbearable for my sister. Marianne's caregiver spirit crashed into the reality that her best friend was dying, and there was nothing she could do to stop it. During Mom's final days, fear, despair and tears were my sister's interchangeable companions. Still, she needed to execute powers of attorney, living wills, do-not-resuscitate orders and more, and all this while trying to balance Mom's final comfort in this life without impeding her departure for the next life. This was a very complex and infinitely painful ordeal for my sister to manage. I felt helpless. Then, I determined that the best help I could be was to be there with my sister—every day, every minute—and reaffirm her life-and-death decisions.

During Mom's last hours, the doctor gave her a shot to ease her torment and pain. Later that night, the angels came for Mom and helped her pass into the next life peacefully.

We buried Mom next to Dad. My sister and I felt so empty and sad standing there. I was hoping Dad was looking down, pleased with my presence at the end of Mom's life. Then, that still-quiet voice came back to me: *That is why you were brought back.* In that moment, I realized I had the answer to the question I had stopped asking. I was not brought back to be a caregiver to Mom. My blessed destiny in all this was to be a rock, a refuge, a comfort to her caregiver, so she could finish her Divine assignment.

John Black

Raising Evan

Children are God's apostles, sent forth day by day, to preach of love, and hope and peace.

J.R. Lowell

Raising a child with autism was not what I had imagined ten years ago as I walked down the aisle in my white dress toward my Columbia-law-graduate husband. The thought never crossed my mind that the children of two such well-educated people would be anything other than above average intellectually. And, at first, it seemed as though it would be that way.

Our son Evan was a beautiful baby with sky-blue eyes and a smile that lit up an entire room. During his first year and a half, everything seemed fine. He met all his developmental marks on time or before. But by the age of two, it became apparent that something was horribly wrong. When other children talked and babbled, our son was strangely silent. When other children laughed and played together, our son sat alone in a corner, endlessly rolling toy cars back and forth. After a year of shuttling him around from doctor to doctor, we finally were given a diagnosis for his silence and strange behavior: autism.

After the diagnosis, we did what all parents do when they learn their child has a problem: We searched to find a remedy, something that would lift the clouds that seemed to fog his mind. We were urged to try intensive behavioral therapy, and he responded well. Four years later, seven-year-old Evan was mainstreamed for part of the day into a typical first-grade classroom.

But while Evan was doing well, I found that I needed answers. I looked for the reason why I was chosen to be the parent of such a special child. What had I done, I wondered, to deserve having a child like Evan?

Solace came from another parent of a child with disabilities. "I knew God does everything to perfection," this parent stated, while I wondered, *Where is the perfection in my child?* The father went on, "My son can't understand things like other children do and can't remember facts and figures," he said. "The answer is that the perfection of such a child is not within the child. When God brings a child like ours into the world, the perfection that He seeks is in the way people react to this child."

And so, I sought out God's perfection and found it.

I discovered it in children who extend their hands to Evan, trying to include him in their games, even though he doesn't usually understand them or how to play. I've seen it in other parents who pointedly make play dates for their children with my son, knowing that exposure to a child like Evan will make their children better human beings. I have seen God's perfection in teachers who refuse to see my son's disability as a handicap or believe that he is capable of anything less than any other child. And I have seen it in churches, schools and camps that welcome Evan into their programs with open arms and whatever support he needs to participate.

I have often felt that people pity me for having a child

with a disability. But, I have never believed I deserved that pity. It's been a long, hard road, and there are many more battles to be fought. Never, though, has there been a day when I did not rejoice that Evan has come into our life. At night, Evan often lies down with his head in my lap. We talk and laugh, as I stroke his hair and look into those beautiful, clear, blue eyes. Never, I say in these moments, has God created a more perfect child than this.

Elayne Robertson Demby

9

UNEXPECTED BLESSINGS

He that does good to another does good also to himself, not only in the consequences, but in the very act; for the consciousness of well doing, is, in itself, ample reward.

Seneca

A Heart to Give

The generous who is always just, and the just who is always generous, may, unannounced, approach the throne of heaven.

John Casper Lavater

As I lay in bed on Thanksgiving Day 1989, my body wracked with pain, I found little to be thankful for. Some months earlier, I had broken my foot. Having been a world-champion steer wrestler on the rodeo circuit in my early years, I certainly didn't worry over broken bones. The main problem was the inconvenience of the cast. But as the weeks went by, I began to experience intense pain. Finally, the cast was cut away, and the source of pain revealed. Somehow, the cast had cut the bottom of my foot, and since I was a diabetic, gangrene had quickly set in. After several days of intravenous antibiotics, I went home, but the wound never healed. The searing, throbbing pain was unbearable, and my temperature escalated. I knew what the next step would be.

The following morning, an emergency surgical team prepared to amputate my right leg, just below the knee.

Though I had protested in the beginning, now I just wanted to live and to be out of pain. After the surgery, I gradually moved from a wheelchair to crutches and often hopped around on my good leg, until a blister appeared on my foot. Six months later, I was a forty-four-year-old double amputee. I had felt sorry for myself after the first amputation, but it was nothing compared to the anger and rage I experienced with the second.

When I was a youngster, I had joined a little country church and thought that took care of my religion. I didn't talk to God the way some people claim to. I took care of myself and figured most folks would be better off if they did the same. What I learned about God growing up was that He was to be feared, and I had experienced enough fear in my own home. I certainly didn't need more from some deity.

But now, as a grown man trying to cope with two "stubs" instead of legs, I even lost my fear of God. As I sat in the middle of the bathroom floor, unable to raise myself up, I cursed God violently. So what if He struck me with lightning, could that be much worse? Maybe I wasn't the best person in the world, but I didn't deserve this.

Eventually, I was fitted with two prostheses and spent time in rehabilitation learning to walk again. By 1995, I was back to a fairly normal lifestyle, with a good job, wife and family. Then, I began having chest pains. The pain was familiar. When I was thirty-one, I had quintuple heart bypass surgery. Years later, stints were placed in the arteries. What else could they possibly repair? Increasing pain and total exhaustion forced me into the hospital. Finally, the doctor recommended a heart transplant, even though my medical problems posed a great risk. Having been a gambler in my rodeo days, I didn't like the odds they were giving me, but I saw no other option.

Being accepted by a transplant team was no easy task. As a diabetic and double amputee, some teams wouldn't even consider me. And even if I was accepted, I would have to go on a waiting list, which could take months or years. Even if I got lucky and received a heart, there were no guarantees that the surgery would work.

When I had the bypass surgery years earlier, I was put on a heart-lung machine to keep my heart pumping during surgery, and then an electrical impulse restarted my heart to function on its own. But this time, someone else's heart would be placed in my body. It didn't take a genius to figure out that the only One who could make a brand new heart start beating was Almighty God, and I figured I had alienated Him completely the day I cursed Him. I was tired of the anger and bitterness, and didn't want to live what life I had left raging against my circumstances. So, I made my peace with God.

Eventually, I was accepted as a transplant candidate, and on the day after Christmas, I went into the hospital with hope and apprehension to wait for a new heart. It was like living with life and death at the same time. One minute I thought of being healthy again; the next minute the reality surfaced that I might die.

Finally, on January 22, the doctor told me a heart had been located. I gathered my family together. As they prepared me for surgery, I felt complete peace.

Suddenly, the doctor came in and told us there was a problem. Hesitantly, he said, "We have a seventeen-year-old boy on a ventilator who probably won't make it through the night without a heart." He paused awkwardly. "I don't know how to ask you this, but would you consider giving him the heart?" He emphasized that the heart was originally intended for me, and it was my choice. I could keep it, since there was no way of knowing when another heart would become available or how long my body would make it without one.

From the moment I was notified a heart had been donated, I had gone from disbelief to elation, to apprehension to acceptance, and now I wasn't sure what I was feeling. How do I choose who lives or dies?

The tough part was knowing what my family would go through if I didn't receive another heart. I didn't want to make my wife a widow. I wanted to live and see my grandchildren grow up. The easy part was knowing who needed the heart most.

It was the toughest and the easiest decision I ever made.

The young man survived the surgery, and one week later I received my new heart, an even better physiological match for my body than the previous one. Several months later, one of the doctors told me that he knew of no one in medical history who had chosen to give up a donor heart to someone else.

That was seven years ago. Today, it takes extra energy for me to walk, but I enjoy going places and meeting people. I wear shorts everywhere I go, no matter what the season or weather. I want people to see my prostheses and ask questions, so I can tell them about my medical miracles. When they ask, I tell them that God gave me new legs so I could walk with Him. Then, I explain how He gave me two new hearts—this physical heart transplanted into my chest cavity and a spiritual one deep in my soul, which overflows with His love.

John Patterson as told to Louise Tucker Jones

Just Me

Therefore whoever humbles himself as this little child is the greatest in the kingdom of heaven.

Matthew 18:4

As my grandmother lost her memory and independence, I watched my mom and aunt face the great dilemma of finding appropriate care for her, and I listened to their worries and concerns. I was a twenty-one-year-old newlywed. My husband, Marty, and I had just moved into our first home, a fixer-upper that definitely needed some love and attention, so my income was needed to help with the monthly mortgage and repairs.

The idea of placing my grandma in a care facility bothered me. Although I knew she might be happy there with all the activity around her, I wasn't ready to let her go. I needed some extra time with her.

"I've got it," I said to myself one afternoon while scraping ancient wallpaper from my dining room wall. I prayed as I picked up the phone and called my mother. "Mom, I've found just the right place to help you with Grandma. It's a loving service that will come to your house, fix her breakfast, dress her and then take her on outings. They'll love Grandma, Mom. You've got to say yes!"

"What is the name of this service? Who are 'they'? How much does it cost?" Mom questioned all at once.

"It's in Orange," I piped back, citing the location of my new home. "And the cost—well, I'm not sure."

There was a moment of silence before I continued. "There is no 'they,' Mom. I'm the service. It's just me! Grandma needs me, and I would love extra time with her. I can care for her in the daytime, and she can live at home with you and Dad at night!"

Within days, I quit my job, and my new job began. My parents arranged to pay me the same salary I had walked away from, eliminating financial concerns for Marty and me.

Each morning, I arrived at Mom's, kissed her good-bye as she left for work then prepared toast and coffee for Grandma and me. While we ate, Grandma often said, "You're Janet, aren't you?"

I'd smile, thinking of how close we'd always been, and then answer, "Yes, I'm Janet, and you're my grandma."

Our mornings often began slowly, but by noon we were out on the town doing errands, window shopping, pausing for lunch and then returning to my house for a nap. Periodically, she'd ask, "You're Janet, aren't you?"

"Yes," I'd respond lovingly. "I'm Janet, and you're my grandma."

Late afternoons we'd go for a walk down my street and around the corner. We often walked past a church and stood along the fence of its preschool to watch the children play. After many days of watching, the teachers and children got to know us by name. After many more days of watching, Grandma and I were offered jobs! One small class needed a teacher every afternoon from three o'clock until five. With my preschool background, I was asked to teach and told to "Bring Grandma along! It will be great for the kids and your grandmother," the director insisted.

So Grandma and I began our two-hour-a-day job. While I worked with the children, Grandma sat quietly in a maple rocker, slowly swaying back and forth. They drew her pictures, sat on her lap and even gave her kisses. It didn't seen to bother them that more than once Grandma asked them their names.

One day, I watched her hug a little boy. "Sweetheart, I can't remember. What's your name?"

"Adam. My name is Adam."

"That's right," Grandma said as she patted the little boy on the back. Pointing to him and then to me, she said proudly, "You're Adam, and I'm her grandma."

I smiled to see that Grandma finally knew who I was, at least for today. But I also realized, it wasn't "just me." There were now twelve little "theys" in the loving service of helping Grandma.

Janet Lynn Mitchell

The Image of Gramps

As winter strips the leaves from around us so that we may see the distant regions they formerly concealed, so old age takes away our enjoyments only to enlarge the prospect of the coming eternity.

Jean Paul Richter

"Okay, we go now."

That phrase always signaled a decisive end of my grandfather's visit when I was a kid. With those words, he rose sharply from the couch, sneaked dollar bills into my hands and the hands of my siblings, and drove off, more often than not, in the paint-encrusted, white Chevrolet station wagon he used in his work as a painting contractor.

A decidedly handsome man, he reminded everyone of a Romanian Cesar Romero, with dark, thick, wavy hair that, in later years, turned shock-white, all the while maintaining its thick texture. I can still sense his smells—the aftershave mingled with the lingering scent of lacquer and paint thinner, whichever he was using last.

Gramps came to this country in the 1930s, yet, he never lost his luxurious Romanian accent. He was a man of great contradictions, wearing jackets mismatched to pants, but always jacketed and always elegant. He never hesitated to kiss a woman's hand as she entered his room. He was strong, firm and direct, but a kidder of the first degree.

His strong, sure hands were those of a true artisan, chiseled and firm, as only a man who had used them in labor for decades would possess. Yet at the same time, they were gentle, passionate and artistic. They were like those of a painter on the Left Bank of Paris who gestures in the air to judge the scope and shape of a scene about to be painted. Gramps could paint anything from the side of a house to his own self-portrait, which he lovingly gifted to me.

Once, I went home for a visit to celebrate his eightieth birthday. As I entered my mother's house, I saw my grandfather standing on a chair placed on top of a desk in my childhood bedroom. He was painting the house—the *entire* house—alone. Why? "Because it should look good for the celebration."

A few years later, Gramps started showing signs of Alzheimer's disease. This was a devastating blow to the entire family. Our goal from that point forward was to create a sense of what I call "transparent caregiving." We constructed a world where he felt he was still in charge, but where he was also safe from harm. The adult day-care center where he spent the day became his "job." He stood outside his apartment complex and waited for the bus to take him to "work." On days off, he was on "vacation." The magnificent caregiver who ran the center took him under her wing, but to Gramps, his boss was the activities director. In Gramps' time, the bosses were usually men, so Gramps called this man "Boss."

As his disease progressed, he was moved to assisted living and eventually to a nursing home. I loved to sit for long periods holding his hand and talking with him about what, I will never know. I savored the times we spent together and cherished the occasions he would smile and point to his mouth, asking for a kiss, which I cheerfully bestowed. He would tap his head repeatedly, as if to say, "I know I am not thinking as well as I should, and I am no longer in control," as though he could beat his mind to be better, like hitting the side of a soda machine when the drink fails to appear.

One day before I left for a business trip, I looked at my watch—9:45. I sat on the couch in my apartment, looking at a picture on the wall behind me, the self-portrait of Gramps. When he painted it, the face he saw looking back at him was vibrant, kind and handsome. At that instant, the image replaced the face afflicted by advanced age and illness, the one I had become used to over these past few years.

I left the house with this new image of Gramps brightening my heart. On the way to the airport, I got a call from my brother. Gramps left for heaven—at 9:45.

This time, he didn't press dollar bills into my hands, but he left me a treasure far greater. I smiled as I recalled the vibrant man in his self-portrait. "Okay, we go now."

Gary Barg

More Blessed

Marriage is the strictest tie of perpetual friendship.
Samuel Johnson

"It wasn't supposed to happen this way," Russell said in his hospital-weary voice as a tear splattered on the arm of his wheelchair. "Thelma isn't supposed to die before me. She's everything to me; what will I ever do without her?" His voice trailed off as his thoughts collected seventy years of memories together, the last good ones of which were already past, unless God performed the miracle for which he prayed.

Perhaps Russell was recalling Christmas Day 1931, as the Great Depression destroyed most everyone's fortunes and stole their hopes—but not his. He and his beloved Wakarusa High School sweetheart, Thelma, began a marriage adventure together that day, one in which they would conquer trials and tribulations for the better part of a century. Neither considered the day when their journey as one might end.

Perhaps Russell was thinking back over just the last five years, when his dependence on Thelma increased as his lack of equilibrium confined him to a wheelchair. But now, his ninety-year-old chauffeur and lover lay fighting for her life, and seemingly losing the battle. Her quintuple-bypass heart surgery had gone better than could be expected for an elderly, petite patient. But the recovery had not. Infection had claimed her vitality, forcing an additional emergency surgery, and now the illness was lurking to claim the very life Russell had walked beside for seven decades. The family had been called.

What will I do? was his question, and *What will I do?* was mine.

At not quite half his age, I was suddenly alone many nights, due to an isolating divorce. I, too, was on my own. As his friend, I welcomed the warmth with which Russell received me and the wisdom I saw in his gentle spirit. I had been married twenty-three years; Russell and Thelma marked exactly three times that long. This man had experiences I valued, a love I admired and advice I wanted about how to grow a loving until-death-do-you-part marriage. If I ever married again, I wanted a marriage like Russell and Thelma's.

Since all his family members were out of town, I took joy in the fact that I was the logical choice to accompany Russell to the hospital and stay with him in his home when others were not available. I learned to operate his wheelchair-accommodating van, almost as well as Thelma. Although he never complained, I know Russell preferred her company to mine, even when she was gravely ill. I observed this as he spent hours by the side of a woman who couldn't even respond, as he caressed her legs, held her hand and prayed for her recovery.

Yet, Russell didn't understand why I wanted to be with him, why I had "nothing better to do." What better deed is there than to lend a hand to a friend in a time of need? I considered it a privilege to be in the presence of a man I so respected, to have the honor of assisting him. I looked forward to blocks of time to soak in his wisdom and his attitudes.

On weekdays, I took him to the hospital then went to work. Each evening we'd stop for a bite to eat before returning to their home. Before we crawled into our beds at night, he encouraged me that God continues to be faithful and bless us, no matter what life has thrown at us. He often repeated the same thing I had heard from his lips in his quiet, gentle manner during happier and healthier times, "Well, I can tell you one thing. If God blesses you only half as much as He has me with Thelma, you will be a fortunate man."

Then, reality of the present would take over for Russell. "I thought she looked better today, didn't you?" I assured him I agreed.

"When she comes home, we will have to make some changes, so it's easier for her to get around the house and into bed." I promised that when we knew she was coming home, we would create a custom-made habitat just for Thelma.

That time finally came, one that few ever thought would. Thelma came home, weak and in pain, but her husband insisted he would care for her, as she had for him all those years. So from his wheelchair, he vacuumed floors, put guy-scattered things away and made sure the dishes were washed, although he couldn't quite get them up to their Thelma-appointed place in the cupboard. He asked me to raise their mattress up on concrete blocks to make it less painful for Thelma to get out of bed. However, she discovered his plan and threatened me. "You can't raise our bed. Russell won't be able to get into bed from his wheelchair if it's that high. Leave it alone; I will manage just fine."

Thelma had told me, "In all those years, we never had

a real argument," but it seemed to me this just might be the issue, an argument over who could love the other one more.

Russell's examples began to bear fruit for me. God brought a loving wife for me to cherish like Russell demonstrated. I may not have seventy years to perfect it, so I was thankful for a good teacher to speed my learning. Carol and I spent as much time as possible with Russ and Thelma, as couples.

Amazingly, Thelma made a full recovery, and it's a good thing. Not long ago, Russell fell, fracturing his pelvis and leg, forcing him into the hospital. Thelma visited daily, stayed for dinner with him, then hurried home before darkness fell. At ninety-one, she tried not to drive after dark anymore.

One evening, as my wife and I visited Russell, he suddenly stopped. He looked worried. "Are you two going to stop by and see Thelma on the way home?" When I assured him we would, the worry disappeared as he said, "Oh good. Tell my wife I love her."

When we did a few minutes later, a proud, blushing Thelma responded, "Oh, he forgot to tell me that tonight before I left. He *always* tells me he loves me, and he forgot tonight."

It always amazes me when Russell claims, "I don't know why a young couple like you would want to spend so much time with old folks like us." He tells everyone about how blessed they are that we want to come spend time with them. I guess after ninety years, there are still some things Russell just can't understand. Doesn't he know that we're the ones more blessed?

Jeff Keplar

Sunrise

Although the world is full of suffering it is full also of the overcoming of it.

Helen Keller

Ray was the first terminal patient I visited as a hospice volunteer. He was dying alone in a world that promised to ignore his passing. A shy man with no close circle of friends, Ray's few acquaintances had distanced themselves, as people often do when life presents its most challenging trials. When I arrived at his home, he met me at the door.

"Are you Ray?" I asked.

I'll never forget his answer. He peered up at me through smudged glasses, and with a trace of mischief in his eyes, he said, "What's left of him."

"I'm new at this," I told him.

"Likewise," he said.

At first, I didn't know what to make of this quiet little man. Our first conversation was filled with awkward silences as we struggled to find our places in this new relationship. I don't remember what we talked about that day, but as we came to know each other during the visits that followed, we became close friends.

In the course of time, Ray told me about his life. He told me about losing his job, because he'd become too feeble to work. He told me about the shock of being diagnosed with cancer. And he told me how his wife of thirty years had abandoned him the week after he'd received his diagnosis.

He could no longer drive, so sometimes to brighten his day, I took Ray for rides through the countryside in my pickup. We talked about our lives and our dreams. We shared our hopes and aspirations, and the fear and uncertainty of death. We watched as summer surrendered to fall, and we talked about the seasons and cycles of life. We swapped jokes and laughed together. He told me he hadn't laughed for months. And we prayed together, often sitting for extended periods in silent communion.

Sometimes, under the weight of this terrible thing that was happening to him, Ray would hang his head and the tears would come, but he always pulled himself together. He had a dignity about him that would not allow self-pity. And Ray never lost the hope that his doctors were wrong, that he would live, and that he could someday return to work.

"Hope is the key," he once told me. "Hope is stronger than the pain. And it's stronger than the fear. Hope is my secret weapon."

The two things that struck me most profoundly about Ray were his toughness in dealing with the pain associated with his cancer and his frustration at not having accomplished certain things in life. He never came right out and broached the subject, but, on occasion, when he turned the conversation to the topic of personal achievement and fulfillment, I felt he was challenging me to live *my* life more deliberately. Although I had come to assist him, it sometimes seemed as though he was mentoring me.

Then, just as I was about to begin construction on my dream house, a devastating back injury turned my life upside down. In one day, I was changed from being the king of my world to being a helpless victim of chronic pain. I was bedridden with pain so intense that I could not even read a book. My eyes scanned the page to the end, but pain so permeated my being that I had no idea what I had just read. So I lay and stared at the ceiling day in and day out, while sinking deeper and deeper into depression.

Pain ruled my life. I lost track of Ray and his condition as fall gave way to winter. I spent thousands of dollars on diagnostic tests and medical treatments that I could not afford, but nothing seemed to help. Then, four months into my ordeal, I woke in the predawn twilight, as usual, racked with pain and consumed by dread. Dread of facing another day of agony. I despised consciousness, with its reminders of what my life had become. I lay awake for an hour and realized that I couldn't stand the thought of going through another day. I prayed for death to come. All I wanted was relief from the pain, and if that meant death, then so be it. Then my thoughts turned to Ray for the first time in months. I remembered the toughness and courage he had shown despite the debilitating pain of the cancer that was destroying him. I wondered if he was still alive. And I wondered if he could help me cope—if only I could talk to him one more time.

At that very moment, the sun rose above the horizon, and a thin finger of light entered obliquely through my bedroom window, illuminating a single word in the title of a book on my shelf. That word was "hope."

Call it random chance. Call it coincidence. Call it whatever you want. But that beam of light started me thinking about the spirit of hope that my friend Ray had always maintained. Did this ray of light, resting on the word "hope," represent the communication I so desired? Was my friend speaking to me on that cold and pain-filled morning? I looked at that word, and I thought about Ray. I could feel hope grow within me. It was almost as if I could hear Ray's voice. "Don't let the pain beat you. Don't let me down. You know it can be done, and you know you can do it."

In the weeks and months that followed, when it seemed the unbearable suffering would never end, my eyes often turned to the word "hope" on the jacket of that book, and I'd hear Ray say, "Hope is stronger than the pain." His words gave me the determination to hang on.

My recovery from the back injury was slow, but there finally came a time when I was able to walk across my yard. Then, there came a time when I could again put on my own shoes. I phoned hospice to reconnect with Ray, only to learn that he had passed away shortly after my visits were interrupted.

In the eight years that have elapsed, not a season has passed that I haven't thought about Ray and what I like to think of as his personal message to me. In the meantime, I have fulfilled my dream of building a house with my own hands. But more important, I have dedicated my life to living each day as deliberately as possible and to following my dreams. Ray had hoped he could return to work. For me, he is still working. I will never forget my Ray of Hope.

Steven Beach

The Last Gift

The manner of the giving shows the character of the giver more than the gift itself.

John Casper Lavater

On a bright June afternoon, my world turned upside down. Mom called to tell me she had malignant masses in her lungs and was scheduled for surgery the next day. Hundreds of miles away, I felt helpless, but I attempted to comfort my ailing mother. "It will be okay, Mom. I will be there for you." But something told me that it was *not* going to be okay. Silently, I complained, *Why, God? Haven't we endured enough tragedies?*

It was hard enough losing my father when I was sixteen. Five years later, a prison escapee murdered my brother.

As I packed hastily to be with Mom, the irony of the moment hit me: I was expecting our second child, while my mother just received a death sentence. What comfort could I bring her in her final weeks?

As I peered around the corner and into her hospital room, I found Mom puttering around as if she were perfectly well. A powerhouse of energy, faith and enthusiasm, this lady was going to hang tight for as long as she was able. Her defining attitude was one of simplicity and grace. As we hugged and talked, it became clear to me that she had put her things in order with no trace of fear or bitterness. I came away feeling small and unnecessary, as if nothing I did could impact her life.

After her surgery, I stayed to help Mom transition back to her home. She deteriorated rapidly. It became apparent that additional care was needed, so a hospice nurse joined our team.

My sister Jill came to give me a break, so I could return to my husband and eighteen-month-old son for a while. I struggled with the idea of leaving Mom, yet I knew she was in the very best hands.

Summer turned to fall and then to winter, then Jill called to tell me Mom's time was drawing close. I took the first flight out, hoping to share Mom's last hours with her. Mom recognized me and gave my hand a squeeze. She faded in and out of consciousness, but her lips moved constantly, as if she were talking to someone. As I drew closer to her bedside, I gasped realizing she was repeating the Lord's Prayer over and over.

On December 23, she called everyone to her side. "There's no Christmas present that I need, however, I want to make a request. Will you adopt a needy family as your Christmas gift to me? Buy them some groceries and Christmas presents, and please be as generous to them as you would to me," she whispered lovingly.

Suddenly, our mournful Christmas had a purpose! My brother, Bucky, scurried off to find a needy family through Mom's church. With names in hand, we were off shopping like there was no tomorrow! Each of us went our separate ways with individual grocery baskets, filling them to the brim with ham, turkey, yams, green beans and cranberry sauce. Then came the rolls, stuffing and butter, along with lots of lavish trimmings. The next stop was the toy store, for a doll, a ball, a bat, a jump rope and jacks.

Driving up to the tiny clapboard shack, we wondered who and what we would encounter inside. After knocking lightly on the door, it took a few moments for someone to answer. Finally, a little face with wide eyes peered around the door at us.

"Hello," Bucky cautiously greeted the little boy with the tousled blond hair. "We have some Christmas gifts for you. Is your mother home?"

The door slammed shut. We didn't know whether to run or wait. In an instant, a young girl opened the door. Her mother stood behind her. "Please, come in," they chimed. As we brought in the baskets and boxes, the children's faces wore looks of astonishment. They smiled and chattered among themselves, "Now we'll have a *real* Christmas!"

A warm feeling of heavenly accomplishment filled our souls. We felt blessed. For months, I had wondered what I could do to comfort my dying mother. Now it had been done with her simplicity and grace. Our Christmas gift to Mom was also her last gift to us.

Janice Jackson O'Neal

Love from Beyond

All I ever am, or hope to be, I owe to my angel mother.

Abraham Lincoln

Mother was vivacious, funny, clever, loving, talented and caring. I didn't place her on a pedestal, but she stood close. The one thing that kept her off that foundation was her smoking. For forty years, she burned up a pack and a half a day. Then, her dependency caught up with her. She got to the point where she couldn't even walk across her living room without struggling for every breath. After doctor visits and hours of testing, Mother faced the fact that she had advanced emphysema.

Too soon, we started to see symptoms that Mom tried to hide. She lost bladder control and started to fumble a bit. Her words seemed dark and far away. She'd slouch in her chair or crawl into bed just wanting to rest.

One Saturday morning, I visited Mom and found her taking a fistful of pills. I stopped her hand from going to her mouth when I noticed that the week-at-a-glance pillbox George had set up the night before was half gone.

When I quizzed her, she didn't know what day it was.

Within a week, Mother moved into a treatment center, where her meds were regulated and she received twenty-four-hour care. For the next few months, Mother and I talked every day, and I saw her about every third. During those encounters, we talked about death, God, afterlife, recipes, history, future grandchildren and how much we loved each other. One of those conversations led her to ask, "Do you want to be here when I die?"

I shook my head "No." I didn't want her passing to be my last vision of her.

One morning, the nursing home called—Mother was deteriorating. When I arrived, she was propped up in bed with half-dozen pillows. She gasped to take shallow breaths, even though oxygen was flowing into her through nose tubes. Her skin was pale and onion-paper thin. Her feet were dark and blotchy.

I leaned over her bed. "I'm here."

"It's hard," she groaned.

"I know." My tears dripped onto her mottled arm. I crawled into bed and held her head to my chest.

"I'm so tired of fighting."

"I know." I took a deep breath for both of us. "It's okay to let go."

I couldn't believe I said that. Was I hoping that she'd pass on so that I wouldn't have to watch her suffer anymore? I wanted to retract every word I'd just said, then I looked down at her face. Her eyes were closed, and a slight smile wrinkled her lips. I relaxed into her cool body, held her close and stroked her long salt-and-pepper hair.

For the next three days and nights, I ate, slept and prayed in her room. Mother went in and out of consciousness. During one of her lucid moments, she strained out the words, "Are you sure . . . it's okay?"

"Yes."

She wheezed, "You have . . . a wonderful . . . husband and . . . I won't be . . . leaving you . . . alone."

"That's right."

"You're gonna . . . miss me."

I swallowed hard. "Yes, I will."

"I . . . wanted . . . to be . . . here when . . . you adopted your child . . ." Tears puddled in her glassy eyes.

I took her thin hand in mine. "George and I've been talking about that. We think you need to be on the 'other side' to help us locate our child. We think you're our child's guardian angel."

Mother's body relaxed and melted into the bed. "You . . . could . . . be . . . right. Maybe . . . it's . . . time . . . to . . . go. I'm . . . so . . . tired."

"Remember to send me a redheaded one," I teased through tears, "like I always wanted to be when I was a little kid."

"Okay," Mom whispered.

That night, George stayed with me until late. Mother appeared to sleep better than she had in months. But a few days later, she fell into a deep coma. I watched her chest rise and fall in rhythm with her breathing machine.

I decided to go to work that morning. I gave Mother a big kiss on her forehead and told her I loved her, and that I'd be back on my lunch break. I pulled out of the parking lot at 8:00 A.M. At 10:00 A.M. the nursing home called. Mother was gone.

Granting my wish, she'd waited until I was gone before she transitioned.

Almost one year to the day Mother died, our son Keefer arrived. His birth father is Filipino and his birth mother Indian, but he has bright red hair—and a guardian angel on the other side.

Candace Carteen

"I'm your guardian angel,
I CAN'T mind my own beeswax."

Reprinted by permission of David Cooney

God's Answer to Prayer

I've been driven many times to my knees by the overwhelming conviction that I had nowhere else to go. My own wisdom, and that of all about me, seemed insufficient for the day.

Abraham Lincoln

Within a matter of minutes, our lives were transferred from happy and healthy to sad and hopeless. My husband and I barely survived a horrendous motor-home accident that would change our lives forever. The first week, I was in a drug-induced fog, on the live or die list with a shattered back and 48 percent of my body burned. My husband was 68-percent burned and in a coma two rooms from my own with a 9-percent chance of living. During my two-month stay, I had many skin grafts and a surgery to fuse my back. I would lie in the hospital, wondering how I was ever going to be able to care for myself again, let alone care for him. I prayed for God to send someone to help me when I was released.

He sent my niece, Vikki, a home-health aide, to be with me twenty-four hours a day for the next five months, while my husband remained in the hospital. When she first came to live with me, we were not close, but because of her expertise in nursing and my need for her help, our relationship grew into an everlasting bond.

In the beginning, I re-learned to do the simplest of human chores, like walking and eating, so there were many other caregivers in and out of our home too. Each morning, a nurse came to change my bandages, which took two hours. In the afternoon, a physical therapist arrived. There were usually five or six people in the house to help out. There were heaps of laundry each day and good meals, which were usually provided by the neighbors. There were appointments to make and keep, and a lot of therapy and exercise to do on our own.

In the midst of it all, Vikki was my protector, mentor and healer.

I had weekly burn-doctor appointments and weekly back-doctor visits, which usually took two to three hours because of overcrowded doctor's offices. Vikki taught me how to solve this problem. She put me in the wheelchair, puffed a little powder on my face and told me to drool, as if I didn't look pathetic enough already! It seemed to work, because they started taking me right in. Through it all, we laughed a lot, and Vikki kept everything going, thank God.

Every fear I had in my life reoccurred with the trauma of this accident, so she not only had to deal with my physical injuries but also with my psychological needs. I was such a mess. She taught me to be strong and wouldn't allow others around me to baby me. She taught me to do things for myself again and many times had to say, *"Just do it!"* I couldn't believe her persistence and perseverance. She taught me well that love must be tough, and I remember not liking her many times because she made me do things that hurt. At times, other family members seemed jealous of our relationship. We shared the pain, tears and sense of humor that it took for me to recover. I trusted the Lord to send me the right person to help me through this experience, and He definitely did.

While all of this was going on at home, my husband was still in the hospital. It took two months for him to wake up from the coma, and more months to be in recovery. He had fifteen fractures of his head, and he lost four fingers of his left hand, his left eye and the left side of his face. I knew how hard and painful it was learning to take care of myself, and I knew he would have to go through the same process. I longed for the day I could help him.

It took nine months for me to be able to be his caregiver. Thanks to my niece, I was able to take care of myself, so we no longer needed a caregiver living with us when he came home from the hospital. He was declared legally blind, and at first I was very frightened to be on our own. Vikki had taught me how to help him by making him realize that he is a survivor, not a victim. It was so difficult to watch him struggle learning to dress himself and putting on his shoes with one hand. At times, I felt more like his mother than his wife, and I had little patience. Every movement seemed to be in slow motion. When I felt like giving up I would tap into all the kindness but firmness Vikki had taught me. He had to learn to do things for himself again, and many times I had to say, *"Just do it!"* I couldn't believe *my* persistence and perseverance.

By the grace of God, we made it through those challenging eight years of healing and rebuilding, and now we are closer than ever. We wear our scars as badges of courage, and we're proud to tell our success story.

My husband often shares how he, too, had laid in the hospital praying that God would send the right person to help him. Then, he kisses my cheek and says, "He did. He sent me you."

Susan Lugli

Two Grannies in the Kitchen

*P*atience is the companion of wisdom.

St. Augustine

It was time for Pat to redecorate the bedroom. She'd put it off for years, always using the money for something else—Tom's college tuition, Cathy's nursing school, Jim's diving classes, Mike's trip to Mexico.

But now the children were grown, and it was her turn. First, Pat and her husband, Al, bought a century-old black-walnut bedroom set at an auction. The seven-feet-tall headboard, ornate dresser and matching chest of drawers were splendid, especially after they painted the room bright white to show off the beautiful dark-wood furniture.

Next, Pat hired a decorator, who designed the most magnificent blue and white draperies. Thick pale-blue carpet picked up tones from the multi-colored sunburst quilt. The pillows, pictures, knickknack shelf—everything was perfect. Now that their parenting years were ending, it was time now to enjoy life and each other.

Camelot lasted two months.

In May, Al's eighty-seven-year-old mother, Mabel,

came to live with them. She'd moved into a lovely nursing home a month earlier, but each time they visited, Mabel lamented, "I can't stand this place! There's no kitchen! How do they expect me to entertain my friends? I'll come live with you. At least you have a kitchen."

It wasn't a problem for Pat to take Mabel in. As a full-time nurse, Pat knew Mabel's medication needed to be better regulated, and she could do that easily if they lived together. Plus, Mabel had driven the five-and-a-half hours to their home in Milwaukee many times over the years to stay with their children when Al and Pat took trips together, and for weeks at a time when each of the four children was born. Mabel had been Pat's support system, caring for her children, mending their clothes, cooking their meals. She was always there when Pat needed her.

Now, Mabel needed them.

The only room large enough for Grandma's treasured pieces of furniture that she insisted come with her was the newly decorated master bedroom. The elegant walnut bedroom set was moved into the small room down the hall, the room with the race-car wallpaper.

When Grandma arrived, she made it clear that the kitchen was her domain. By the time Pat arrived home from work at 4:30, the potatoes were boiled, and a lettuce and mayonnaise salad was cooling in the refrigerator.

"Supper's ready, except for the meat. Didn't know what you had planned," was Grandma Mabel's daily greeting. Pat started hiding the potatoes.

That summer was one of ups and downs while they learned to adjust to Grandma Mabel's fierce independence, her memory failures ("I already took my pills!"), her old-fashioned way of cooking and dominance of the kitchen, her increasing urinary problems and her threats whenever the slightest thing upset her ("I'll get my own apartment!").

In the meantime, problems started developing with Pat's mother, Olive, also in her eighties, who lived alone in a small farmhouse just fourteen miles from where Mabel had lived. First, Olive developed Parkinson's disease, then she fell and broke her hand. A small nursing home was her next home, but, like Grandma Mabel, she hated it.

"There's no life in this place! I'm all cooped in. I just can't stand not doing anything."

Pat and Al realized that both Mabel and Olive belonged in their home. After all, they'd known each other and compared Mother's Day and birthday gifts for twenty-five years. They'd talked on the phone regularly—Mabel from her elegant city home, Olive from her farmhouse. Mabel was forgetful but in pretty good shape, physically. Olive was mentally sharp but confined to a wheelchair. Each one could do for the other what the other couldn't do for herself.

So, just five months after Pat and Al had redecorated their master bedroom, they had two grannies in their kitchen. Since Al and Pat both left for work early, they hired a woman to help get both grandmas up, dressed and ready to go to a day care for the elderly, where they were treated to a full day of physical and occupational therapy, aerobics and continuing-education classes.

When Olive's little house finally sold, she insisted they move more of her things into Pat and Al's home—chests of drawers, books, tables, pictures and ancient mementos of her life on the farm.

Grandma Mabel followed suit by demanding that her treasured collection, all two hundred pieces, of Haviland china be brought in so she could "entertain her friends properly." Soon, Pat had delicate pink and white china all over her house.

Other problems appeared as the months ticked by. Both Olive and Mabel developed arthritis. Sometimes, the pain made them cranky. Pat's mother, especially, often became depressed and manipulative. "I'm pitiful and such a bother. I'm no good anymore." Al would give her a hug of reassurance, yet, Olive would say, "I don't know how you can stand it with me here."

Grandma Mabel lost control of her bladder but refused to wear the necessary protection. She'd wet her clothes then hide them under the bed or hang them back in the closet, hoping they'd dry by morning so she could wear them again.

Pat felt like a young mother with mounds of laundry. Only, she wasn't young. She was tired. Sometimes friction developed between her and Al. She'd come home from work, tired from a long day in the pediatrics ward, and both grannies would be floundering about in their small kitchen. When Pat finally shoo'd them both out of her way, Al would come on the scene with "Let Mom do it. She's just trying to help." Cooking had always been Pat's favorite household duty, and now it seemed she was doomed to a life of meat and boiled potato dinners.

Pat wanted it to work. And, with a great deal of organization and patience, it usually did. But sometimes when she was really down, the nursing home seemed mighty tempting. Pat prayed. She remembered the days when both grandmas were saving her life when she had four preschoolers.

One night when the frustrations mounted, Pat retreated to the race-car wallpapered bedroom and sat with her head in her hands. Then, from the room next door, Pat heard Mabel reading her Bible to Olive. Mabel was a staunch Methodist; Olive a strict Roman Catholic. Here they were, the city mouse and the country mouse, sharing the one thing they had in common.

Mabel read her favorite verse, John 3:16: "For God loved the world so much that he gave his only Son, so that anyone who believes in him shall not perish but have eternal life."

Pat smiled and whispered to herself, "If these two exasperating, wonderful old women can have such hope for life eternal, then I can certainly have hope for today, tomorrow and next week." She stared at the race cars for awhile, and promised herself once and for all that she would never send them back to nursing homes. That promise was hard to keep. About a year later, Olive had a severe stroke and died. Two months after that, Mabel died peacefully too.

The weekend after the second funeral, Al and Pat moved their antique walnut bedroom set back into the master bedroom. On the shelf by the bed, there's a picture of Grandma Mabel and Grandma Olive sitting together, holding hands.

"Somehow," Pat said to her husband as they stepped back to admire it, "this room feels much better now than it did before we had to move out of it. I feel better, too. Growing old doesn't seem too scary anymore."

Patricia Lorenz

A Ray of Sunshine

*In every child who is born, under no matter what
circumstances, and of no matter what parents,
the potentiality of the human race is born again.*

James Agee

Ray-Ray was born to a drug-addicted mother with full-
blown AIDS, and both problems were passed on to her
newborn son. She could not care for the infant due to his
illnesses, so he remained in the hospital, where they
simply waited for him to die. When he didn't die the first
year, he was placed in a hospice-type foster home, where
again they waited.

At age eighteen-months, little Ray-Ray was still hanging on to life, and significant delays in his development
entitled him to special educational services. As an early-
childhood specialist, I was sent to the home to provide
him with therapeutic services.

The moment I looked into his chocolate-brown eyes, he
melted my heart. My evaluation showed Ray-Ray's delays
were not caused so much by his illness as by his environ-
ment. His medical and physical needs were met, but not

much more. The clock ticked away the minutes of his life as everyone stood by, still waiting for him to die. I was mortified to think that this child's life would not be filled with the comfort of a mother's arms, the joys of childhood, and the love of family and friends. My focus shifted from being Ray-Ray's teacher to being his advocate. I was sure that God was asking me to find this little angel a home.

I begged social workers to find him a family. The response I got made me sick to my stomach. "He's not worth the paperwork. No one would want a drug-addicted child with AIDS." I was outraged, but my rage quickly turned to love for this little boy who had nothing going for him. I knew that God was asking *me* to be his mother. I fought with myself, wondering how I could possibly do this. I was, after all, single and barely able to pay my bills. In the end, my heart won out over any of my worries. I applied to become Ray-Ray's foster mom, with the intent of adopting him.

I never dreamed how this decision would change my life. There was no day care available for Ray-Ray, so I had to quit my job and move. Expenses increased. Everything went on the credit card, and I accumulated huge debts. Many friends deserted me, thinking I was crazy to take on such a burden that could only end in heartache. Steadfast in my calling, I gave my fears to God and became focused on letting Ray-Ray know that he was loved, and that he would not die before he had a chance to live.

At three-and-a-half, Ray-Ray could not speak and knew nothing of toys or the outside world. He still drank from a bottle and had never called anyone his friend. That all changed as we filled our days with fun and adventure.

New friends came into our lives, and Ray-Ray blossomed into a delightful little boy with a very energetic spirit and a contagious smile. He learned to speak, ski, swim and ride a bike. He went to Disney World and the ocean. He met his hero, Garth Brooks. He went to birth-day parties and played with friends. He had a real Christmas at his grandma's house, surrounded by aunts, uncles and cousins. He learned how to live. He learned that he was loved. Our days were also filled with chronic illness, frequent visits to the doctor, awful medication, fear and rejection from people who didn't want anything to do with this disease, and the reality that each day together could be our last.

Ray-Ray experienced the world for the first time, and I got new perspective as I saw the world though his eyes. The first time he saw the mountains, tears streamed down his face as he exclaimed, "Did God make these just for me?" I replied, "Yes, Ray-Ray. God loves you this much and more." God had proven He loved me that much too— He had chosen me to be Ray-Ray's mommy.

Just eleven short months later, Ray-Ray became vio-lently ill. I rushed him to the hospital and watched help-lessly as he was hooked up to intravenous tubes and a ventilator. I could hardly bear watching as his little body swelled from the medications and his limbs turned black. In desperation, I begged God, "Don't take my son! Don't let our lives together be in vain!"

After three days in intensive care, Ray-Ray passed away peacefully in my arms, on the tenth anniversary of my father's death. I felt my dad there as the angels lifted my little boy into heaven. Although I was deeply sad-dened, I knew that it was part of God's plan and He wasn't done with me yet. I prayed for direction. "Now what? Why did you give me this little boy only to take him away from me?" The answer came in the sweet voice of my very own angel, as Ray-Ray's words from one of our mountain visits echoed through my head: "Mommy, you need to bring the kids up here."

I inquired, "What kids?"

He answered, "The kids with AIDS. You need to show them how to have fun." "But we don't know any kids with AIDS," I objected.

"You will, Mommy, you will . . ."

I knew what to do. I would start a camp for children with AIDS.

One year after he went to heaven, we held the first annual Camp Ray-Ray. Fifteen families enjoyed an all-expenses-paid, peaceful and fun weekend at Ray-Ray's favorite resort in the beautiful Colorado mountains.

Angels Unaware, the organization that sponsors the camp as well as other monthly activities, continues to grow, reaching out to more than seventy families. Currently, we are planning the tenth-annual Camp Ray-Ray. Each year, we bring more families to be pampered with horseback riding, fishing, hiking, entertainers, massages, makeovers, crafts and the joy of being with friends. We have become a big family as we spend the weekend remembering to live, laugh and love. This disease that isolates us in society is the bond that holds us together here.

Angels Unaware/Camp Ray-Ray is run solely by volunteers who work hard all year to raise thousands of dollars and then give up the last long weekend of the summer to work some more. They are true angels, unaware of how deeply they affect families by making Ray-Ray's dream a reality.

The world may have looked at Ray-Ray and seen a boy who would be nothing more than a burden to society, but he was more than "worth the paperwork" and the inevitable heartache. He spreads his rays of sunshine bringing renewed hope to us all.

Barbara Johnson

Hanging Up the Cape

Every thread of gold is valuable. So is every moment of time.

John Mason

"Put on your cape, Superwoman! You think you can leap tall buildings in a single bound?" one of my sisters asked sarcastically when the four of us girls were discussing my mother's care after her stroke. As a happily married mother of three teenagers, full-time childcare provider, aspiring author and a volunteer, my life was very full. Yet, I was convinced that having Mom stay with my family was best for her recovery.

To say it had been a difficult year was an understatement. We had pulled together through the death of my brother-in-law, Dad's quadruple-bypass surgery, Mom's spleen-removal surgery and now a major stroke, which had paralyzed the left side of her body. After much prayer, I'd closed a lucrative cake-decorating business in order to pursue God's call to write, and I could hardly believe that within months He'd rewarded me with the sale of the first book I'd ever written. Mingled with many layers of ongoing grief and stress was the excitement each stage of publication brought.

A week after Mom's stroke, she'd come to a rehabilitation center a few miles from my house. Within two months, she had mastered the skills necessary to go home, but the handicap-access renovations at her own house would not be completed for six more weeks. Since I worked at home, my husband, Dave, and I insisted Mom stay with us, even though I was swamped with my child care job and a second book deadline.

"You've lost your mind," one sister warned.

"You aren't Superwoman, you know," the youngest chimed again.

"I can't believe you're going to do this," another said.

Despite my sisters' warnings, my determination never wavered.

We moved Mom into our master bedroom and most of the furniture out to make space for her extra equipment. My family learned to juggle more than ever before, and our lives became a precisely timed chorus. Each day began and ended with making and unmaking the hide-a-bed sofa in the living room, where Dave and I slept. We choreographed fitting Mom's home-healthcare visits and therapy into our schedules, while I continually strived to maintain our usual routine.

Initially, Mom still needed a great deal of assistance dressing, standing and walking. Since watching preschoolers often took me to the other end of the house, I gave Mom a brass bell to ring if she needed help, just as she had done during my childhood when I was sick and she managed our family-owned motel.

Mom loved the company of my preschool charges as well as the opportunity to visit with her children and grandchildren. Despite the physical and emotional demands on my time, I felt comforted knowing she was making progress and growing stronger each day. Yet, niggling in the back of my mind was the contract I'd signed just days before her arrival. Since I still considered selling one book a miracle, telling my editor my work situation never seemed a wise option. I never doubted that I could fit writing another book into my already overwrought routine.

Each afternoon, I helped Mom into bed for a rest then took the children downstairs for quiet time. Day after day as they napped, I anticipated diving into that magical world of fiction. I couldn't wait to escape from the challenges of reality to a world where "happily ever after" would overcome anything I tossed at my characters. I always began the same way—after a short prayer, I turned on music, read the previous scene and tried to write.

It never failed that about the time the children fell asleep and I'd finished reviewing what I'd previously written, the bell rang. Day after day, it rang. Day after day, I ran up the stairs to my mother's side, the writing momentum lost. On a few occasions, I was puzzled to discover her dozing, but more times than not, her eyes popped open, and she began to visit. I hadn't the heart to walk away. I simply hoped I would have energy left at the end of the day, once my kids were in bed and Dave asleep, to escape to my office and write. Instead, I found myself exhausted and craving a few minutes alone with my husband, desperate for a glimpse of normalcy. Instead of staying up to write, I reviewed the kids' events and schedules with Dave, set the alarm to get up with Mom every two hours throughout the night, and drifted into a deep slumber. After several days of this overwhelming frustration, I realized my sisters were right. I wasn't Superwoman. I couldn't do it all.

I finally adjusted my goals to do what was most important. Instead of writing, I devoted the time to Mom, praying fervently that God would help me meet my deadline once she was back home.

Together, we experienced the frightening and humorous first shopping trip with Mom at the controls of an electric wheelchair. Side by side, we celebrated her "first steps." As a family, we returned to "prairie living" when a freak blizzard left us without electricity. And Mom and I even survived patching her delicate skin in the middle of the night when determination to regain her independence ended in calamity. We learned to relinquish our traditional roles as mother and daughter, to rely on more than our own strengths and accept that which we could not change.

Finally, renovations were completed, and my mother returned home. My family moved the furniture back to their proper rooms, we closed up the sofa bed, and my husband and I slept through the night in our own bed for the first time in nearly two months. I opened my doors for the preschoolers on Monday morning, excited to return to my ordinary routine, and I looked forward to writing during naptime.

Joyfully, the kids and I played, ate lunch, read several books and, finally, the lights went out for quiet time. Everything was going just as scheduled. I closed my eyes to pray, turned on the music, reviewed my last chapter and, as regular as clockwork, the bell rang.

It couldn't be! Mom was three hours away.

"My sisters were right! I've lost my mind." I looked around. The kids were asleep. The dogs were quiet.

The bell rang again. *Who could be ringing Mom's bell?* I ran up the stairs and realized the clanging bell I'd heard everyday wasn't Mom's brass bell at all, but the Noah's ark wind chimes blowing outside my office window. Half-laughing, half-crying, I heard its message.

Today, I sit in my office completing the contract for my eighth book, and listening to the bells that remind me, still, to do what is really important.

Carol Steward

Grandpa Harold

Only the brave know how to forgive; it is the most refined and generous pitch of virtue human nature can arrive at.

Lawrence Sterne

Grandpa Harold's family shed quiet tears at his funeral, which bespoke a legacy of friendship and family.

Now, I'd be surprising no one if I said that Grandpa's youngest son, Uncle Tom, was the black sheep of the family. He'd been a drifter most of his life and had frequent minor scrapes with the law. He divorced thirty years ago and had no permanent relationships since then—none, that is, except for his mom and dad. Uncle Tom had settled near them, in Florida, twenty years ago. He tried to help them when he could, and they certainly did the things parents do for their children—a little money from time to time, Sunday dinners, a place to crash when things went wrong, as they often did for Uncle Tom. It would be an understatement to say that he had alienated the rest of his family. His brothers and sister worried that he was taking advantage. There was no trust. Oh, but his daddy loved him so.

Two years after Grandpa Harold passed, Uncle Tom was in a motorcycle accident. He was comatose for several days and remained on a ventilator for over a month, 2,000 miles away from any family, family he hadn't spoken with for over two years. Who would direct his care?

So it was that, out of the blue and in the middle of May, I got a call with news of my uncle and his dire situation. A chain of events was set in motion, and I can only believe that Grandpa Harold had something to do with it all.

Word spread through the family quickly, and we began a telephone relationship with the ICU staff. As the nurse in the family, I was elected spokesperson, while my father, his brother and his sister consulted from both sides of the continent. While their feelings were mixed, their upbringing wouldn't let them ignore a blood relative. After two weeks of teleconferencing, with more dialing than dialogue, it became apparent that this situation needed face-to-face attention. Uncle Tom wasn't getting better, and no one could really say why. And I couldn't understand why a sixty-year-old man with no prior medical history couldn't be weaned from the ventilator by now. The nurse in me told me I needed to be there. The granddaughter in me heartily agreed.

My decision to travel to Uncle Tom's bedside in Florida set off a reaction within the ranks that I was not prepared to deal with. "What difference will it really make?" "Are you out of your ever-lovin' mind?" "What did he ever do for us except bring trouble to our door?" After Uncle Tom's lifetime of bad decisions and turning away from family, they were concerned about my safety, physical and fiscal.

Grandpa Harold.

His face kept coming to my mind. I could not ignore the special way that he loved his rebellious, ne'er-do-well son. If I turned my back on Uncle Tom, I turned my back on my grandfather's son. That is something I simply would never do, no matter what it cost me. I just knew that going was the only thing to do.

My father and his siblings pledged their support, financial and emotional. I felt for their pain and guilt, knowing this entire circumstance opened old wounds and let ghosts out of closets. Although I had dark memories of my own, I could operate on two concrete principles: honor my grandfather's memory and the nurse's Nightingale Pledge. I admit I was more than a little apprehensive. I did not want to go!

Grandpa Harold.

In the days before I left, his memory comforted me and kept my anxiety at bay. He understood. He would have been pleased.

Funny how un-nurse-like a nurse can feel when she's "the family." The corridor leading to the ICU of this strange hospital so far from home seemed endless. I felt alone and unsure. I talked quietly to myself, "This is right, keep walking, breathe, go through those doors, remember who sent me."

In the last conversation with Uncle Tom's physician, he said Uncle was minimally responsive and frequently combative. I prepared for the worst, and it met me head on when I arrived at his room. Uncle was in isolation, so I had to don a gown, gloves and mask to enter the room. Great! Like I wasn't already sweating and feeling trapped!

As un-nurse-like as I felt, the noises, the strange equipment and the restless man in the bed were overwhelming. *Dear God, I hate this!*

Then, Grandpa Harold gently touched my shoulder.

I walked slowly to the bedside, took Uncle Tom's crusty and swollen hand in my own, and spoke his name.

He didn't respond. "Uncle Tom . . . it's Debbie . . . your niece . . . from Ohio." I waited. Why were tears streaming down my cheek? Why was everything suddenly quiet?

His eyes opened halfway and slowly found their way to mine. The moment hung in the air for what seemed a lifetime. I called his name a third time. Suddenly, his eyes flew open, and he began to tremble. I quietly told him, "You've been in an accident. You need to wake up. You are in a hospital." I touched his face. "Harold sent me." He began to cry and gripped my hand tightly.

From that moment, Uncle Tom was back. No more lack of responsiveness, no more combativeness. He was weaned off the ventilator two days later. I knew I had witnessed the real miracle. Love from heaven. Grandpa Harold.

When I called my dad and aunt, there was quiet on the other end of the phone. Each softly said, "Thank you." I could only thank them in return, for making it possible for me to be Harold's messenger.

That evening, I went to John's Pass, on Treasure Island, an area so familiar to me from childhood visits. The last time I saw my grandpa, we had driven there and shared an ice cream cone together on the Boardwalk. I knew then, down inside, they were our last moments together. I adored him so; it had been a bittersweet evening. I climbed the ramp to the Boardwalk and the ice cream shop. Trembling, my mind raced. *Are you here, Grandpa? I did the right thing, didn't I? What will become of Uncle Tom?*

I reached the top of the ramp and looked out over the water, my mind wrenching with memories and questions. Then, my eyes beheld the answer: a majestic rainbow arched over the bay. Enormous soft, gray clouds were its background. The wind gently whispered to me. The tensions of the past month and days rushed from me, and I cried tears of joy and sorrow.

The next day, I arose early to make the short walk to the hospital. I was homeward-bound later in the day, and I wanted to say good-bye and help make plans for Uncle Tom's remaining hospital stay and rehabilitation.

As I strolled through the quiet neighborhood, I enjoyed the sense of peace that had settled with the rainbow the night before. I turned the corner for the walk up to the main entrance, and my eyes were drawn to the sky. My heart paused, and my breath caught in my chest. My magnificent rainbow was back! Glorious in its splendor, arching perfectly over the hospital, with those same soft, gray clouds as its background!

Grandpa Harold.

The wind repeated its message. "All is well. Thank you for loving me and my son this way."

Debra Oliver

A Time to Heal

Sorrow's crown is remembering happier things.
Alfred Lord Tennyson

As I rummaged through papers on Jim's desk, I laid my head atop a stack of files and wept. My loving husband of fifty-one years had died suddenly of a heart attack the month before, leaving me a grieving widow enmeshed in settling estate affairs. A few weeks later, our eldest daughter, Kathy, was diagnosed with multiple sclerosis. When I thought I could bear no more, the call came. Our younger daughter, Kerry, fell and fractured her foot in four places.

As I drove the fifty miles to Denver to comfort her before surgery, I felt my faith was being tested. After successful surgery and her release, Kerry struggled with crutches in her tri-level home. My house is on one floor, so I suggested she stay with me awhile. Her husband agreed, and soon she was settled in my guest bedroom.

With a cast up to her thigh, Kerry couldn't take tub baths, so I installed a flexible showerhead and seat so she could sit while showering. It seemed like old times as we shampooed and styled her hair, and recalled days of pigtails and bunny barrettes. As I prepared her favorite foods, it felt good to cook for two again and share meals with a person instead of a book.

During warm afternoons, we took short strolls while she mastered walking with crutches. I loved the companionship as we sauntered neighborhood streets that Jim and I had walked so many times. Afterward, we relaxed on the patio, recalling her coming-of-age years. We phoned her sister, Kathy, in Seattle and soon they were reminiscing. On my extension phone, I heard Kerry chuckle. "Remember when we were little and jumped on Mom and Dad's bed every morning and chanted, 'This is the day the Lord hath made,' and repeated it until we woke them up?"

"Yeah," Kathy tittered like she had years ago. "We didn't stop until they responded, 'Let us rejoice and be glad in it.' Then we got hugs and kisses to start the day."

I leaned back in my chair and visualized happier times with Jim, as our daughters rambled on about our numerous camping trips and how he had helped teach them to swim, camp, water ski and pilot our boat.

As Kerry's foot healed, I took her shopping and introduced her to electric carts. My spirits rose as she tooled around stores, recounting stories about how patient Jim had been when he taught her to drive. "He took me to the empty school parking lot and taught me how to park between lines. Back and forth, and back and forth—it must have taken me a hundred times to get it right!"

As we swayed together on the porch swing one evening, I almost felt Jim's presence there. Kerry piped up, "Remember when we misbehaved? You bought two flyswatters, one red and the other yellow. Whenever I deserved a swat and Dad grabbed the yellow one, Kathy yelled, 'Run, Kerry! He's got *your* flyswatter!' " She tossed her head back and howled with laughter.

I joined in, laughing harder than I had in months. "And

by the time he caught you, he didn't need to use it, because you apologized."

She flashed an impish grin. "I'm glad you disciplined us."

Three weeks later, Kerry returned to her own home, and I sat at Jim's desk, alone again, but with a lighter heart, revitalized, cherishing the time she and I had spent together healing.

Sally Kelly-Engeman

Veterans

All, everything that I understand, I understand only because I love.

Leo Tolstoy

I served as a registered nurse in Vietnam during the height of the war and came home tired, disillusioned and burned out. I couldn't do it anymore. Yet, I still wanted to help. So I returned to college and graduate school and figuratively began a new life as a clinical social worker. No matter where I worked, that old "pull" from the war veterans—my brothers and sisters—tugged at me. And so it was, in the summer of 1989, I began a new social work job at a rural Pennsylvania veteran's hospital.

Most-recent hires traditionally got the poorest assignments. So there I was after years of practicing psychotherapy, behind the locked door of a urine-smelling ward full of old, mindless men, who at best shuffled the halls, rattling locks or anything shiny, and at worst were confined and restrained to hospital beds with feeding tubes protruding from their stomachs.

What could I possibly do here?

All the patients died. My department chief expected me to farm them out to local nursing homes for their end, making room for more hopeful cases, the ones who could be Band-Aided and sent home. My predecessor, I learned, became so depressed that she went "off the deep end."

Well, I figured, these are human beings. They have souls in there beyond the stone faces and lifeless eyes—*somewhere*. I'll find a way to make lemonade from lemons.

One old gentleman seemed to attempt suicide nightly by pressing a pillow over his face. Never was his family told of this behavior. The physical strength he exerted to effect these apparent suffocation attempts kept him in constant danger. A death wish?

Another, a formerly prominent professional, had his wife's visits accurately timed and, somehow knowing she would visit me first, urinated against my office door right before she came. Territory marking, I guessed. Instinctual?

Others just groaned, wandered, or became mute and bedridden.

What could I possibly do here?

Still, a steady stream of spouses, friends, siblings and children appeared daily. Some visited regularly, others only once, never to return. I was struck by the selflessness in their simply showing up, knowing they would not be acknowledged by their loved one. I was totally over-whelmed by the wives who came and bathed, turned, trimmed, sang, read to and thoroughly cared for these shells of the men they once had been.

That's when I realized the families could use a bit of nurturance and support themselves. So I engaged another staff member and trained her in group therapy, and together we instituted weekly sessions for signifi-cant others.

They came timidly and sporadically, at first. Then the concept took hold. Every Monday afternoon, people filled all the chairs I could appropriate and even sat on the floor of my little office. They told me of their love, their guilt, their anger, their grief, their fear.

Stories unfolded.

The fellow who pressed a pillow over his face nightly had lived in rat-infested trenches during World War II. He learned to cover his face, lest his ears and nose be bitten off. His military career was brilliant and heroic.

The man who urinated on my door before each spousal visit was a veterinarian. His still-beautiful wife and he had a lengthy, fairy-tale marriage. He was not letting that go. She was *his*, and he marked his territory.

During these years of family meetings, I learned many lessons of the goodness of man, but mostly of the goodness of love. There was much for me to do there. Love was in them, and it is now in me.

Rhona Prescott

Grandma's Caregiver

*Like a morning dream, life becomes more and
more bright the longer we live, and the reason of
everything appears more clear.*

Jean Paul Richter

His mom had called in tears. "Rich, I am so afraid I have
to break my promise to your grandmother. I know I
promised her she would die in her own bed, but it's harder
than I thought. She needs constant care now and won't let
me stay with her. . . ."

He didn't let her finish. "Mom, I've had enough of
Canada, and I'm ready to come back to Colorado. I can
stay with Grandma. I'll work during the day when she's
got help, and I'll be there at night. Mom, I can do this. We
don't have to break our promise to her."

Our promise.

"I can do this."

By April, he and Grandma had a happy routine. Every
night, he'd peek into her dim room, where she was awake
listening to talk radio playing softly near her bed.

"Do you need anything, Grandma? Would you like
another Tylenol or a milkshake?"

"No, Rich, I'm fine. Just come sit near me and tell me about your day." He'd sit gently on her big bed, knowing her arthritis caused her constant pain, which she tried to hide. Any movement was agonizing, and no painkiller would help. He'd chat on about his day at the health club and his clients—funny stories to make her smile. She chatted on about what she'd heard on talk radio that day—the Bronco's training camp and life after John Elway. Eighty-five years old, and she knew more about sports, politics and current events than most of his friends. All without leaving her house, her bed.

Now here he was, twenty-eight years old and living with his grandmother, so she could stay in the home she loved. He wondered if she thought of herself as a prisoner to her body. The rheumatoid arthritis had gnarled her once-elegant fingers and crippled her feet. She couldn't walk and could hardly even hold a spoon. Except for visits to doctors, she hadn't left her house since he graduated from college, almost four years before. He had pushed her wheelchair the few blocks to campus, so she could watch him in his black cap and gown.

They'd always been close, and even now he loved to talk with her, to gear down and get a new perspective on life. She was always his cheerleader, encouraging him to do what made him happy, to not worry about making lots of money, but to do what he loved. She was the reason he acquired his degree in sports medicine and why he was so content helping others as a personal trainer. Maybe that was why he was so frustrated that all his skill and knowledge couldn't help this wonderful, frail old woman he adored.

He knew she was sliding, losing a bit more each day, eating a bit less, sleeping a bit less. But she seemed to come alive when he came into her room. Every night, he asked her if she wanted to go for a ride in her wheelchair.

He'd lift her frail, bony body gently out of the bed, understanding the agony it caused her. Two pillows in the wheelchair didn't help much. "I'm like the princess and the pea, aren't I?" she'd joke, trying not to cry in pain. He'd wheel her though the big house, and she'd talk about times long past—the holidays, his mom and dad getting married in the living room, the parties and her rose garden. She didn't seem to notice that this house, once filled with laughter, had faded, scuffed walls and drapes frayed at the hems.

When she was exhausted by her adventure, he gently helped her back into her huge bed. "Sing to me," she said, smiling past the pain. She loved music, and his songs about dreams, loves and life lulled her to sleep, at least for a while.

By summer, they knew their time together was growing short. They toured the house less often, and now he carried her from room to room. She didn't weigh a hundred pounds, and it was almost like carrying a child. Sometimes he'd say, "Grandma, would you dance with me tonight?" And he gently swayed to the music and sang verses he made up as they waltzed about the house.

By August, it was harder to keep her comfortable, and the visiting nurses said it was time to call in hospice. He was exhausted, and watching her die was taking its toll on him. When his friends asked, "How can you do this, Rich? It must be so hard." He replied, "This is a gift I can give her. She should be in this place that's brought her happiness."

When his mom was there, she too would ask, "Are you sure you can do this?" And he'd answer, "It's not easy, Mom, but I can do it. I learned I'm capable of doing so much more than I thought I could. Grandma makes it easier than I feared it would be. I've learned from her that you focus on what's good, not on what's bad."

As he closed the front door and waved good-bye to his mom, he thought about the brave words he'd just uttered and how they were so close to being lies. Oh yes, it was so hard, but not because he was repulsed by this gaunt old woman, or because he had to take care of her as if she were a baby. No, he felt selfish because he already missed her so much. And it hurt him to realize that all the love in the world couldn't stop her grinding, painful, daily slide.

But then he smiled. *Oh, Grandma. The lessons you've taught me,* he thought. He realized he was a far different person than he had been in April. She taught him the essence of duty, of sacrifice and the importance of keeping a promise. He had learned patience and compassion, and hoped someday he could teach his own kids to be as caring as his folks had taught him to be. He was proud that nobody broke their promises to his grandmother—she would die at home, in her own bed, surrounded by memories, knowing she was loved and cherished, and not alone.

He slipped quietly into the bedroom. "Grandma, how about a song?"

He held her hand as he sang the lullaby that he'd heard her sing so many times when he was tiny. His voice cracked, but the words and music flowed with his tears as he sang what would be their last song. His mind echoed *her* voice and *her* words, and he hoped the gentle notes brought her the same feelings of being safe, protected and loved that they had brought to him so long ago. By the end of the song, she seemed to feel the peace that enveloped him. He knew he could finally let her go. *Ah, Grandma, I didn't know if I could do this. But I did. And I wouldn't have missed it for the world.*

Ann Clarke

What God Would Say to Caregivers

Amen I say to you, whatever you did for one of these least of my brothers, you did for me.

Matthew 25:40

I want to thank you for all the love, kindness, hope, comfort and dignity you give to those you care for. It is your strength and caring that make a difference, for without you their lives would be unbearable. I know because I hear from those you care for. They thank me that you are there for them. They tell me they don't know what they would do without you. They ask me to watch over you. They tell me of their love for you and about your sacrifices for them. You bring joy into their world and you comfort them in a way no one else can.

I thank you.

I know that you not only care for their bodies but care for their spirits as well. You strive to make their days as pleasant as can be, despite the pain, by doing their hair, painting their nails, putting up drawings from their grand-children, bringing flowers from your yard, listening to a ballgame with them, taking them for a walk . . . you do anything you can think of to bring a smile to their faces. I know you will never give up.

I love you.

I know your rewards are the little things you experience each day, the grateful look you see in their eyes, the occasional laugh that brightens your day, the warm hug you receive when you leave, and the gentle squeeze of your hand as they thank you for being there. These rewards are the small heartfelt things that allow you to go on.

I am so very proud of you.

I want you to know that I have been with you and will be with you always to give you strength as you perform the endless duties of a caregiver. I have felt your despair and loneliness. I am the one who whispers in your ear when your heart is breaking and you feel you can't go on. I am the one who gives you strength when you are exhausted physically and mentally. Know that I will always be with you. Lean on me. I will always wrap my loving arms around you and give you hope, and love, and comfort and the strength to go on.

I thank you, I love you, and I am so very, very proud of you.

Paula Ezop

Who Is Jack Canfield?

Jack Canfield is one of America's leading experts in the development of human potential and personal effectiveness. He is both a dynamic, entertaining speaker and a highly sought-after trainer. Jack has a wonderful ability to inform and inspire audiences toward increased levels of self-esteem and peak performance.

He is the author and narrator of several bestselling audio- and videocassette programs, including *Self-Esteem and Peak Performance, How to Build High Self-Esteem, Self-Esteem in the Classroom* and *Chicken Soup for the Soul—Live*. He is regularly seen on television shows such as *Good Morning America, 20/20* and *NBC Nightly News*. Jack has co-authored numerous books, including the *Chicken Soup for the Soul* series, *Dare to Win* and *The Aladdin Factor* (all with Mark Victor Hansen), *100 Ways to Build Self-Concept in the Classroom* (with Harold C. Wells), *Heart at Work* (with Jacqueline Miller) and *The Power of Focus* (with Les Hewitt and Mark Victor Hansen).

Jack is a regularly featured speaker for professional associations, school districts, government agencies, churches, hospitals, sales organizations and corporations. His clients have included the American Dental Association, the American Management Association, AT&T, Campbell's Soup, Clairol, Domino's Pizza, GE, ITT, Hartford Insurance, Johnson & Johnson, the Million Dollar Roundtable, NCR, New England Telephone, Re/Max, Scott Paper, TRW and Virgin Records. Jack has taught on the faculty of Income Builders International, a school for entrepreneurs.

Jack conducts an annual seven-day Training of Trainers program in the areas of self-esteem and peak performance. It attracts entrepreneurs, educators, counselors, parenting trainers, corporate trainers, professional speakers, ministers and others interested in developing their speaking and seminar-leading skills.

For further information about Jack's books, tapes and training programs, or to schedule him for a presentation, please contact:

Self-Esteem Seminars
P.O. Box 30880
Santa Barbara, CA 93130
phone: 805-563-2935 • fax: 805-563-2945
Web site: *www.jackcanfield.com*

Who Is Mark Victor Hansen?

In the area of human potential, no one is more respected than Mark Victor Hansen. For more than thirty years, Mark has focused solely on helping people from all walks of life reshape their personal vision of what's possible. His powerful messages of possibility, opportunity and action have created powerful change in thousands of organizations and millions of individuals worldwide.

He is a sought-after keynote speaker, bestselling author and marketing maven. Mark's credentials include a lifetime of entrepreneurial success and an extensive academic background. He is a prolific writer with many bestselling books such as *The One Minute Millionaire, The Power of Focus, The Aladdin Factor* and *Dare to Win,* in addition to the *Chicken Soup for the Soul* series. Mark has made a profound influence through his library of audios, videos and articles in the areas of big thinking, sales achievement, wealth building, publishing success, and personal and professional development.

Mark is the founder of the MEGA Seminar Series. MEGA Book Marketing University and Building Your MEGA Speaking Empire are annual conferences where Mark coaches and teaches new and aspiring authors, speakers and experts on building lucrative publishing and speaking careers. Other MEGA events include MEGA Marketing Magic and My MEGA Life.

He has appeared on television (*Oprah,* CNN and *The Today Show*), in print (*Time, U.S. News & World Report, USA Today, New York Times* and *Entrepreneur*) and on countless radio interviews, assuring our planet's people that "You can easily create the life you deserve."

As a philanthropist and humanitarian, Mark works tirelessly for organizations such as Habitat for Humanity, American Red Cross, March of Dimes, Childhelp USA and many others. He is the recipient of numerous awards that honor his entrepreneurial spirit, philanthropic heart and business acumen. He is a lifetime member of the Horatio Alger Association of Distinguished Americans, an organization that honored Mark with the prestigious Horatio Alger Award for his extraordinary life achievements.

Mark Victor Hansen is an enthusiastic crusader of what's possible and is driven to make the world a better place.

Mark Victor Hansen & Associates, Inc.
P.O. Box 7665
Newport Beach, CA 92658
phone: 949-764-2640
fax: 949-722-6912
Visit Mark online at: *www.markvictorhansen.com*

Who Is LeAnn Thieman?

LeAnn Thieman is a nationally acclaimed professional speaker, author and nurse who was "accidentally" caught up in the Vietnam Orphan Airlift in 1975. Her book *This Must Be My Brother* details her daring adventure of helping to rescue three-hundred babies as Saigon was falling to the Communists. An ordinary person, she struggled through extraordinary circumstances and found the courage to succeed. *Newsweek* featured LeAnn and her incredible story in its "Voices of the Century" issue.

Believing we don't have to rescue orphans to be caregivers, LeAnn inspires audiences to care for themselves while caring for others by balancing their lives physically, mentally and spiritually—truly living their priorities while still making a difference in the world.

After her story was featured in *Chicken Soup for the Mother's Soul,* LeAnn became one of Chicken Soup's most prolific writers, with stories in eleven more *Chicken Soup* books. That, and her devotion to thirty years of nursing, made her the ideal co-author of *Chicken Soup for the Nurse's Soul.* Her lifelong practice of her Christian faith led her to co-author *Chicken Soup for the Christian Woman's Soul.* All of the above earned her the honor of now co-authoring *Chicken Soup for the Caregiver's Soul.*

LeAnn and Mark, her husband of thirty-four years, reside in Colorado, where they enjoy their empty nest. Their two daughters, Angela and Christie, and son, Mitch, have flown the coop but are still drawn under their mother's wing when she needs them!

For more information about LeAnn's books and tapes, or to schedule her for a presentation, please contact her at:

LeAnn Thieman
6600 Thompson Drive
Fort Collins, CO 80526
970-223-1574
www.LeAnnThieman.com
LeAnn@LeAnnThieman.com

Contributors

Sandra P. Aldrich, president and CEO of Bold Words, Inc. in Colorado Springs, Colorado, is a popular inspirational speaker who wraps humor and encouragement around the serious issues of life. She is also the author or co-author of sixteen books and contributor to two dozen more. Please reach her at *BoldWords@aol.com.*

Sharon Armstrong is a freelance writer from Yuba City, California, who has been in the childcare business for almost twenty years. She also spent many years counseling for a women's crisis center. She can be reached by phone at (530) 673-4130 or by e-mail at *sharon-armstrong@sbcglobal.net.*

Holly Hutson Baker received a Bachelor of Science in Biology from Texas Tech University in 1981 and resides in Texas with husband, Brad, and their three teenage children, Gregory, Amanda, and Jessica. She has Chronic Progressive MS, and enjoys riding through the park in her wheelchair with companion dog, Moose. Writing for a Chronic Pain and Illness Web site, *www.restministries.org,* she loves bringing glory to God.

A noted speaker, writer and publisher on caregiving issues since 1995, **Gary Barg** is author of *The Fearless Caregiver: How to Get the Best Care for Your Loved One and Still Have a Life of Your Own* and editor-in-chief of *Today's Caregiver* magazine. Please reach him at: *gary@caregiver.com*

Barbara Bartlein, R.N., L.C.S.W., is a professional speaker, author, and consultant. She sends a loving thank you to Stephanie Brosky for sharing her inspirational story. A motivational humorist, Barbara helps companies sell more goods and services by developing people. Her column, Success Matters, appears in numerous publications. Her latest book, *Why Did I Marry You Anyway? 12.5 Strategies for a Happy Marriage,* was released in 2003. She can be reached at *barb@WhyDidIMarryYouAnyway.com* Or visit her Web site at: *www.successmatters.org.*

Teri Batts—Lover of Life and Collector of Memories. Teri is a "Life Writer". She writes of family, fun, travel, adventure and inspiration. Teri's goal is for you to remember and feel. Teri invites you to become more familiar with her work by contacting her via e-mail: *tbaccutrans@aol.com.*

Steven B. Beach is an award-winning author, a magazine editor, copy writer, and a literary critic for the *Winston Salem Journal.* He is currently writing a novel entitled *Refugees in the Backyard,* the story of a young boy and an old man. You can visit his Web site at *stevenbbeach.com.*

Dale Berry is a certified prosthetist and the Vice President of Clinical Operations for Hanger Orthopedic Group Inc., the nation's largest provider of prosthetics and orthotics. Dale is also a professional motivational speaker and author of *RESULTS, There's No Such Word as Can't.* Dale can be contacted at *Dale@ResultsCoach.org.*

John Black is a financial professional, business consultant and Certified Public Accountant. He also holds a masters degree in business administration degree and is insurance licensed. When John is not working, he enjoys spending time with his wife, Susan, and their three children. John can be reached by e-mail at *blackjo@cox.net* (Please reference "Chicken Soup" in the subject line.)

Irene Budzynski is a medical/surgical nurse at a Connecticut hospital. She became a nurse at age 40; at 50 she learned to ride a Harley and has her motorcycle license. A volunteer at her library's used bookstore, Irene is passionate about books and writing about unsung heroes.

Candace Carteen started writing at age eight. It wasn't until she married her bestfriend, George, that she discovered she could "touch people's hearts with her words." She resides in Washington State with her husband and son and is seeking to adopt a daughter. Please contact her at *scribe@aemail4u.com*.

Emily Parke Chase is the author of *Why Say NO When My Hormones Say GO?* (Christian Publications, 2003) and a popular speaker to teens and women's groups. Emily enjoys playing dominoes with her father-in-law who, after a heart attack, now lives with the family. Contact her via *www.emilychase.com* or *emilychase@juno.com*.

LindaCarol Cherken is a lifelong Philadelphian. Her writing has taken her from an interview with the Beatles for her school paper to weekly food and health columns for the *Philadelphia Daily News* to a syndicated advice column. Today, she writes features for newspapers and magazines including *Family Circle*.

Ann Clarke has been an award-winning photographer, writer, and consultant. Today as a speaker she peppers her presentations with lessons learned from her heroes—her family. Ann and her husband, Dick, live in the Colorado foothills near their son Rich and his family. Contact Ann through her Web site at *www.AnnClarke.com*.

Helen Colella is a wife, mother, former teacher and freelance writer of stories and articles for adults and children. She has been published in *Chicken Soup for the Expectant Mother's Soul* and *Chicken Soup for the Grandparent's Soul*. Her new interest is in e-publishing and she offers her services and experience to those also interested in self publishing. Please reach her at: *HCCOLELLA@aol.com*.

Sharon L. Cook of Beverly, Massachusetts, has an MFA in writing. A freelance writer, she formerly worked in healthcare as a certified OT. "Waiting for Mother" is taken from her manuscript titled *Waiting for Mother: Tales from a Nursing Home*, a book both poignant and humorous, which she hopes to publish. She can be reached at: *Cookie978@aol.com*.

David Cooney's cartoons and illustrations have appeared in numerous *Chicken Soup for the Soul* books as well as magazines including *First for Women* and *Good Housekeeping*. David is a work-from-home dad, cartoonist, illustrator and photographer. David and his wife, Marcia, live in the small Pennsylvania town of Mifflinburg with their two children, Sarah and Andrew. David's Web site is *www.DavidCooney.com* and he can be reached at *david@davidcooney.com*.

Esther Copeland received her Bachelor of Arts from the University of Denver. She continues her twenty-third year of teaching in Denver, Colorado. Besides volunteering for hospice, she enjoys walking with her husband and dogs. She is almost finished with her first non-fiction book. You may e-mail her at: *Copelandbooks@aol.com*.

Mary Kerr Danielson began her writing career by joining a local writer's group at age fifty-something. (Known within a small circle of family and friends as the "Ditty Lady"—original verses for any and all obscure occasions—she's positive Hallmark isn't worried!) She and her husband, Kay, are parents of six daughters—one of whom is deceased. (After they all "left the nest," the nest was recently moved from Loveland, Colorado, to Riverdale, Utah.) Writing mainly about her life experiences, she also does poetry, plays and children's stories. E-mail address: *danielson_l@msn.com*.

Alfred H. "Skip" DeGraff, Ph.D. candidate in human rehabilitative services, University of Northern Colorado, enjoys presenting multi-media classroom lectures and conference seminars on disability-related topics. His recent book, *Caregivers and Personal Assistants: How to Find, Hire and Manage the People Who Help You (Or Your Loved One!)*, is available in bookstores. *www.saratoga-publications.com*

Elayne Robertson Demby is a freelance writer and mother of two living in Weston, Connecticut. She has a B.A. from Boston University, a J.D. from Fordham University School of Law and an LL.M in taxation from New York University School of Law. She writes for both trade and consumer publications. She can be reached at *edemby@ix.netcom.com*.

Peggy Eastman is the author of *Godly Glimpses: Discoveries of the Love That Heals*, and editor of *Share* magazine, an inspirational quarterly. Her work has appeared in many periodicals, including *Guideposts, Washingtonian, Ladies' Home Journal, SELF, The Living Church* and *Working Mother*. Visit her Web site at *www.bookviews.com/BookPage/godlyglimpses.html*.

Loretta Emmons has been an animal behaviorist/trainer for 20 years. Now an AKC judge, she trains Service/Therapy dogs in Georgia. Loretta enjoys drawing, writing and teaching. She has written a children's novel. and is a member of the Society of Children's Book Writers and Illustrators. She can be reached at *eemmons5@comcast.net*

Paula M. Ezop is an Aquarian and professes to have entered the age of wisdom. She has written a book titled *A Personal Message From God,* which is yet to be published. Her fanciful children's stories appear online. You can reach her at *pmezop@cs.com*.

Alice Facente has been an RN for almost 30 years, and recently earned a master of science degree in nursing education, from the University of Hartford.

She has been working as a community health nurse for the past 15 years. She and her husband have two grown children and live in Connecticut.

Kerrie Flanagan is a freelance writer from Colorado. Her articles have appeared in various publications, including *The Chicago Tribune, Woman's World,* and *Colorado Homes & Lifestyles.* She is the author of the children's book *Cornelius Comma Saves the Day.* She enjoys playing video games with her husband and two kids, dodging snakes in the prairie with her good friend, and drinking chai tea. She can be reached at *kerrief@frii.com.*

Debbie Gallagher is now a registered nurse, living in Georgia. She writes children's books and enjoys spending time with her husband and two children.

John Gaudet lives in Prince Albert, Saskatchewan with his wife Chantalle and their Daughter Charisa. He is a creative writer for a network radio station and is currently seeking a publisher for his first book. When he is not out in the forest with his family he can be reached at *drmrjohn@hotmail.com.*

Nancy B. Gibbs is the author of four books, a weekly religion columnist and freelance writer. She has been published in several *Chicken Soup for the Soul* books, including the *Chicken Soup for the Nurse's Soul, Christian Woman's Soul* and *Romantic Soul.* Nancy may be contacted through her Web site: *www.nancybgibbs.com* or by e-mail: *Daiseydood@aol.com.*

Pamela Gordon is a former school principal. Today she speaks professionally about adult learning and teaches graduate school at The University of Denver. An avid scuba diver, Pam clears her mind while swimming along a coral reef. On land, Pam enjoys the elegance of high tea. Please reach her at: 3969 East Arapahoe Rd., Bldg. 2, Suite 200, Littleton, Colorado 80122. Phone: 303-779-0227. E-mail: *PGLearn@aol.com*

Beverly Haley, a former teacher and author of articles and books in the field of education, now focuses on writing personal essays, family and human interest pieces, poetry, and books for young people. You may reach her by mailing to: 3904 Benthaven Street, Fort Collins, CO 80526.

Ruth Hancock has been published in magazines, hospice journals and newspapers, most recently in *Chicken Soup for the Volunteer's Soul,* and *Chicken Soup for the Grieving Soul;* is writing short stories based on her life and interests in hospice volunteer; is the wife of an Episcopal priest, and a mother; and has had extensive career in the fashion industry. E-mail: *Rahancock@worldnet.att.net.*

Jonny Hawkins is a freelance cartoonist whose work has appeared in over 285 publications and dozens of books and products over the last 19 years. His latest books, *The Awesome Book of Heavenly Humor, Laughter from the Pearly Gates* and *Wild and Wacky Animal Cartoons for Kids,* along with his cartoon-a-day calendar, *Laughtershocks,* are in bookstores and online. He can be reached at P.O. Box 188, Sherwood, MI 49089 or at *jonnyhawkins2nz@yahoo.com.*

Sue Henley has been a nurse for 30 years in all areas of patient care. She attended Tennessee Tech University. Sue now works full time with special needs adults and loves her job! She lives in Tennessee with her husband of 27 years and has two daughters who bring her constant joy! You may reach Sue at: *Doupray2@charter.net.*

Alicia Hill is the Executive Director of Tyler Day Nursery in Tyler, Texas. Since 1936, the Nursery has been providing child care for low-income children. Alicia published her first children's book, *I Chose You,* in 2001. Alicia speaks on behalf of children in poverty. Please contact her at: *Agmhill@yahoo.com.*

Mary Hjerleid makes her home in the Colorado Rockies with her husband. She is the author of fiction and non-fiction short stories and articles about love and life, which have appeared in a number of regional and national publications. Her writing goal is to publish a novel-length romantic fiction.

Beverly Houseman is a retired RN, wife, mother, grandmother, writer, singer, speaker, author of *Rusty And Me, A Mother's Story,* contributor to *Chicken Soup For The Nurse's Soul,* right-to-life counselor and childbirth educator at Osceola Pregnancy Center in Kissimmee, Florida.

Married for a quarter of a century to her high school sweetheart, **Carole Howey** has two wonderful and exceptional children and a loving and supportive, if small, extended family. Her historical romances move hearts, but her non-fiction moves mountains. When you just can't find the right words, contact: *carole.howey@verizon.net.*

Vera Huddleston grew up in New Mexico and now lives in Texas. Huddleston is an RN, with an MBA, and holds a pilot's license. She is a full time writer of Christian fiction, using the name Vera Inice. *A Time to Mourn or a Time to Dance* was published in 2002.

Ellen Javernick is a first and second grade teacher in Loveland, Colorado. She writes books and articles for children. She is active in her church and community. She can be reached at *javernicke@aol.com.*

Shirley Javernick is an LPN who graduated in 1966 from St. Francis Hospital in Colorado Springs, Colorado. She has worked in the medical field since graduating, both as an office nurse and a staff nurse at the hospital and presently at a nursing home. She enjoys working and being kept busy with children, grandchildren and great-grandchildren.

Amy Jenkins writes creative nonfiction and articles related to healthcare, parenting, writing, and more. She's currently studying to attain her MFA in Creative Writing and writing a book of essays about baby boomers. A lover of anthologies, she serves as editor for *www.AnthologiesOnline.com.*

Barbara Johnson is the founder of Camp Ray-Ray and author of *Ray-Ray's Dream.* Her book emanates the worth of every human being, regardless of their circumstances. Barbara enjoys sharing this important message through her inspirational talks. To find out more about Barbara's works go to *www.heavensentbooks.net*.

Louise Tucker Jones is an award-winning author and inspirational speaker. Her books include *Dance from the Heart* and *Extraordinary Kids* (co-authored), along with contributions to over a dozen compilation books and numerous magazines, including *Guideposts* and *Angels on Earth*. Louise resides in Edmond, Oklahoma, and can be contacted at: *LouiseTJ@aol.com*.

Sally Kelly-Engeman is a freelance writer who's had numerous short stories and articles published, and is currently writing a historical novel. In addition to reading, researching and writing, she enjoys ballroom dancing and traveling with her husband. She can be reached at *sallyfk@juno.com*.

Jeff Keplar exchanged an international corporate communications career in presentations, photography, and writing to work with those less fortunate at rescue missions. Now he communicates people's images and their emotions visually and on paper, and encourages positive change through his enthusiastic teaching of practical life lessons and biblical principles. E-mail: *jeffkeplar@yahoo.com*.

Roger Dean Kiser, Sr. is the author of the book, *Orphan, A True Story of Abandonment, Abuse and Redemption*. Roger also writes non-fiction short stories that he displays on his Web site, *The Sad Orphan*, located at: *www.rogerdeankiser.com*. Roger's short stories have also been published all around the world and in publications such as *Chicken Soup for the Grandparent's Soul* and *Chicken Soup for the Horse Lover's Soul*.

Darlene Lawson and her family live on a farm in Atlantic Canada. Her mother who will be 90 in January also lives with them. Darlene enjoys listening to stories from her mother's past and is currently writing a book about her mother's rich experiences of life. You can contact her at *antenna@nb.sympatico.ca*.

Flo LeClair received her associate degree in nursing in 1978 from Quinsigamond Community College and a bachelor's degree in nursing from Assumption College in 1988. She has practiced oncology and hospice nursing in Worcester, Massachusetts since 1981. She finds it an honor and a privilege to be at the bedside of those passing from this world to the next. Please reach her at: *leclairf@ummhc.org*.

A native of California, **Linda S. Lee** and her husband reside in Indiana, near their grown children and grandchildren. Her work has been published locally and nationally by Comcast and in magazines and newspaper columns. The story of her marriage miracle was published in the 2004 book *For Better, For Worse—Devotional Thoughts for Married Couples*, edited by Marlene Bagnull. Linda also writes fiction. Roles are reversed as Linda now serves in a caregiving role for her husband, while he confronts his own battle for life. Linda can be reached at *linda@daves-place.net*.

Karen Davis Lees lives in Middle Tennessee with her husband, Dan. Along with her five brothers and sisters, she is a caregiver for her mom and dad. She enjoys homemaking, volunteering for her church and art.

Patricia Lorenz, who enjoys all the nature she can cram into her busy writing/speaking life, is one of the top contributors to the *Chicken Soup for the Soul* books with stories in seventeen of them. She's the author of over 400 articles, a contributing writer for 15 *Daily Guideposts* books, an award-winning columnist, and the author of four books. Her two latest, *Life's Too Short To Fold Your Underwear* and *Grab The Extinguisher, My Birthday Cake's On Fire* can be ordered through Guideposts Books at *www.dailyguideposts.com/store*. To contact Patricia for speaking opportunities, e-mail her at: *patricialorenz@juno.com*.

Susan Lugli is a Christian speaker and published author. She is an active member in the Phoenix Society for burn survivors and works helping burn survivors and their families. Susan and Rusty Lugli live on a ranch with their family in Lompoc, California. Please reach her at: *suenrusty@aol.com*.

Claire Luna-Pinsker resides in New York. She's an author, wife, mother of three and pediatric nurse. With a sense of humor and a personality that hasn't lost the inquisitiveness of youth, she has published multiple romantic shorts, essays and a novel, *Ebony Blood.* Contact Claire at *Lunarose22@hotmail.com*.

Martha Larche Lusk is a native Texan, although she has lived in other states. She currently lives in Dallas. First published when ten years old, she has authored four books and many short pieces. Credits also include publication in two anthologies.

The father of two sons, **Steven Manchester** is the published author of *The Unexpected Storm: The Gulf War Legacy, A Father's Love, Jacob Evans* and *At The Stroke of Midnight,* as well as several books under the pseudonym Steven Herberts. He may be reached at *shmanchester@statestreet.com*.

Jacqueline Marcell is an author, publisher, radio host, speaker, and advocate for eldercare. Her bestselling book, *Elder Rage, or Take My Father . . . Please! How to Survive Caring For Aging Parents,* a Book-of-the-Month Club selection, is being considered for a feature film. Jacqueline hosts *Coping with Caregiving* on *www.wsRadio.com/CopingWithCaregiving/* an Internet radio program. *www. ElderRage.com*.

After marrying and raising three children, **Mrs. Marvin** returned to college and later taught high school and middle school children for 22 years. She began her writing career at age 57, and published her first short story at 59. In 1994, she won the coveted Milkweed Editions prize for children's literature for her novel, *A Bride for Anna's Papa,* for which she was nominated for a Minnesota Book Award in 1995. She published 11 novels and hundreds of short stories. "Sisters" was written when she was about 55; shortly after she wrote it, her father came to live with her until he passed away in 1983.

Christina Miranda-Walker, a graduate of Holy Names College in Oakland, California, is a wife, mother and "granny-mom" who is happily spending her retirement years writing short stories and articles, going to PTA meetings and dance classes. Grown-up conversation is welcome at *SpiritEnterprise@aol.com*.

Janet Lynn Mitchell is a wife, mother, author, and inspirational speaker. She is the co-author of *A Special Kind of Love, For Those Who Love Children with Special Needs*, published by Broadman and Holman and *Focus on the Family*, 2004. Janet can be reached at *JanetLM@prodigy.net* or faxed at (714) 633-6309.

Janet Nicholson writes humorous articles and children's books including the Leon Chameleon P.I. stories. She volunteers in the SPCA bookshop (book heaven), writes a neighborhood watch newsletter and is a member of ITC. She lives in South Africa with her husband, three cats and two dogs. Contact Janet on *jannev@mweb.co.za*.

Debra Oliver lives in Stow, Ohio with her children, Adam and Corinne, and her best friend and husband, Greg Lee. Believing it is a rare privilege to be invited into one's soul, she is honored to share her story of faith and forgiveness with you. You can contact Debra at *do122961@aol.com*.

Janice Jackson O'Neal has taught kindergarten and second grade for many years. She has published poetry entitled, *Faith in the Shadows*. Currently, she is writing an inspirational children's book, *Duncan the Dragon Discovers the Kingdom of Love*. Her favorite pastimes include gardening, traveling, and reading. Please reach her at: *janoneal@bellsouth.net*.

Mark Parisi's *Off the Mark* comic panel has been syndicated since 1987 and is distributed by United Media. Mark's humor also graces greeting cards, T-shirts, calendars, magazines (such as *Billboard*), newsletters and books. His cartoons can be found in the pages of many *Chicken Soup for the Soul* books. Lynn is his wife/business partner and their daughter, Jenny, contributes with inspiration (as do three cats).

Denise Peebles resides in Rogersville, Alabama, with her husband, Keith, and children, Ashley and Jonathan. She has written for magazines, local newspapers and *Chicken Soup for the Soul* including the lead story in *Christmas Treasury for Kids*. Her goal is to someday write a children's book. Contact her at *Speeb47489@aol.com*.

Kim Peterson earned her B.A. at Grace College and her M.A. at Wheaton College. She has authored numerous articles for newspapers and magazines and currently reviews books for *CBA Marketplace* and *Salem Press*. She serves as Writer-in-Residence at Bethel College in Mishawaka, Indiana. Find her on the web at: *www.bethelcollege.edu/users/peterson*.

Rhona Knox Prescott, R.N., L.I.C.S.W., completed nurses training at Flushing Hospital in New York, and graduate work at the University of Houston, Texas. She is retired from the federal government. Rhona served in Vietnam during the war. She co-authored *Another Kind of War Story*, has a chapter in *Chicken*

Soup for the Nurse's Soul and is currently writing her first fictional work, *Street of Flowers*. Contact her at *Rhona41@hotmail.com* to purchase *Another Kind of War Story* at $12 plus shipping.

Virginia Beach gastroenterologist **Patricia Raymond, M.D.**, leads nurses and physicians to resuscitate their passion for their medical careers. Her stimulating books, *Don't Jettison Medicine and Colonoscopy: It'll Crack u Up* are available through *www.RxForSanity.com*, where you may request her complimentary *Rx For Sanity* eNews, brimming with medical humor and stories.

Carol McAdoo Rehme, one of *Chicken Soup's* most prolific authors, finds her niche—inspirational writing—is the perfect avenue to share life's lessons. As founding director of Vintage Voices, Inc., a non-profit agency that provides engaging, interactive programs in eldercare facilities, she witnesses caregiving in its purest form . . . among the aged. Contact: *carol@rehme.com* or *www.rehme.com*.

Daniel James Reust lives with his wife in Colorado. He is an observer of nature and human nature and is cursed or blessed with a dictate to wrestle with the wily word, which one day he hopes to do well. He can be contacted at *danreust@msn.com*.

An award-winning writer and editor, **Ramona Richards** has more than 300 publications to her credit, including a single parent column for *Special Education Today* magazine and an article on Internet pornography in the September/October 2003 *Today's Christian Woman*. She can be reached at *RamonaRichards@hotmail.com*.

Lisa Rossi has her master's degree in elementary education and is a Curriculum Generalist for Poudre School District. She is the mother of three children (Cody - 16, Chris - 13, and Elizabeth - 10) and the wife of Michael. She can be reached at: *LisaRayRossi@aol.com*.

Julie Schneider resides in North Dakota. She has an extensive background in the travel industry. Currently, she homeschools her two children. Julie enjoys home decorating, craft projects, cooking, and writing. Her future plans include pursuing a writing career. Please reach her at *justjewelhere@hotmail.com*.

Deborah Shouse is the daughter of a woman with Alzheimer's. She has performed her work at caregiver's gatherings and aging conferences. Her work has appeared in publications such as *The Washington Post, Spirituality and Health, Woman's Day* and more. Her latest book is *Making Your Message Memorable: Communicating Through Stories*. Visit her Web site at *www.thecreativityconnection.com*.

Lula Smith received her high school diploma from Brookland, Arkansas, in 1951. She has also attended many seminars and workshops over the past 37 years in Indiana, where she owned and operated a licensed day care center for 30 years at the Jack & Jill Day Care Center. She worked 13 years at her daughter's A.B.C. Childcare Learning Center. In October 2003, at the age of 71, she ended her full-time employment there. Many of these years, she worked at both places.

Dorothy Snyder, a retired administrative secretary, is the mother of four adult children. Her husband suffered from Alzheimer's disease and she cared for him in their home. She is a freelance writer and is currently working on a book about her caregiving experience. She can be reached at *Dotmyree@aol.com*.

Carol Steward is a multi-published romance author and hopeless romantic. She has retired from family child-care and now works at a state university in addition to her writing. Carol loves traveling, camping, crafts, and spending time with her family. She would love to hear from you at *csteward37@aol.com*.

Melodie Lynn Tilander transitioned from a corporate career to pursue her dream of writing. She resides in Oregon earning publishing credits in several mediums. Melodie enjoys being near the water and creating stained glass/stone design. She is co-authoring an inspirational book on God's Ministering Angels. Please reach her at: *lynnmelodie@hotmail.com*.

Lori Ulrich is an elementary teacher in rural Saskatchewan, Canada. Writing poetry in her spare time is her passion. Along with her husband, Perry, she encourages her children to live life and be "real." Active in her local Canadian National Institute for the Blind, Lori is an advocate for blind children and youth.

John A. Vanek is a physician, writer and poet, with works published in *Heartlands, Common Threads, The Vincent Brothers Review, Tattoo Highway, The Journal of the American Medical Association (JAMA)*, and *Medical Economics*. His poem, "The People's Republic," is part of the George Bush Presidential Library and Museum.

Suzanne Vaughan (B.S. Education), author of the book *Potholes and Parachutes*, is a motivational speaker who has delivered personal growth programs to corporations and associations for over 25 years. She is past-president of the Colorado Speakers Association. To contact her call toll free 866-303-7222 or visit her Web site at *www.suzannevaughan.com*.

Amy Ross Vaughn—"Christmas Eve Devotions" is Amy's debut story for *Chicken Soup For the Soul*. She graduated from Hannibal-Lagrange College in 1992, with a bachelor of arts' degree in human services. Since that time, she has worked extensively with the geriatric population. Amy enjoys spending time with her husband, Robert, writing, playing the piano and singing. She hopes to continue her writing career and branch out into motivational speaking. You may reach her at *amyvaughn.1@juno.com*.

Maryella Vause graduated from Duke University School of Nursing and is certified as a Family Nurse Practitioner. She and her physician husband of 46 years enjoy their Christian faith, with five adult children, eight grandchildren, their cat, dogs and horses. They also work for Excel-telecommunications. You may reach her at *maryella@myexcel.com*.

Bobbie Hamblet Wilkinson is a freelance writer and artist. She has edited and illustrated several books, including the original edition of her sister's book, *My Beautiful Broken Shell*. Her passion is sharing the beauty and blessings that surround her. Visit *www.artbybobbie.com* or e-mail Bobbie at *bobbiewilkinson@earthlink.net*.

Thomas G. Williams graduated high school in 1955. He enlisted in the US Navy and was assigned to USN Ceremonial Honor Guard, followed by assignments: Navy Hospital Corps. School, Operating Room Tech. School, USS *Dash*, USS *Morongshelia*, USS *Maury*, Jungle Training Philippine Islands, Hunter Angel 7 Helicopter Squadron. Assigned Search Air & Reconnaissance Udorn Thailand, Insertions and Extractions in Cambodia, Laos, Viet Nam and Gulf of Thailand.

Bret Wright lives in Colorado where he writes both fiction and non-fiction stories. His work has appeared in *InformArt* Magazine, *Futures Mysterious Anthology* Magazine, *EOTU*, *Grit*, and a host of others. He is a copublisher of *Apollo's Lyre Ezine*, the 'zine for writers, by writers. You may reach him at *www.apolloslyre.com*.

Dorothy Palmer Young grew up in Baltimore and graduated from the University of Maryland, but now calls Edmond, Oklahoma, home. Dorothy and her husband have four adult children. She is the full-time caregiver for their disabled daughter and writes for her church and other publications. Please reach her at: *dorothypalmeryoung@cox.net*.

Wendy Young, MSW, BCD, a Child and Family Therapist, maintains a private practice in Bessemer, Michigan. She is the creator of Kid-lutions™: Solutions to kids' everyday problems. Kid-lutions™ offers resources to assist children in dealing with such issues as grief and loss, anger management, self-esteem and more, as well as workshops for parents and educators. Contacts: *www.kid-lutions.com* or *wyoung@up.net*.

Thousands of **Bob Zahn** cartoons have been published in all the major magazines. Seven collections of his cartoons have been published. His e-mail address is *zahntoons@aol.com*.

Permissions

We would like to acknowledge the many publishers and individuals who granted us permission to reprint the cited material. (Note: The stories that were penned anonymously, that are in the public domain or that were written by Jack Canfield, Mark Victor Hansen or LeAnn Thieman are not included in this listing.)

That's Why I Am Here. Reprinted by permission of Loretta Anne Emmons. ©2002 Loretta Anne Emmons.

The Day Wishes Came True by Lula Smith as told to Kim Peterson. Reprinted by permission of Lula Mae Smith and Kimberly T. Peterson. ©2003 Kimberly T. Peterson.

A Musical Eye-Opener. Reprinted by permission of Nancy B. Gibbs. ©2001 Nancy B. Gibbs.

Christmas Eve Devotions. Reprinted by permission of Amy Ross Vaughn. ©2001 Amy Ross Vaughn.

Daddy's Dance. Reprinted by permission of Louise Tucker Jones. ©2002 Louise Tucker Jones.

My Sunshine. Reprinted by permission of Suzanne Vaughan. ©2001 Suzanne Vaughan.

Caregiver's Handbook. Reprinted by permission of Beverly Ann Jones Haley. ©2002 Beverly Ann Jones Haley.

When All Hope is Lost. Reprinted by permission of Janet Lynn Mitchell. ©2002 Janet Lynn Mitchell.

Daddy's Little Girl. Reprinted by permission of Ruth Hancock. ©2001 Ruth Hancock.

Saving Him. Reprinted by permission of Roger Dean Kiser, Sr. ©2002 Roger Dean Kiser, Sr.

In the Sack. Reprinted by permission of Carol McAdoo Rehme. ©2003 Carol McAdoo Rehme.

Lunch with Grandma. Reprinted by permission of Teri Batts. ©2003 Teri Batts.

Too Late. Reprinted by permission of Esther Copeland. ©2003 Esther Copeland.

Love in the Land of Dementia. Reprinted by permission of Deborah Shouse. ©2001 Deborah Shouse.

Love's Own Language. Reprinted by permission of Dorothy C. Snyder. ©2002 Dorothy C. Snyder.

Dear Precious Husband. Reprinted by permission of Holly Hutson Baker. ©2002 Holly Hutson Baker.

Earning Her Wings. Reprinted by permission of Sally Kelly-Engeman. ©2003 Sally Kelly-Engeman.

The Killing Streak. Reprinted by permission of Debbie Gallagher. ©2002 Debbie Gallagher.

Waiting for Mother. Reprinted by permission of Sharon Love Cook. ©2003 Sharon Love Cook.

No Response. Reprinted by permission of Donna J. Parisi. ©2003 Donna J. Parisi.

Good Night, Harry. Reprinted by permission of Daniel James Reust. ©2003 Daniel James Reust.

Brothers. Reprinted by permission of Thomas G. Williams. ©2003 Thomas G. Williams.

The Little White Box. Reprinted by permission of Roger Dean Kiser, Sr. ©2003 Roger Dean Kiser, Sr.

On the Line. Reprinted by permission of Carol McAdoo Rehme. ©2002 Carol McAdoo Rehme.

The Package by Shirley Javernick as told to Ellen Javernick. Reprinted by permission of Shirley Javernick and Ellen Javernick. ©2003 Ellen Javernick.

I Can't Do a Thing. Reprinted by permission of HEARTPRINTS. Copyright ©1999 by Sandra Picklesimer Aldrich and Bobbie Valentine. Used by permission of WaterBrook Press, Colorado Springs, CO. All rights reserved.

Long-Distance Vitamins. Reprinted by permission of Emily Chase. ©2002 Emily Chase.

Food for Thought. Reprinted by permission of Carol McAdoo Rehme. ©2003 Carol McAdoo Rehme.

Time Flies. Reprinted by permission of Dorothy Palmer Young. ©2003 Dorothy Palmer Young.

The Magic of Making a Difference. Reprinted by permission of Barbara Bartlein, R.N., L.C.S.W. ©2002 Barbara Bartlein, R.N., L.C.S.W.

Fostering Memories. Reprinted by permission of Janet E. Nicholson. ©2002 Janet E. Nicholson.

The Eraser. Reprinted by permission of John Joseph Gaudet. ©2003 John Joseph Gaudet.

May Day. Reprinted by permission of Carol McAdoo Rehme. ©1999 Carol McAdoo Rehme.

In Over Their Heads. Reprinted by permission of Carol McAdoo Rehme. ©2003 Carol McAdoo Rehme.

Lost & Found. Reprinted with permission of *Family Circle* magazine.